T0075000

Unwired

Our society has a technology problem. Many want to disconnect from screens but can't help themselves. These days we spend more time online than ever. Some turn to self-help measures to limit their usage, yet repeatedly fail, while parents feel particularly powerless to help their children. *Unwired: Gaining Control over Addictive Technologies* shows us a way out. Rather than blaming users, the book shatters the illusion that we autonomously choose how to spend our time online. It shifts the moral responsibility and accountability for solutions to corporations. Drawing lessons from the tobacco and food industries, the book demonstrates why government regulation is necessary to curb technology addiction. It describes a grassroots movement already in action across courts and legislative halls. Groundbreaking and urgent, *Unwired* provides a blueprint to develop this movement for change, to one that will allow us to finally gain control.

Gaia Bernstein is the Technology, Privacy and Policy Professor of Law, Co-Director of the Institute for Privacy Protection, and Co-Director of the Gibbons Institute of Law Science and Technology at Seton Hall University School of Law. She writes, teaches, and lectures on subjects at the intersections of law, technology, health, and privacy. Professor Bernstein developed a nationally recognized outreach program on technology overuse for school-aged children and their parents. She is also a mother of three children who grew up in the era of smartphones, screens, and social media.

Unwired

Gaining Control over Addictive Technologies

Gaia Bernstein

CAMBRIDGE
UNIVERSITY PRESS

Shaftesbury Road, Cambridge CB2 8EA, United Kingdom

One Liberty Plaza, 20th Floor, New York, NY 10006, USA

477 Williamstown Road, Port Melbourne, VIC 3207, Australia

314–321, 3rd Floor, Plot 3, Splendor Forum, Jasola District Centre,
New Delhi – 110025, India

103 Penang Road, #05–06/07, Visioncrest Commercial, Singapore 238467

Cambridge University Press is part of Cambridge University Press & Assessment,
a department of the University of Cambridge.

We share the University's mission to contribute to society through the pursuit of
education, learning and research at the highest international levels of excellence.

www.cambridge.org
Information on this title: www.cambridge.org/9781009257930

DOI: 10.1017/9781009257954

First published 2023 (version 2, May 2023)

Printed in Great Britain by CPI Group (UK) Ltd, Croydon CR0 4YY

A catalogue record for this publication is available from the British Library

Library of Congress Cataloging-in-Publication data
NAMES: Bernstein, Gaia, author.
TITLE: Unwired : gaining control over addictive technologies / Gaia Bernstein,
    Seton Hall University.
DESCRIPTION: Cambridge, United Kingdom ; New York, NY : Cambridge University Press,
    2023. | Includes bibliographical references.
IDENTIFIERS: LCCN 2022031304 (print) | LCCN 2022031305 (ebook) | ISBN
    9781009257930 (hardback) | ISBN 9781009257947 (paperback) | ISBN 9781009257954
    (epub)
SUBJECTS: LCSH: Internet addiction. | Social media addiction. | Video game addiction. |
    Compulsive gambling.
CLASSIFICATION: LCC RC569.5.I54 B47 2023 (print) | LCC RC569.5.I54 (ebook) |
    DDC 616.85/84–dc23/eng/20220713
LC record available at https://lccn.loc.gov/2022031304
LC ebook record available at https://lccn.loc.gov/2022031305

ISBN   978-1-009-25793-0   Hardback

To my loves, Yonatan, Daniella, and Ytamar

CONTENTS

PROLOGUE

On a summer evening in 2019, I met a friend for dinner in an Italian restaurant in the Village in Manhattan. About halfway through dinner, our conversation turned to her 15-year-old daughter. Her daughter was always on her phone. When they had gone on a family ski trip that winter, she spent every moment posing for Instagram photos, editing them, and deciding which to post. She refused even to take a break during dinner to interact with the family. When her father took her phone away, she flew into a rage because she did not finish posting that day's skiing photos. My friend brought this up because she was planning a family trip to Los Angeles. She asked me what I thought of asking her daughter to leave her phone at the hotel and use it only at night before she went to bed. Would this be a good method?

Many people at that point expected me to have answers. A couple of years earlier, I had launched an outreach program about technology overuse and potential solutions. My friend thought I would support her idea and maybe offer some tweaks. But unfortunately, I couldn't. I had never thought I would find myself in this position. I had started out as a staunch believer in using methods to help ourselves and our children reduce our time on screens. But, on that summer evening in 2019, my answer was: "It is unlikely to work. It's too late to ask her to disconnect when Instagram and messaging are her whole world." It was a truth I didn't even want to admit to myself until I said it. My friend looked confused and asked rather impatiently, "So what is the solution?" Deep down I knew the answer, but I was not yet ready to share it.

Our world has changed gradually, beginning around 2009 when smartphones and social networks became popular. I didn't pay attention at first. I lived a very hectic life, working as a law professor and raising three small children in Manhattan. Around 2015, something clicked, and I started noticing more. The way I put my phone on the table whenever I sat with a friend to grab a cup of coffee, expecting and accepting its distractions. How I watched my kids' end-of-year performances through rows of held-up phones and iPads. Eventually, I realized our reality had changed. We sit next to our loved ones, our friends, but we often do not talk. Our kids stare blurry-eyed at their screens. They barely glance up to respond to us, returning quickly to their phones. We are too rarely present; too often elsewhere.

I tried making different choices for myself. But by 2017, I wanted to do more than fight my personal battles. In my role as the director of the Institute for Privacy Protection at my law school, I launched an outreach program for school-aged children and their parents, which went beyond privacy to tackle technology overuse. I hoped to help kids and parents realize how much time they spent on screens and the price they paid for it. When I started speaking to parents, my main goal was to bring awareness to the topic. But by the second year, I had encountered a sense of guilt and helplessness I had not anticipated. Parents came to hear my talks because they were desperate. They felt personally responsible for losing their children to their screens.

I was conflicted about what should be done. Like many, I liked a lot of things about online technology. I opened every lecture pointing out the advantages of connectivity. I talked about kids speaking to grandparents on Skype; the convenience of shopping online; and the wonders of having so much information at our fingertips. I did not believe, and still do not believe, that technology is bad. I did think, though, that we needed a better online–offline balance. So, faced by despair, I offered self-help methods, suggesting ways to limit kids' screen time. I suspected that technology companies purposefully designed their technologies to make sure we spend more time online.

Still, I did not explicitly say this in my lectures. I was a lawyer who shied away from conflict and opted instead to become a law professor. Unsurprisingly, I was reluctant to come out and say that Facebook, who sought "to connect the world," or Google, whose motto was "Do no evil," were the bad guys.

But then things changed. Inside information from the tech titans leaked out. Whistleblower after whistleblower explained how tech companies use known principles of psychology to manipulate our brains to addict us. They lure us to spend longer time online by giving us rewards intermittently, on an irregular schedule. When rewards are unpredictable, our brains release stronger surges of dopamine – the brain neurotransmitter responsible for pleasure. For example, tech companies designed the popular "pull to refresh" feature. On Facebook, we keep pulling to check if we got our "reward": a like or a comment. Every time we get a "reward," we receive a burst of dopamine; we then keep pulling to refresh in anticipation of our next dopamine infusion. Tech companies also took away our stopping signals. One of their popular design features is "autoplay." On YouTube, when one video ends, the next automatically begins. This makes it harder to stop. These are just a few of the tools in tech companies' kits to ensure we stay hooked.

While information trickled out about how the tech industry manipulates us to prolong our time online, data accumulated about the harms of extended screen time. Researchers published significant findings, based on psychological studies and brain scans, of how excessive screen time affects kids' cognitive development and mental health; of how some of us become addicted and many, while not qualifying as clinically addicted, still manifest symptoms of overuse that resemble addiction. Other investigations uncovered the impact on our ability to connect with one another, and even worse the disconnection and social division. With all we now know, it seems increasingly unlikely that we would have opted for all of this, had we known this information around 2009, when we had the opportunity to choose.

This shed light on what I had observed. Our self-help efforts mostly failed to reduce our time online. The parents I lectured to felt desperate and powerless because their efforts had not helped their families. Self-help measures gave us the illusion that we were in control, while in fact we were not. Surveys reflected this, showing that screen time had not decreased; if anything it was on the increase. I realized that, while we kept blaming ourselves, we were not really the choice-makers. The technology industry was calling the shots.

During the fall of 2019, following the dinner conversation with my friend, my lectures to parents changed. I wanted to alleviate their sense of helplessness, but I realized I should not reinforce their illusion of control by focusing on self-help strategies. I knew then that real change could only come if we shifted from focusing on personal responsibility to making technology companies accountable for their addictive design choices. I started talking more and more to parents, not about what they should do at home, but about what they could do in the outside world to pressure the technology industry and the government to fix the problem.

Then came 2020 and the COVID-19 pandemic. While technology preserved a semblance of normal life as we went into lockdowns, days spent on screens also underscored the harms. They illuminated the future we had mindlessly approached before the pandemic. We painfully felt the cost of no face-to-face interaction. We could no longer deny the price our children were paying. At the same time, the extremes of pandemic life also highlighted the possibility of a different trajectory. The option of changing tracks and taking action to prevent a future we never intentionally chose for ourselves.

Selecting the right moment to end scientific debate and formulate law and policy is always difficult. Making decisions too early, before all the facts are in, could be premature. But the pandemic underscored the other danger: we may err toward waiting too long and missing the window of opportunity for change. The realizations brought on by the pandemic occurred simultaneously with alarms from medical professionals and journalists alerting us to the escalating social and public health crises. Experts explicitly warned that we are running a dangerous uncontrolled experiment on a whole generation of children.

In this book I spell out what I was not ready to tell my friend that summer evening in 2019. I wrote this book to empower readers by laying out the other option: the collective action alternative to failing individual battles. Connectivity is here to stay. It has many advantages. But to regain what we have lost, we need to stop blaming ourselves and engage in concerted legal action to exert pressure on governments and the real choice-maker – the technology industry – to redesign products and spaces in a way that will put us back in the driver's seat.

This book interlaces the human with the legal. While taking an in-depth look at what has happened to us, I outline the most promising legal strategies for developing a movement that would reassert our control over our time. This kind of movement could not depend on lawyers alone. We who pay the price of technology overuse need to push for change for ourselves and for our children. Change is possible. Today, we cannot picture a bar without phones consuming the attention of every patron. Neither could we imagine smokeless bars in the 1980s. But by the beginning of the twenty-first century, that had become our reality.

To envision the paths for the future I delve into the past – into the battles against tobacco and junk food. I show that our history of self-blame is repeating itself once again. We are still telling ourselves the same story. We blame ourselves for smoking too much, for eating too much junk food, for spending too much time on our phones. As I describe the figures who led these battles and the legal strategies they employed, I identify those that would transcend time and subject matter and will likely be part of the fight to contain technology overuse. Indeed, some of these strategies are already in play. The picture that emerges from this book is that no single course of action can serve as the magic bullet. Raising awareness is a first step, but it is insufficient by itself. Different players attempting diverse measures will be the best tactic to bring about change.

While outlining a framework for future action, I tell the story of the new movement that has already taken off. I describe the activity taking place in court houses and legislative halls across the country and around the world, sowing the seeds for a major movement for change. From parents suing game-makers for addicting their children; to anti-trust authorities acting to tame the titans of Big Tech; to governments outlawing addictive features and legislating to limit kids' time online. Doing nothing carries the danger of neglecting a whole generation of children. But if we fight, we do so for our kids and for ourselves: to preserve our own free will. This book is not just a call to arms; it is also a call to join those who are already in the trenches.

Part I

THE PRICE OF THE ILLUSION OF CONTROL

1 BECOMING THE CHOICE-MAKERS

Up to Our Necks

I always had a complicated relationship with technology. I would like it, then realize I like it too much, and then try to disentangle from it. I went through several cycles of this. As a young girl in the 1970s, I spent far too much time playing video games. Then in the 1990s, I spent every spare minute during one college semester playing a dungeon treasure hunt computer game. I stopped only after I convinced a friend to place a password on the game to prevent my access. Then came email. I simply could not stop checking it. In my first apartment in New York City as a graduate student, I endlessly connected and disconnected my modem to check my emails. But for me and for many others, 2009 was the year when things started changing. This was the year that smartphones and Facebook became popular.[1] Suddenly, we could text, email, access the Internet, and engage in social interactions practically anywhere and anytime.

These days, I am an academic. I spend much of my time researching and writing on my laptop. I am also the mom of three kids. I value efficiency. I can't really afford not to. For over a decade, I often sat down to write at my regular table at the coffee shop near my apartment. I took out my laptop, my iPhone, and my Kindle. I wrote down my list of tasks for the day. But then two and a half hours later, with little writing done and feeling drained, I wondered what happened. The answer was usually texts and emails, but more than anything, uncontrollable Internet browsing: news sites, blogs, Facebook. Every click triggered another.

I no longer do this. At least, I try my best not to. It started in 2015, when I walked out of a yoga class into a busy New York café. About fifteen people stood in line in front of me. Everyone was looking down at their phones. Normally I would have pulled out my phone as well. Perhaps it was the impact of the yoga class. But for once I didn't. Instead, I looked at the people around me. No one met my glance. Many people crowded in the café's small space, but there was no talking, no smiling, not even eye contact. This was the first time something felt very wrong to me.

By now I know many feel the same way. They wish they did not spend so much time online. They keep surfing, texting, swiping, and playing. They report feeling drained and unsatisfied, but they seem unable to stop.[2] Some actually tried to restrict their time. Still, resisting screen time was practically futile. Despite increasing talk about maintaining a healthy online–offline balance, little has changed. Our self-help attempts did not work. Companies promised to add features that will help us help ourselves. These promises, unsurprisingly, did not offer much relief either.

The Illusion of Control

We spend five hours every day on our phones. But when asked: "Do you want to spend five hours a day on your phone?" for most of us the answer is "no." Still we just do it over and over again. Day in and day out. What would happen if we paused and reflected on what we want to do with our time? Do we want to mindlessly squander our moments, hours, days, and years, or would we prefer to intentionally decide how we spend our time?

Of course, we do contemplate large life choices. Do I want to pursue a degree in social work? Do I want to get married? Do I want to work outside the home or be a stay-at-home mom? But when decisions seem less significant involving free-time and entertainment choices, we are likely to reflect less. This may seem rational. We cannot dedicate significant decision-making resources to every small decision. And not all decisions are made equal. But what happens when we think we are only making small choices, but inadvertently we are making a huge one?[3]

My path to the café table surrounded by beeping and tempting screens was gradual. It was not one I paid much attention to. I got my first smartphone – a red Blackberry – in 2008. My oldest son was then 6 years old and my twins were infants. I lived in Manhattan and worked as a law professor at Seton Hall Law School in Newark, New Jersey. During workdays I left my children with different caregivers. I initially got a smartphone to text and coordinate my kids' days during my train commute. Replacing time-consuming phone conversations and phone tags with texts was a huge time saver. I then realized that using it to answer work emails on the train helped me maximize my workday once I reached the Law School. That year, I also joined Facebook because I wanted to keep in touch with other academics in my field. All of these were seemingly small decisions, but they started my trajectory toward a life immersed with screens.

Many of us made these small choices that led to a larger one. The numbers are quite staggering. Even leaving out time spent on tablets or computer screens, American adults spent 5.4 hours a day on their phone before the pandemic. This is 1,971 hours a year. Teens spend even more time online than adults. Forty-five percent of teens say they are "constantly online."[4] Through these seemingly small decisions we unintentionally completely transformed how we spend our time and how we interact with one another. Instead of interacting through conversation, eye contact, and a smile with those in our physical proximity, we are more likely to engage with others not present, through letters, symbols, and game strategies. While treating each small choice along the way as insignificant, we have unwittingly made a huge decision defining who we are and how we relate to one another. We felt in control as we opted for one app after another, but, unwittingly, we were lured into a place we may have never intended to reach had we really considered our options.

We fall into these traps too often in life. We make choices, intentionally or not, that may even seem in line with our goals at that moment. We assume we are in control, but these choices accumulate into a reality we never imagined for ourselves. The illusion of control blinds us from seeing where we are.[5]

Autonomy and Making Our Own Choices

Autonomy is a big word that is often tossed around. People mean different things when they talk about autonomy. For many people, and for me too, autonomy means making independent decisions about our lives. I have autonomy when I write my life story by making my life choices. In a perfect world, I would have the opportunity to think about each option, evaluate if it fits with my beliefs, desires, and commitments, and ultimately make a decision based on my own reasons.[6] This is the ideal. Some people's decision-making lies in the other extreme. They lack autonomy to a point that they become a mere puppet. Their environment is so highly constructed their free will evaporates. This becomes evident when they can no longer give their own reasons for their choices. A wife whose abusive husband prohibits her from seeing her friends and family would often voice his rationales for staying away from her loved ones, but cannot articulate her own.[7]

How about my choices to use my devices? At least initially I was making small deliberate choices. I assessed how little time I had as the mom of three small kids and a law professor on the tenure track. I made choices to text and email during my commute that made sense in terms of efficiency and convenience. I chose to join Facebook because I realized that many colleagues in my field were active on the social network. I was a new academic and decided it was an effective way to get to know people better in between conferences. I could articulate my reasons for these specific choices. But, a decade later, as I tried to work, and realized I had wasted hours online, I could no longer express my reasons for my actions. My acts were no longer in line with my goals and preferences. The design choices of the devices, websites, and apps I was using influenced my actions.

In reality not all our decisions are ideal independent decisions, nor do we usually become puppets unable to make any decisions at all. Still, we are often constrained by our circumstances, our background, and the people that surround us. The question is how much? At what point do we lose our autonomy? A key indicator is whether we reflect upon a decision. We are autonomous as long as we exercise our will considering our choices.[8] At some point, I stopped reflecting upon my choices. I then crossed over from the gray zone to the lack of autonomy zone.

Manipulating Choice

When someone manipulates us, they interfere with our ability to author the story of our lives. They decide for us how and why we ought to live. A unique feature of manipulation is that it is often covert. We are not aware that someone else is, in fact, controlling our decision-making.[9] Businesses have strong incentives to manipulate consumers. The behavioral economist Dan Ariely described humans as "predictably irrational."[10] Businesses rely on this predictable irrationality and use human vulnerabilities to increase their revenues.[11]

Legal scholar Cass Sunstein said: "Manipulation takes multiple forms. It has at least fifty shades."[12] When I walk into a drugstore, and hear a song I like playing in the background, I tend to linger a bit longer and sometimes even end up buying a product I did not plan on purchasing when I walked in. This is no coincidence. The store owners hope to achieve exactly this result by playing music targeted at their clientele's age and background.[13] Some marketing strategies are more intricate, like advertisers' use of subliminal advertising. They incorporate sounds and images that do not enter our consciousness but affect us. Both the music in the drugstore and subliminal advertising somewhat impair our ability to reflect on our decisions. But just as many decisions are not perfectly independent, neither does every commercial action aiming to influence consumer choice threaten human autonomy.[14] At what point, then, does manipulation affect reflection to an extent that it is unacceptable?[15]

Highly manipulative actions are particularly unacceptable. These are actions that are hidden and hard to detect or fully grasp even once exposed. Covert manipulation is, unfortunately, central to the Internet economy. Its business model feeds on two crucial resources: users' personal data and time. Online services are often offered for free to users. We do not pay for our basic Gmail account or to subscribe to Facebook or Instagram. But these companies sell our personal data to advertisers who use it to target us with ads we are more likely to respond to. Using and selling personal information for advertising is most effective when users maximize their time online and increase their exposure to the ads. Internet companies obscure their use of data and time because, unlike automobile manufacturers, they do not mine their resources underground. Instead, they harvest them from their customers and their customers' social network, without these individuals' explicit consent and even awareness of the harvesting process. In Chapter 3, I discuss in detail the ways in which tech companies take advantage of our cognitive vulnerabilities to hijack our time. We believe we are making the choice to spend hours on Instagram, while, in fact, unseen and powerful mechanisms keep us hooked. Tech companies use technology to covertly influence our decision-making of how to spend our time. They tempt us, through the likes, the endless scrolls, and the unexpected rewards. They influence us in ways we are consciously unaware of and cannot fully comprehend. We lose the opportunity to reflect autonomously on how we spend such a large part of our time. We make decisions that seem like they are our own, while they are driven by corporate decision-making.[16]

Manipulation though does not always dictate the result. Even when manipulation takes place, it is rarely that absolute. It seldom means that we have no say at all and completely lose self-control.[17] Even though tech companies' product design manipulated me into spending much more time than I intended online, I could make some choices. When I had to prepare a class for the next day or to finish a draft of a paper for a conference or publication, I could resist the allure of the online world. It is actually the remnants of choice that are so misleading and reinforce the illusion of control.

We Are the Frogs in the Water

How did we get there? How did we give away our power to decide how we spend our time? People often bring up the fable of the frog in the boiling water.[18] It is very relevant here. According to the famous fable, if you throw a frog into boiling water, it will jump out and stay alive. But if instead, you put it into tepid water and then slowly bring the water to a boil, it will not realize the danger and will be cooked to death.

How did we become the frog in the water? Many of us stepped into the lukewarm water when smartphones, texting, and social networks gained popularity. I started texting and emailing during my commute to maximize efficiency. But, the more I texted, the more texts

I seemed to receive. The topics became less urgent and more miniscule. Within a month I rarely took my eyes off my phone throughout the commute. I was often surprised to find out as I got off the train in Newark that a student or a colleague was on the same car throughout the ride. By the time I started thinking of writing this book, I had already made many small decisions that accumulated into a different lifestyle. I rarely took my eyes completely off my phone anywhere, whether I was standing in line to buy coffee or even having dinner with a friend. A doctor's waiting room was a signal to take out my laptop. My head was usually buried elsewhere.

Like me, many people gradually changed how they use their devices. We viewed our smartphones initially as communication devices for calling, texting, and emails. We never imagined we would use them for so many other functions, including social media, news reading, shopping, games, or even making payments. And that all of these options would be available everywhere and at any given time. Deciding to start using a new app often led to adopting a new habit. Many of these decisions made sense, either for convenience or to alleviate boredom. But we made each decision separately. We never contemplated the whole picture, nor did we reflectively endorse this way of life. Sometime, around 2009, we voluntarily stepped into the tepid water and under the illusion of control we adopted a very different way of being. We endorsed a choice many of us would have rejected had we reflectively evaluated it.[19]

We often become frogs in the water through small gradual changes. I did not decide in 2009 to prioritize screen time over live relationships. I did it gradually, and at least initially, through a series of specific decisions. But over time, I ended up spending an alarming part of my waking hours online. Technology makes us especially vulnerable to finding ourselves in unanticipated places. Once we get used to technology it often becomes invisible. It may be a refrigerator, a toaster oven, or a smartphone. We just stop paying attention to the device. We also usually do not see how they operate. This is particularly true for digital technologies, where much more is hidden than is seen. We are more likely to miss digital manipulation than other technological influences.[20]

The Value of Making Choices

Why do we care about autonomy? Why throughout history have so many thinkers written books about autonomy? They did so because they considered autonomy crucial for human flourishing regardless of the specific political or economic system. To this day, many believe that autonomous people will make better decisions for themselves because they know themselves best and consider their own interests. Not only that, the hallmarks of our society – democracy and free market – rely on a collection of autonomous individuals. Markets are efficient because we are rational. Democracy works because people think for themselves and do not abide by the whims of an autocratic leader.

So would people choose differently if they had the opportunity to reflect and consider the detrimental impact of excessive screen time on their personal life? Would they try to minimize online interaction? Was our role as autonomous citizens in a democracy diminished when social networks used hate and incitement to prolong our time online? In Chapter 2, I examine the evidence that can help answer these riddles. But for now, I look at what we are losing by giving up the ability to be the choosers, regardless of the choices we end up making. To say it another way, even if maximizing time online would benefit our psychological well-being and democratic participation, would it still matter that we do not decide how much time we spend online?

Philosophers addressed this question early on. Aristotle wrote that the ability to choose is an important way in which humans are different from animals.[21] Animals act voluntarily, but they do not choose. As a teenager, I used to feed my dog under the table. My dog would snatch the piece of chicken I handed it as soon as it could. I wanted the chicken just as much as my dog (my mother is a great cook), but decided to eat part of it and give up some to try and lose weight. My dog's actions were voluntary, while mine involved choice.

Humans are different because they can shape their own lives. Making our plans and shaping our lives according to the plans, regardless of the specific choices we make, gives meaning to our lives.[22] The philosopher T. M. Scanlon wrote:

I want to choose the furniture for my own apartment, pick out the pictures for the walls, and even write my own lectures despite the fact that these things might be done better by a decorator, art expert, or talented graduate student. For better or worse, I want these things to be produced by and reflect my own taste, imagination, and powers of discrimination and analysis. I feel the same way, even more strongly, about important decisions affecting my life in larger terms: what career to follow, where to work, how to live.[23]

Others emphasized the psychological benefits of personal growth and daily charging of emotional resources that come from the very act of choosing and striving to implement the choice.[24] Viktor Frankel, a psychiatrist and Holocaust survivor, explained how autonomy fosters personal growth. He stated: "... between stimulus and response there is a space. In that space lies our freedom and our power to choose our response. In our response lies our growth and our happiness."[25] Frankel points out that by taking a pause and contemplating a situation, we can avoid making automatic decisions. We can instead make decisions that expand our psychological growth. By pausing we can refrain from making choices that are thoughtlessly triggered by external pressures (like a knee-jerk reaction to a mother-in-law's repeated nagging) or an internal one (a hounding memory of a past failure). By taking this pause we can make decisions that reflect ideas that we personally endorse.

We all struggle with choices we make, large and small. Even when we do take a pause and make a reflective decision about our preferences, we often have a hard time sticking by it. During the Coronavirus lockdown phase, I was cooped up in my Manhattan apartment. I made a plan that every afternoon, after I finished working on this book, I would complete a vigorous yoga set. It did not always work out. Too often, I just could not bring myself to do the yoga. By dinner time I realized I had instead wasted many hours aimlessly reading the news and scrolling through Facebook and Instagram. But on other days, I did follow through and completed my yoga set. On these days I felt better – not just because I exercised, but because I followed through on my decision. I had the satisfaction of fulfilling my original goal for the day, even though it was a struggle. Acting with intentionality gave me a sense of fulfillment and recharged my emotional resources, despite the dreariness of life during the pandemic.[26]

Studies also show that autonomous decision-making is important independent of the quality of the decisions that are made. Many people actually care about making their own decision even if they are not the most qualified people to make that decision. The importance of being the decision-maker increases when the stakes of the decision are high.[27] Some life decisions carry much more weight than others. For example, some years ago I taught a law student called Alice. Alice decided at the age of 40 to leave her career as a nurse and attend law school full-time. She gave up a solid career with a steady income and took student loans to pursue her dream of becoming a lawyer. For Alice, it was especially important that she independently considered all her options and costs and still decided to make this leap.

Being the authors of our life stories is precious. Regardless of how well we do it. This means that manipulating someone's decision-making process is harmful because it disrupts this important process. Tech companies designing products to maximize our time online are committing a wrong. It is a wrong even if eventually it turned out that spending extensive time online is beneficial for us. Hijacking our time is inexcusable because these companies are manipulating our decision-making powers. By taking advantage of our cognitive vulnerabilities, they are robbing us of our ability to pause and reflect. Instead, they intentionally expose us to stimulus designed to generate a predictable response. For example, getting likes on a Facebook post, which trigger us to react automatically by wanting more and waiting for the next like. Tech companies' actions to erode our autonomy are especially troubling because the stakes are high. We may be making small acts each time we install an app. But altogether through our online activity we are making a high-stake choice about how we spend huge increments of our time.

The Wound Is Where the Light Enters

The Sufi poet Rumi wrote: "The wound is the place where the light enters you."[28]

Bad things happen to all of us. But sometimes they also serve the purpose of waking us up. We tend to be habitual creatures. We do not like change. These disruptive events, as painful as they may be, can force us to make changes we would not voluntarily make. They can make us see things differently and move on.

Some years ago, I read a book called *Accidents of Marriage*. The story stuck with me. Maddy, the main character, lives with her children and verbally abusive husband. At home she walks on eggshells fearing that she will cause his next outburst. Although she works as a social worker helping abused women, she fails to see how their stories reflect her own. But then a seemingly catastrophic event happens. Her husband's reckless driving causes a car accident. Maddy is injured and wakes up without any memory of her past life. Slowly she pieces her life back together. She finds her bathroom closet full of the sedatives she used to take to cope. She wonders why anyone would do this. As she regains her memory, she finally sees her old self and decides anew what life she will tolerate.[29]

Not only individuals but also societies resist change. Jews remained scattered in the diaspora for 2,000 years until World War II and the Holocaust instigated the creation of the State of Israel. Some compare the Coronavirus pandemic to World War II. Like World War II, the Coronavirus pandemic destroyed lives and economies. We all wish it did not happen. Many blame governments for not preparing for this devastation. But regardless, it happened. We cannot choose the bad events or circumstances that come upon us, but we can change our attitude to them. We can acknowledge that sometimes catastrophic events can bestow sudden clarity.

In 2020, the Coronavirus pandemic accelerated our path into a technology-dominated future. We started using technology much more and in new ways. Live classes became online classes, work and social meetings became video conferencing. Cooped at home, with little to do, some adopted new technological pursuits, like playing online games or participating in e-sports. Others increased the time they spent on their favorite online pastimes. Teens and young adults, for example, spent significantly more time on YouTube and TikTok each day.[30] Reports indicated that kids' average time online doubled from three to six hours, with 26 percent of kids spending eight hours online compared to 4 percent previously.[31]

These trends could be here to stay. We are likely to continue operating remotely much more than before the pandemic. Consumption of online videos and entertainment activities boomed during the pandemic and users expected to maintain their viewing habits. Businesses also planned on keeping many employees working remotely from home to save on commercial rental space. The unique surge in the value of Big Tech companies' stocks during the pandemic reflected their revenues' increase and investors' predictions of future growth.[32]

Even early on in the pandemic when technology showed up as the savior, only about one in four Americans thought remote communication was as effective as in-person contact.[33] When technology completely took over, we starkly felt what we took for granted. The importance of face-to-face physical interactions. A sense of drainage began dominating. It soon got a name: "Zoom fatigue." Experts explained that our brain naturally decodes non-verbal cues, like eye contact or body language. Our ability to do this online is limited. So, we need to intensely focus on the words that are spoken. When we use multiple screens, the task becomes even more exhausting.[34]

By the time the pandemic erupted, online teaching had expanded in higher education for over a decade. Although some parts of academia resisted the trend, economic pressures, working adults' schedules, and the desire to spread education to less privileged groups prevailed.[35] During the pandemic, like every aspect of online life, online classes exploded. Online teaching became the norm for all university students, as well as school kids. Although some applauded the options, critical reactions soon followed. Educators described online teaching as diminishing what they do. It "transforms creative expression into dull repetitive drudgery." How can you share a joke if you can't hear anyone laughing? How can you know if your students understand when their videos are more often than not turned off? What about the loss of impromptu discussions between professor and students after class?[36]

Students also revolted against the impoverished nature of online teaching. Incoming college students deferred instead of beginning their college careers online. The editors of the Harvard students' newspaper *The Harvard Crimson* wrote that education "… simply cannot be replaced by classes over Zoom. Without the physical gathering of students and professors, much is lost. Virtual technologies, no matter how smooth and high-resolution, cannot replace dining hall conversations, the exchanges on the way in and out of classrooms, and the richness of body language. What remains, when you take these out, is a subpar educational, not to mention social, experience."[37]

The pandemic changed the technology overuse problem. On the one hand, it made it much more severe. It placed it on a trajectory that may not recede in the future. On the other hand, it suddenly highlighted the overall limitations of online communications. Like lightning that strikes in the middle of the night setting the skies alight, giving us a moment of clear vision. We may have a chance to reroute from what we thought was an inevitable path. An opportunity to make new choices. Looking back at the frog in the water fable, for the first time in years some of us felt the water boiling. This means that although we are worse off than before, more of us are on the alert. These are people who may want to jump out of the water and help others make the leap.

We spent over a decade obsessing over our screens at the expense of our real relationships. Instead of making ourselves the prisoners of our past technology choices, we can look at where we are and use these extreme circumstances to find freedom. Making a choice does not mean going back in time to a screenless and unconnected world. It means we can find a better balance between our online and offline lives. But we can do so only by finally making an autonomous reflective choice about what it is and how we want to get there.[38]

2 ADDICTION, OUR CHILDREN, OUR BONDS

From Addiction to Overuse

I met Seth, a 23-year-old man, at a meditation retreat in Connecticut. Seth called himself "a recovering tech-addict." It started in high school, he told me, when he spent a lot of time playing online games. But it was in college when things got out of control. For nearly three years, he said he was "a slave to information from the Internet." He spent eight hours a day on Reddit. Reddit users can submit news items and vote them up or down. When enough users give a submission up-votes, the item will make it to the site's front page. Sam told me it was a vicious cycle. He felt isolated in college and used Reddit to fill his time. But then the more he used Reddit, the more isolated he became. He could not stay off Reddit and barely studied. Eventually, the college placed him on academic probation, and he knew then that he had to quit. In our conversation, he used AA lingo. "I have been two years clean," he said. Seth explained that he now religiously limits the time and type of his online activities, but he is always worried about relapsing.

There are others like Seth, who cross the line from overusing technology to addiction. They are often online gamers, though sometimes tech addicts are hooked to other sites. They spend so much time online that they are unable to maintain their relationships, academic work, jobs, or even their basic needs. Extreme cases end in violence. Daniel Petric, an Ohio teen who is now serving 23 years in jail for killing his mom, was one of these.

Daniel got hooked on a violent video game called Halo, in which players shoot alien monsters who try to take over the Earth. He started out playing eight hours a day, but eventually got up to eighteen hours a day. Daniel's father, a priest, decided to intervene and confiscated the game, placing it in a safe that also contained a handgun. But Daniel found the key, walked behind his parents who were sitting on the couch, and said: "Would you guys close your eyes? I have a surprise for you." He shot both his parents, then fled the home, taking only one thing with him: the confiscated Halo game. Daniel's lawyers raised an insanity defense, claiming that video game addiction was the underlying psychiatric condition. Although the judge sentenced Daniel to twenty-three years in jail, he stated when he announced the verdict: "I firmly believe that Daniel Petric had no idea at the time he hatched this plot that if he killed his parents, they would be dead forever." Basically, Daniel had been so addicted, he was living the game.[1]

While stories like Daniel Petric's are thankfully rare, examples of extremely angry outbursts from kids, violently grabbing or even hitting their parents when they take away an iPad or a phone, are unfortunately quite common. The first question we will look at is: when does technology overuse become an addiction?

Addiction used to mean addiction to substances: to drugs, to alcohol, to tobacco. But this has changed in 2013, when the American Psychiatric Association released its latest edition of the manual of mental disorders – the DSM-5 – and included behavioral addictions. The DSM-5 categorized a behavior – gambling – as a non-substance addiction. It also recommended further research on another potential non-substance addiction – Internet Gaming Disorder (IGD).[2] In 2018, the World Health Organization (WHO) went a step further and included "Gaming Disorder" in its classification of diseases.[3]

Not every player who plays video games for long hours is diagnosed with Gaming Disorder under the WHO or DSM-5 criteria. To qualify under the WHO definition of Gaming Disorder, a player needs to act in a way that manifests an impaired control over gaming. This means that playing the game becomes more important to them than other activities in their lives, such as school, work, or relationships with family and friends. They keep going, even when bad consequences occur, like getting bad grades in school or regularly arriving late at work because they spent all night playing. In addition, players who qualify have more than a few small issues in different areas of life. They demonstrate a significant impairment in an important area of life, like work, school, or family. For example, a young man unable to maintain a regular job. Finally, length of time matters as well. This is not about a short-term infatuation with a game. To qualify, a player needs to manifest these patterns for at least twelve months.[4]

Addiction to online gaming is tragic. Lives of gaming addicts get confined to just the game and little else. But psychology studies found that gaming addiction is not just about depleted lives. Gaming addiction is associated with increased risks of depression, shyness, anxiety, poorer impulse control, and ADHD symptoms. Also, males are significantly more likely to be diagnosed with gaming addiction.[5] However, studies also point to a reciprocal connection: those who tend to be lonely, impulsive, or have attention problems are more likely to get addicted to gaming, which then makes these problems worse.[6]

Brain scan studies reflected some of these findings. Scans of individuals diagnosed with Gaming Disorder indicated changes in the regions of their brains that are associated with addiction, rewards, and emotional processing, when compared to scans of a control group.[7] Not only that, but the scans of those with Gaming Disorder also resembled the scans of those diagnosed with gambling addiction.[8] Researchers found an impact of video games on the release of dopamine (the neurotransmitter associated with pleasure, attention, and reinforcement) which was also similar to the effect on dopamine release in brain scans of gambling addicts.[9]

While researchers agree that some people are addicted to gaming, there is disagreement about what percentage of people are afflicted by this condition. Estimates range between less than 1 percent to more than 9 percent.[10] And although most scholars agree that medical authorities should classify video gaming addiction as a mental health disorder, some are still skeptical.[11] Some researchers resist classifying gaming addiction as a mental health disorder, pointing to the benefits of video gaming, including improved working memory, attention, and visuospatial skills.[12]

Video gaming is clearly at the forefront of the addiction debate. But other forms of online addiction exist. Professor Kimberly Young pioneered the study of "Internet addiction." In 1996 she reported on "patient zero." Patient zero was not a "techy." She was a stay-at-home mom in her 40s. She had no prior psychiatric history, but within three months of going online, she was spending sixty hours per week in chat rooms (the social networks of the 1990s). When she was not in front of her computer, she felt depressed, anxious, and irritable. Over time, the patient stopped performing everyday chores like cooking, cleaning, and grocery shopping and no longer interacted with family and friends.[13]

Nearly two decades later, researchers identified "smartphone addiction," when people started reporting anxiety when parted from their phones. Reports of smartphone addiction varied, with the most frequent range being 10 to 20 percent of study participants qualifying as addicted to smartphones. Individuals reported withdrawal symptoms: "I feel restless and irritable when the smartphone is unavailable." Some reported lack of control: "I try to spend less time on smartphone, but the efforts were in vain," or "I find myself engaged on the mobile phone for longer periods of time than intended."[14]

It seems that problematic use of gaming, Internet, social media, and smartphones may co-occur and are not necessarily distinguished. Some view Internet addiction as the umbrella condition that encompasses all the others. While the percentage of people qualifying for addiction ranges widely among studies, it is not negligible. For example, studies measuring Internet addiction show that 4.4 to 20 percent of participants qualified.[15] Facebook's own internal data showed that "problematic use" affects 12.5 percent of Facebook users.[16] Although researchers mostly debate how many individuals are strictly clinically addicted, the data reveals a concerning picture regardless of the answer to this question.

Spending a day without my phone made me realize the role it played in my life. It happened a few years ago. I used to ride the PATH train from Manhattan to work in Newark, New Jersey. During the first part of the ride the train went underground, emerging above ground after it crossed the Hudson River into New Jersey. There was no wireless connection on the train, and I used the time to prepare my classes with no distraction. I vividly remember one day when I reached into my bag for my phone as the train went above ground only to realize I had left it at home. Going back home to Manhattan to retrieve my phone was not an option. I had to get to school and teach my class and stay there for a full day of meetings. I felt extremely anxious. How will anyone reach me? What if my kids' schools or caregivers text or call me and I won't even know? I could not check emails during meetings. I walked around that whole day feeling as though I was missing an arm. I eventually left work early to get home to my phone.

While most people would not qualify for the clinical definition of addiction, many of us manifest at least some of those symptoms. For example, studies of young participants and gaming found that about 5 percent had withdrawal symptoms – such as irritability, anxiety, or sadness – when a game was taken away; about 9 percent developed tolerance to the need to spend increased amount of time on a game; over 9 percent experienced loss of control defined as unsuccessful attempts to control participation in Internet games.[17] It appears that clinical addiction and technology overuse run on a spectrum and share many of the same symptoms. Determining the medical debate about addiction is an important step, but it is only an initial one.

The Changing Face of Childhood

Childhood and growing up have changed dramatically. Although technology has transformed people's lives throughout history, change usually affected different generations rather evenly. For example, the spread of computers, the genetic revolution, and the Internet itself affected both the old and the young. But the upheaval that began around 2009 did not. True, we could all take our screens with us, connect everywhere, and interact virtually. Still these changes most profoundly transformed the everyday lives of children and teens.

The numbers tell it all. Setting aside usage data since the pandemic when screen time skyrocketed for all, surveys taken before the pandemic underscore a disturbing picture. A major national survey in 2018 found that 45 percent of teens said they used the Internet "almost constantly."[18] A 2019 national survey reported that kids aged 8 to 12 spent, on average, five hours on screens per day, while teens spent on average seven and a half hours. These hours did not include time spent on schoolwork.[19] Teens today spend a third of the time partying that their counterparts spent in the 1980s. And the number of teens who get together with their friends has been cut in half from 2000 to 2015. The most significant decline occurred from 2010, when time spent with friends in person has been replaced with time spent socially online.[20]

For me, the change really sunk in during a birthday party I attended in 2016. The guests were mostly adults, but among us were also several 10-year-old kids. The kids' parents were friends, and the kids had grown up regularly playing together in the small garden attached to the host's ground floor Manhattan apartment. That day I noticed for the first time that something was different. The kids remained inside. They sat in a row in front of the television. Each was also holding a phone that consumed most of their attention. Sometimes they raised their heads to look up, but it was not at each other. They glanced instead at the television screen. Eventually the birthday cake came out and the kids got up and started running around, jostling for the first cake slices. I recall sensing relief that things felt a bit "normal" again.

Still, I know that "normal" is a tough word to define. Who should get to decide what is normal? Shouldn't each generation get to say what is its "normal"? An older wise colleague, after hearing me present my initial ideas for this book, stopped by my office to speak to me. He said: "I really liked your project, but then I was thinking to myself when people read huge newspapers on the train on their way to work, weren't they also secluding themselves from other people, just like you say we do with our screens?" And what about television? I wondered as he spoke. For years we heard how television watching makes kids inactive and obese; how it wastes their time; and much more. But I try to convince my kids to watch television instead of spending time on their individual screens. Have we now "normalized" television and, instead, criticize the "newcomer" technology our kids grew up with?

Indeed, many adolescents see online communications as the "normal" way to form and maintain friendships. In 2018, only 32 percent of teenagers said that they preferred to communicate with their friends in person. Kids explain that social media helps them interact with others who share similar interests; that writing, editing, and using images helps them cast away shyness and put forward their authentic selves; it helps them keep in touch with family and friends who live far away; they can share experiences and jokes as a group; they find comfort through friends' comments after stressful events; and some adolescents with autism experience better interpersonal communications online.[21]

What Happened?

A growing body of scientific findings transformed the debate from a discussion about generational differences into a science war. Researchers identified associations between increased screen time and detrimental effects on kids, primarily cognitive and developmental delays; a rise in depression, anxiety, and suicide rates; increased impulsivity; attention difficulties; addiction; obesity; and lack of sleep.[22] These findings surpassed by far concerns about the impact of television watching on children in previous decades.

Screen Time and Cognitive Development

The idea of teaching young kids through screens is not new. When my oldest son was born in 2002, Baby Einstein videos were a hit and a "must do" among well-intentioned parents. I recall the subtitle "Great Minds Start Little" as I sat my toddler in front of "Baby Mozart," excited to expose him to an array of patterns accompanied by Mozart's classical music. I was a bit discouraged by his lack of interest as he walked away after a few minutes. But later, I discovered that not much was lost. Even if my son had stayed watching the videos, he would not have likely learned much about the animals, everyday items, and patterns portrayed.

Since the day my son turned his back on "Baby Einstein," nearly two decades ago, multiple studies have found that screens are not that helpful in teaching babies and toddlers. It turned out that children up to the age of 3 learn much better from a person interacting with them face to face than from screen activities. And this is regardless of how entertaining the screens are. But screens did not just fail to teach. When screen time replaced caregiver interaction, children missed out on face-to-face communications that could help them learn. Why don't small children learn from screens? Researchers discovered that until the age of 3, children did not see videos as relevant to real life. They had difficulty learning different tasks, whether finding an object or learning a word, when watching them on a video. Still, they could learn the very same task when a person in the room with them taught it.[23]

Despite these findings, numerous companies continued to develop learning games for babies and toddlers. Companies and the media reassured parents that while keeping their small children occupied, they also advanced their education. One *Wired* magazine article listing games wrote: "Here are some games that are sometimes called 'edutaining.' Think of them as fun games that also teach something, but in a way your kids probably won't notice."[24] Still, in recent years, new studies examining screens and learning highlighted an even more concerning problem. Not only are younger kids not learning from screens, but worse, there is an association between excessive screen time and impaired cognitive development for both children and teens. The important question then became: what is the chicken, and what is the egg? In other words, does spending more time on screens hinder children's cognitive development, or are parents of kids with developmental delays and behavioral problems more likely to use screens to calm their children?

Sheri Madigan, a professor of psychology at the University of Calgary, conducted a study to answer that very question. She examined 2,441 children over time to determine what occurs first: screen time or cognitive impairment. Madigan and her team found that more time per week spent on screens at 2 years of age, 3 years of age, and 5 years of age was linked with impaired behavioral, cognitive, and social development. The study did not find support for the opposite conclusion: that poor development leads to more screen time. Madigan had answered the chicken and egg question. Excessive screen time leads to developmental issues, but developmental issues do not make parents more likely to increase screen time exposure.[25] But why then did excessive screen time cause developmental delays? We already knew that kids aged 3 and under do not learn well from screens. But it turned out that even older children suffered delays because they remained sedentary. Children sitting down, hooked to screens for hours, did not spend that time practicing walking and running. These children also missed out on opportunities to talk with their caregivers or interact non-verbally, whether through smiles, body language, or eye contact.[26] More and more, it seems that screen time affects kids, at least in part, through what does not happen during these critical developmental years.

Traditional psychology studies had already pointed to a strong connection between excessive screen time and impaired cognitive development, when a new breed of studies entered the arena. Neuroscientists conducting brain imaging studies examined the impact of screen time on kids' developing brain structure. As discussed in Chapter 10, they examined the organization and myelination of white matter tracts, which influence nerve cells' ability to transmit information faster and affect cognitive functioning. The researchers compared scans of areas in the brain related to learning in children exposed to high screen time with those of children who were not. The researchers found stark differences in white matter organization, which linked to performance on cognitive assessments.[27] The brain imaging studies signaled a new stage in the urgent push to limit kids' screen time.

Social Media and Mental Health

Unsurprisingly, the debate over the impact of screens on mental health stands out as the most heated one. Big Tech frequently portrays itself as promoting humanity's well-being. Meta (which owns Facebook and Instagram) prides itself on connecting the world and improving lives.[28] Findings that the opposite is true threaten the very core of these businesses.

Does screen time impact kids' mental health? Some details are becoming clearer. Not all screen time is made alike.[29] A kid reading a book on Kindle or watching news on Vox is not having the same experience as a kid scrolling on Instagram. It is hard to define screen time because it can include so many different activities. But researchers parsing the evidence have uncovered a particularly strong association between time spent on social media and mental health; including anxiety, depression, self-harm, and risk of suicide.[30] By honing in on the data, the findings got even more specific. Gender matters; girls face significantly increased risks to their mental health when using social networks.[31] It also turns out that the amount of time spent online matters. There is little evidence of harm to light social media users, but significant evidence of harm to heavy users.[32]

When asked what about social media makes them feel bad, adolescents pointed to several experiences: feeling excluded when seeing friends getting together without them; suffering rejection and feeling unliked when they don't get feedback on their posts; sensing an atmosphere of negativity, criticism, and hostility; being bullied; experiencing passive forms of relationships; and feeling disconnected.[33]

Once again, we encounter the chicken and the egg question. Does social media cause harm, or are kids who are anxious, depressed, and in need of validation more likely to use social networks? Growing evidence points to social networks as the culprit. Data shows that since 2012 there have been significant increases in the rates of girls' anxiety, depression, self-harm, and suicide. This timing coincides with the widespread adoption of social networks and smartphones.[34] Still, this data by itself does not show that social media caused harmful mental effects.

The perfect experiment to examine this would be to compare two groups of adolescents that are similar, except one does not use social media. In today's world, creating this long-term natural experiment is unlikely. However, researchers conducted similar short-term experiments.[35] In one experiment, researchers randomly assigned college students in the University of Pennsylvania to either limit Facebook, Instagram, and Snapchat use to ten minutes, per platform, per day, or to use social media as usual for three weeks. They found that the limited-use groups showed significant reduction in loneliness and depression over three weeks, as compared to the control group.[36] These experiments, supplemented by inside information leaking from the social networks themselves, strengthen the conclusion that social media contributes to the deterioration in girls' mental health.[37]

Internet Gaming

Nicholas Kardaras wrote in *Glow Kids*: "Video games for the alienated kid and social media for the cheerleader are both just as addicting as heroin is to a junkie."[38] Stories are all too familiar of kids, especially boys, playing video games in a way that becomes disruptive to their own lives as well as those of their families. A kid won't stop playing the game. He stays up late at night. He does not do homework.

He stops hanging out with friends. He is angry when interrupted. His parents remove the game by taking an iPad or blocking access. Kid goes into an intense rage episode. And the cycle repeats itself.[39]

Most kids who play games will not qualify for a Gaming Disorder diagnosis. But they may certainly exhibit some of its characteristics and the confounding problems of depression, shyness, anxiety, poor impulse control, and ADHD symptoms. While studies have shown that video games can have some positive effects on cognition, the important question that Nicholas Kardaras posed is "At what cost?"[40]

Kids play a lot of video games. A 2018 survey found that 90 percent of teens said they play video games. When contrasting gender: 97 percent of teen boys play compared with 83 percent of girls.[41] The impact of video games on kids is particularly significant for two reasons. First, as indicated, most kids play video games. Second, they are more likely to form problematic game tendencies than adults. Research has shown that younger age, male gender, and belonging to certain cultures increase the risk of problematic gaming use.[42]

The Science Wars

Evidence of harm is accumulating. Warning signs of a significant public health crisis for children are intensifying. But the science wars are still on. Parties on each side cast doubt on the other's research methodology.[43] When the WHO added "Gaming Disorder" to its lists of mental health conditions, the video game industry launched a full-blown attack. It claimed the WHO is "scapegoating" games and "jumping to premature conclusions" with "very little scholarly evidence," with the goal to "broadly seek to stigmatize" "billions of players worldwide."[44]

Science wars have happened before and have a predictable cycle. They usually erupt when scientific evidence suggests that corporate actions cause harm. Findings threaten corporate revenues, inflaming the scientific debate. Suggestions of technology overuse invoke fierce science wars, mostly because the monetary stakes are high. The findings threaten a business model, which has flourished for over two decades. As will be discussed in Chapter 3, the tech industry relies on our time as a resource to garner its revenues from advertising. It needs to keep us online for as long as possible.

Another reason for the raging science wars is that the problem is complicated. First, screens are everywhere. Take a school day in the life of my middle-school son before the pandemic. He used Google Maps and a subway app on his phone to get to school and to his after-school activities. He also texted before and after the school day to coordinate plans. At school he used a school computer for certain assignments. Additionally, he watched instructive videos on the teacher's smartboard. At home, my son used his laptop to go on Google Classroom for homework assignments. For entertainment, he alternated playing an online game with friends on his phone, watching Harry Potter movies on the television, and viewing YouTube videos on his computer. My son was not a heavy screen user. Still, many screens and different screen activities dominated his everyday life. This highlights the complexity of research on the impact of screens. Measuring screen time is hard, and screen time encompasses different content. But not all content is created equal.

Other factors further complicate the problem. Many of today's kids are raised by parents exercising intensive parenting. Parents monitor and guide their kids' every move. Studies show that the stifling effects of this parenting style decrease kids' autonomy and creativity and contribute to the development of mental health issues as the children leave home.[45] We also need to figure out whether the intermittent dopamine releases used to keep us hooked are directly producing these effects or are they caused by missing out on real-life benefits while we are online, including sleep, physical exercise, and face-to-face interaction?[46]

Government and professional organizations can end science wars. So can evidence leaking from the corporations at the center of the controversy. Whistleblowers contribute significantly toward ending science wars. For instance, Frances Haugen exposed information from Meta, including its leadership knowledge of how Instagram's algorithms harmed girls' mental health.[47] The WHO's classification of Gaming Disorder as a mental health disorder was another important step. But this addressed only a small part of the problem; it did not address the general problem of overuse. The WHO and the American Pediatrics Association (APA) then took additional action. In 2019, they issued guidelines recommending limiting screen time for children, based on their age. Still, the screen time guidelines mostly focused on children under the age of 5.[48]

Organizations evaluating scientific data face a recurring problem that requires a careful balancing of interests. Making a hasty decision could be overcautious and unnecessarily halt technological innovation. This risk is especially acute when the technologies involved carry many advantages. But waiting instead can create an irreversible situation. Creating change is more difficult as time goes by, once norms become entrenched.[49] Parents accustomed to giving small kids iPads to entertain themselves when they are busy or on long trips may resist change, as would their kids. Still, the impact on kids' development adds an additional concern. The window of opportunity to intervene may be narrower, especially for a generation of kids exposed to years of high screen time.

Disconnection

In 2000, I did not yet use email at work. I only used it sporadically to correspond with out-of-town friends. That year, while on vacation, I read a newly released book called *The Diagnosis* by Alan Lightman. The book described a man whose bodily and mental functioning deteriorated with the advent of the information age. But that was not what struck me about the book and stayed with me for all these years. Instead, it was a sideline story about a mother and a son that caught my attention. The two were together at home, in different rooms, emailing each other instead of talking. The son typed: "what's for dinner? And when's dad coming home?" and the mom answered: "Hi sweetie. I put a pizza in the microwave for you ... I'll be down in a few minutes."[50]

At the time, I was just starting to think about the theme that would later define my academic career – the way technology changes our everyday lives. But I recall feeling appalled by this estrangement between mother and son, finding it hard to comprehend how two people in physical proximity to each other would communicate by writing instead of speaking to each other.

As I write this two decades later, we regularly communicate by emails and messages, even with those near us. I now work at a law school, and for years, etiquette has dictated that we refrain from showing up unannounced – without a good reason – in a colleague's office to avoid disrupting their workday. Instead, we email. And we email a lot.

Sometimes, an email exchange string would consist of dozens of emails, taking up a significant amount of time to resolve issues that could have quickly been solved with a short conversation.[51]

These changes have taken place everywhere. Communicating via text and email with those right by us is not confined to our office walls. As Lightman foresaw in his 2000 book, digital communication has infiltrated our homes. According to a 2017 survey, 45 percent of respondents with children reported texting each other at home instead of speaking.[52]

Many remember November 8, 2016. On that evening, Donald Trump emerged as the unexpected victor in the presidential election. Regardless of political affiliations, few can forget the unexpected turn of events in which President Trump defeated Hillary Clinton – the candidate many believed to be the inevitable winner. That evening will remain forever engraved in my mind, but not just for political reasons. It was on that evening – a time in which we could have been brought closer together by the force of the political events we were witnessing – we were, instead, pulled apart by our screens.

I remember a group of people sitting in front of the television in the living room. None was talking. They glanced occasionally at the television, but were mostly scrolling on their phones, searching for other sources of information, perhaps connecting with others who were elsewhere. Amid this upheaval, there was very little communication among those physically present. Feelings were not expressed in words; instead, eyes were glued to individual screens.

The television has been called the "modern bonfire." Families and friends congregate around it in the same way humans used to historically gather around the bonfire. On Trump's victorious election night, as each person focused on his own screen instead of the "communal bonfire," the silence was reverberating in my ears. As I looked at the multitude of small screens around the room, Sherry Turkle's words "Alone Together" never rang truer.[53]

Even when we are outside our homes or our offices, we just do not see one another. We are somewhere else, buried in our phones. We often forget to look at the waiter who serves us in a café, our eyes glued to our laptop. We sometimes keep our earbuds plugged in as we check out in a store, even asking the salesperson to repeat her words because we could not hear her over the media stream. Brene Brown, in her book, *Daring Greatly: How the Courage to Be Vulnerable Transforms the Way We Live, Love, Parent and Lead*, describes how the attention we invest in our phones transforms our ability to connect with those who serve us. Her words are poignantly clear and deeply disturbing: "When we treat people as objects, we dehumanize them. We do something really terrible to their souls and to our own ... I am not suggesting that we engage in a deep, meaningful relationship with the man who works at the drive-through, but I am suggesting that we stop dehumanizing people and start looking them in the eye when we speak to them."[54]

We do not talk to those who serve us because we are immersed in our devices. Neither do we pay attention to those around us because we can no longer tolerate a moment of doing nothing and aimlessly looking around. Standing in line, we have the immediate impulse to do something and take out our phones. And, even if we battle the instinct, refrain from pulling out our phones, and observe the people next to us, instead of encountering someone's eye contact or a smile, we often see dozens of heads looking down at their phones. Many opportunities for chance encounters or moments of connection are lost.

Hurt, Hate, and Division

"On the Internet no one knows you are dog." This is a famous quote from the early days of the Internet. On the Internet you are anonymous and could be who you want and say what you please. You can also lash out your emotions without repercussions. These were popular sentiments at the beginning of the twenty-first century. And some still live on. But today's reality is that angry emails, hateful texts, and insulting comments for all to see on social networks are aimed at people we know. We can act on our emotions on the spur of the moment, and once we do the words are there to stay. They can no longer be erased by the passage of time or imperfect human memories.[55]

Hurtful messages are abundant, and their impact too often lingers on. Consider a guy standing with some friends in the school hall telling a teenage girl: "You know, you could lose some weight." Unkindness verging on cruelty has always been a part of growing up. But social networks facilitate and increase the frequency of these incidents. Imagine, the very same comment posted under the girl's Instagram photo. It is much easier to write hurtful words on a screen than to speak them out loud while looking at the receiver's face; and when hundreds or thousands of Instagram followers are witnesses to the exchange, at times even joining it, the insult and pain are many times amplified. Kids and adults alike do not see the faces of those reading their text messages. They don't see the impact of their words: the pain, the anger, or tears that may be caused. Empathy is based on perceiving how others feel. Texts and screens make it much harder.

The Internet and particularly social media paved the way from hurtful personal messages and online harassment to group hate and social division. Social networks' goal is to increase users' engagement on their platforms. On Facebook, this is measured through a metric composed of time spent, likes, reactions, shares, and comments. It has turned out, however, that by doing this, social networks like Facebook and Twitter provide people with echo chambers of their own beliefs that increase polarization.[56]

How did this happen? On Facebook we see on our newsfeeds whatever Facebook wants us to see. It wants us to read what will keep us there and engaged for longer. To do so, Facebook assigns points to each post, and the more points a post accrues, the more likely it is to feature on people's newsfeeds. It uses algorithms, which are machine-learning models that keep evolving based on the conclusions they draw. The algorithm learned that anger makes us more engaged, so a post that gets an angry reaction gets five points, while a post that gets a like gets one point. If angry reactions get more points than likes, infuriating posts are more likely to feature on our newsfeeds. It turned out then that the algorithm that maximizes engagement also promotes controversy and extremism. Algorithms can have tragic results. For example, Facebook's algorithms amplified hate speech in Myanmar, which escalated the country's religious conflict into genocide.[57]

Leaked internal reports reveal that Facebook learned in 2016 that its algorithmic recommendation tools like "Groups You Should Join" resulted in 64 percent of extreme group joins. In 2018, an internal Facebook presentation put it bluntly: "Our algorithm exploits the human brain's attraction to divisiveness ... If left unchecked [it would feed users] more and more divisive content to gain user attention & increase time on the platform." And, while Facebook initially sponsored attempts to solve the problem, its leadership diluted the solutions, and eventually resisted the effort altogether because of its negative impact on user engagement. Mark Zuckerberg specifically asked "not to bring something like that to him again" and the leadership notified employees that priorities are "shifting away from societal good to individual value."[58]

Would We Have Chosen This?

Autonomy is important for its own sake. Making our plans and shaping our lives according to those plans, regardless of the specific choices we make, gives meaning to our lives. But autonomy is also vital as a means for achieving a goal. By reflecting on our own choices, we are more likely to select outcomes that advance our interests. The question is then, knowing all we know now, would we have chosen this?

Knowing many of us would become over-users, exhibiting some symptoms that resemble addiction, and some would even become clinically addicted. Knowing that our children would face a public health crisis. And that for all of us, life would change. The ways we relate to one another every day would be different. Hate and social division would escalate. We need to consider now: had we known all of this when it began, around 2009, and had we been given the opportunity to choose a future that would reflect our long-term goals, values, and preferences, would we have chosen this?[59]

3 INVISIBLE CHAINS

Is He an Addict?

Melissa came to speak to me after a lecture I gave to parents at her son's school. Her son Neil was a fifth grader. She told me that Neil was a good student and had friends in school, but he plays Fortnite for many hours a day. At first, Melissa told him to stop playing, but he kept begging for more time. When she insisted, he yelled and got extremely upset. Melissa then installed an app to limit Neil's computer time. After a while Melissa noticed that he was playing Fortnite well into the evening. It turned out that Neil had discovered the password and changed the settings. This happened multiple times. Sometimes Neil asked for extra computer time for homework, but Melissa found him playing Fortnite instead. Melissa told me she thought she was not so good with technology, and that she should have found a better app. She felt that maybe she could have prevented what happened next.

On Sunday night, she told me, the family drove back from the countryside. It was late, so the kids were already in their pajamas. When they started driving, they played on their parents' iPads. But as it was getting past their bedtimes, Melissa asked them to hand over the iPads and try to sleep. Neil refused. Melissa explained again that he should not be playing so late at night and asked again for the iPad. Neil didn't answer. Melissa kept insisting. Neil started crying and whining. Melissa's husband, exhausted from the long drive, asked Melissa:

"Can you do something about this? I can't drive like this." Melissa then turned back and snatched the iPad from Neil. Neil climbed over to the front seat to grab the iPad back. He knocked against his father's arm, which was holding the wheel. The car swayed off the road, nearly hitting a tree. Luckily the family was spared. "We nearly died because of this iPad!" Melissa told me. "I don't know what to do. What should I do? I think Neil is an addict. Do you think Neil is an addict?" Melissa blamed herself, and she blamed Neil. One thing she did not do was point a finger toward the outside actors crucially responsible for Neil's behavior.

Technology as Choice

Too often, we do not know who the true choice-makers are. Our society celebrates innovation, and we believe that technology brings progress.[1] We are also attracted to the idea that technology is neutral. Neutral means that our technologies are the way they are because this is the only feasible option. But our technologies are products of choices and preferences. The words of astronaut Buzz Aldrin are most revealing: "You promised me Mars Colonies, instead I got Facebook."[2] Why did we get fast minicomputers called smartphones, but our planes are flying at the same speed they did when I was born? And yes, what about these flights to Mars we planned in the 1970s?

In the early 2000s, I worked on my doctoral thesis in law and technology at New York University. It was at that early stage of my career that I realized that technology is anything but neutral. I wrote about the technology of artificial insemination in humans. Initially, I thought I was writing about a new reproductive technology. To my surprise, I found out it existed at least since the end of the eighteenth century. Artificial insemination is a very simple procedure. It is performed by injecting sperm into a woman via use of a syringe. Still, infertile couples rarely got to use it, or even know about it, until the second half of the twentieth century. Why? Patients, doctors, and – later – judges were uncomfortable with the idea of implanting the sperm of a donor in the uterus of a married woman. Judges even went as far as to declare that the wife was committing adultery and that the child born through artificial insemination was illegitimate. These intimidating legal decisions further delayed the adoption of artificial insemination.[3]

Creating children through artificial insemination was not technologically difficult, nor was the technology expensive. Yet, it was practically unavailable for many years because social preferences held it back. As I wrote then, the history of artificial insemination is "the story of an abandoned innovation, of a rejected dissertation, of imposed silence, of dark secrets and shame . . . Most of all, it is a tale of lost opportunities for the many infertile people who were sterilized by society."[4]

We tend to assume that we have a certain technology and not another because that is what is technologically feasible right now. But this is not necessarily the case. What technologies we have at our disposable is often a result of covert choices of corporate decision-makers seeking to maximize revenues. The design of our screens and online communications are a perfect example of this. Technology companies designed their products to sustain their business model.

Capturing Time

The Internet economy business model relies on capturing as much user time and attention as possible. Companies like Facebook and Google do not charge fees; instead they sell ads. They collect user data and use it to target ads of products and services they predict these users would most like to purchase. Their ad revenues increase when users spend more time online. More time online means collecting more user data and exposing users to more ads. Design choices prolonging user time online are vital for the Internet economy's business model, but they are business choices, not necessities.[5]

Recently, whistleblowers leaving big Silicon Valley companies exposed how the companies design their products specifically to maximize users' time online. Whistleblowers, like Tristan Harris who defected from Google and later spearheaded the successful documentary *The Social Dilemma*, revealed many of the strategies used by technology companies. Harris warned early on: "Never before in history have the decisions of a handful of designers (mostly men, white, living in SF, aged 25–35) working at 3 companies [Google, Apple, and Facebook] had so much impact on how millions of people around the world spend their attention."[6] Frances Haugen, a former Facebook employee, revealed that Facebook knows its algorithm maximizes user time online by exposing kids to harmful content and provoking hate online. "It chooses to prioritize its profits over people."[7]

Multiple sources have reported on how technology companies keep us hooked online by using techniques that manipulate our deepest human vulnerabilities. These include our biological craving for the release of the pleasure-enhancing neurotransmitter, dopamine; our desire to be liked and socially accepted (a desire felt especially strongly during middle school and high school); and our ways of perceiving and reacting to stimuli.

One popular strategy underlying many design features is based on the Intermittent Reward Model. When we get on an unpredictable schedule for food, social appreciation, money, or any reward we desire, our brains release more dopamine than when we receive rewards on a regular anticipated schedule. This is what makes the slot machine so addictive. We never know when we will win, and the coins will roll out. So, we keep pulling the handle, lured in by our brain's expectation of a dopamine infusion. The more we do it, the more we want it. Similarly, our favorite websites, apps, and devices are so successful in retaining our attention because they imitate unpredictable rewards offered by slot machines.[8]

Notifications are one form of intermittent reward. We pick up our phones repeatedly all day to see if we have received any notifications. The "pull to refresh" feature is another direct implementation of this method. We pull to refresh Twitter, Facebook, or Instagram to check what new likes we got or whether there is an interesting new post or photo. Sometimes we get them, and sometimes we don't. But, regardless, we keep pulling to refresh. On Tinder, we swipe time and again. Sometimes Tinder rewards us with a dating match. On games, sometimes we find surprise treasures that enhance our characters' abilities, but often we are disappointed and go on searching.[9]

Technology companies created these features to enhance our dopamine releases so we will extend our time online. Sean Parker, the founding president of Facebook, admitted the intentional design of features to trigger dopamine release. He said:

> The thought process that went into building these applications, Facebook being the first of them . . . was all about: "How do we

consume as much of your time and conscious attention as possible?" And that means that we need to sort of give you a little dopamine hit every once in a while, because someone liked or commented on a photo or a post or whatever. And that's going to get you to contribute more content, and that's going to get you ... more likes and comments ... The inventors, creators – it's me, it's Mark [Zuckerberg], it's Kevin Systrom on Instagram, it's all of these people – understood this consciously. And we did it anyway.[10]

Another set of design features targets our desire to be socially accepted and our fear of missing out (FOMO). Tweens and teens are particularly susceptible. Snapchat's use of streaks illustrates how technology companies manipulate these social vulnerabilities. A Snapchat user can create a Snapstreak by sending a streak back and forth with another user within twenty-four hours. Maintaining a Snapstreak depends on both parties not missing the deadline. An hourglass emoji delivers the message: "Your Snapstreak is about to end. Quickly send another snap to keep it alive." The Snapchat app lists the name of the person on the Snapstreak with the number of days it is maintained and special emojis for long streaks. Kids view accumulating many long streaks as a sign of popularity. Losing a streak because someone failed to send one within the allotted time is devastating. They go to great lengths to avoid losing their streaks.[11]

Abby Rogers, a 15-year-old from California, came to the rescue of a friend in need whose phone had been confiscated by her parents. The friend accessed a library computer and sent Abby her Snapchat username and password. Every day for two weeks, Abby logged into Snapchat and sent short picture messages back and forth between her friend's account and her own. The content of the pictures did not matter as long as it kept the daily streak alive. Maintaining streaks has become so important to Abby that she checks her Snapchat app on her phone roughly every fifteen minutes.[12]

A third type of design feature manipulates our perception of stimuli and reaction instincts. A common design eliminates stopping cues. Tech companies derived this design from the famous bottomless soup bowl experiment. In that experiment, researchers served one group of subjects a normal bowl of soup where the subject could accurately perceive the amount of soup they had eaten. They served another group of subjects a self-refilling bowl that prevented them from correctly perceiving how much they were eating. As a result, subjects who ate from the refillable bowl consumed 73 percent more soup, and they had no idea that they had eaten more. Members of the second group ate more because they lacked a stopping signal.[13]

Many of our favorite apps and websites resemble the refillable soup bowl. Consider the infinite scroll. When we scroll through news-feeds like Facebook or Twitter, there is no natural stopping point. The newsfeed never ends, so we keep going for much longer than we may have intended. Similarly, the autoplay function on YouTube and Netflix plays the next video or episode with no break or option to pause. The intentional absence of a stop signal is not the only design that manipulates our perceptions and reactions. Push notifications are another example. Device makers set them as the default option on our phones. We receive these pop-up notifications unless we change the settings. These notifications interrupt us to get more attention, reminding us to come back to an app.[14]

Self-Help

Together with whistleblower reports came a flurry of books and websites suggesting how to unplug, control our urges, and limit our time online. Once we knew the problem existed, wherever we turned the onus was on us to resolve it. Advice to parents flourished: "Limit your child's time online"; "Use time restricting apps and parental controls"; "Do not allow devices during family meals"; "Do not allow use of screens in your child's bedroom before bedtime"; "Discuss with your kid what online activities and screen times are most important to them"; and "Model, model, model. If you are constantly on your phone so your child will be when she gets one."

Writers targeted both adults who felt the impact on their own lives and parents who worried about their children. One leading author is Cal Newport, who advocates *Digital Minimalism*: the idea that less can be more.[15] Newport acknowledges that "compulsive use . . . is not the result of a character flaw but instead the realization of a massively profitable business plan."[16] He still puts the burden on the individual, though, to first detox from all technology for 30 days and then re-examine each app, device, and website anew to decide whether to keep it in her life.

Newport quotes one of the participants in the detox study as he undergoes the thirty days of technology detox. These words reveal the reverberations of self-blame and personal responsibility:

> The first few days were surprisingly hard. *My addictive habits were revealed in striking clarity.* Moments of waiting in line, moments between activities. Moments of boredom, moments I ached to check in on my favorite people, moments I wanted to escape, moments I wanted to "look something up," moments I just needed a diversion. I'd reach for my phone and then remember that everything is gone.[17]

Nir Eyal goes further in his book *Indistractable: How to Control Your Attention and Choose Your Life.* He argues that we turn online because we are always seeking distractions to escape our internal discomfort. Eyal is well versed in how tech companies created technologies to lure us in; he wrote the manual. In his best-selling 2014 book, *Hooked: How to Build Habit-Forming Products,* he advised companies how to design addictive products.[18] By now, Eyal recognizes that technology overuse is a problem. Still, he places responsibility on the user, writing: "Anything that stops discomfort is potentially addictive, but that doesn't make it irresistible. If you know the drivers of your behavior, you can take steps to manage them."[19]

Eyal breaks down his philosophy into specific advice. He instructs us to look for the discomfort that precedes the distraction and to focus on the integral trigger. Why are we turning to technology? He then suggests strategies on how to resist our urges. I like his tech-niques. We are both "Googlers." He describes how he sits to write and often has an urge to Google something. I share this urge. When I read something interesting for work, I am often overwhelmed by the desire to Google the author: to check out what else she has written, her life history, her career. I sometimes follow Eyal's advice to "surf the urge" by using the "10-minute rule." I promise myself that I can Google, but

I need to wait ten minutes. Ten minutes later I am often preoccupied with work again and the urge is gone.[20]

"Hacking back" our phones and devices is another component of Eyal's solution. He suggests technology itself to make it easier for us to resist temptation. For example, he proposes resisting Facebook's algorithm-driven, seductive newsfeed by using a technology called Todo-book. Todo-book replaces Facebook's Newsfeed with a user's to do list. Instead of scrolling the feed, the user now sees tasks that they planned to do that day, and only when they have finished them does the newsfeed unlock.[21] But, hacking back our phones – fighting one technology with another – in what could be an endless battle, seems futile. It reminds me of the "Anti-Eraser" of my childhood.

I grew up in Israel, watching black and white television. Color television was commonly available outside Israel, but the first Israeli prime ministers disfavored the idea of television generally. As a compromise, when Israel started broadcasting television programming, it rejected color programming. The government ordered the erasure of colors. I recall watching my favorite show "Little House on the Prairie" featuring Laura Ingalls running through black and white fields. Eventually a commercial solution arrived: consumers could buy an "anti-eraser" for their television. I was thrilled to see Laura appear on my screen in full color. Still, the fight was not completely won. More often than not, Laura appeared only in stripes of pink and green. Users tried to combat one technology with another. Eventually the Israeli government gave up and color broadcasting became the norm.[22]

While Todo-book is a neat idea, the question becomes "why take this circular route?" Why erase color only to restore it? Why invent technologies to combat the addictive features of other technologies? This brings us to the question of efficiency and outcomes. People have tried using different self-help methods for years, but no accounts have shown that screen time has gone down – among youth or adults – even before the pandemic began in early 2020.[23]

Beyond the question of efficiency lies the danger of unintended consequences. Authors alerting the public to the dangers of technology overuse also placed personal responsibility at the center of the stage. As Eyal wrote: "If we believe we're short on willpower and self-control, then we will be. If we decide we're powerless to resist temptation, then we will be."[24] Unfortunately, advice prescribing self-help to resolve technology overuse became a double-edged sword. It increased public awareness, but it also motivated technology companies to jump on the personal responsibility wagon. The technology industry did not invent this wheel. Large corporations regularly fend off public criticism by placing responsibility on the consumer. They then offer tools to facilitate individual self-discipline. These tools create the illusion of control, while rarely ameliorating the problem.

The food industry, criticized for the low nutritional value of its products, heavily utilized this strategy. Food manufacturers added products called "Eating Right" and "Healthy Choice." They offered diet product lines that very often made little improvement over the original products. Unilever manufactures processed foods, including ice cream. It bought SlimFast to improve its image, but SlimFast's products were barely distinguishable from the ice creams. Kraft and Pepsico created a group called the Health Weight Commitment Foundation, which pledged to cut 1.5 trillion calories from its products. But a follow-up study revealed that these trillions saved only seventy-eight calories per person per day. It also attributed most of the progress to a decline in soda sales that had started decades before. The project quickly tapered off.[25]

Turning to Personal Responsibility

The technology industry jumped on the personal responsibility wagon by using the slogan "Digital Well-Being" to implement this strategy. Google led the way. In 2018, one mantra resonated through the keynote speech of Google IO – Google's annual developer meeting: "Give Users Back Time." The conference's keynote speaker pointed out that "over 70% of people want more help." Google presented the idea that with the right discipline, technology will empower not burden you.[26] On its Digital Well-Being site, Google elaborated:

> As technology becomes more and more integral to everything we do, it can sometimes distract us from the things that matter most to us. We believe technology should improve life, not distract from it. We're committed to giving everyone the tools

they need to develop their own sense of digital wellbeing. So that life, not the technology in it, stays front and center.[27]

Digital well-being tools (or digital self-control tools) became the trend. A 2019 study, which reviewed forty-two digital well-being apps and analyzed 1,128 user reviews, concluded that these apps mostly support self-monitoring. They track user behavior and provide feedback.[28] Apple's Screen Time led this trend by providing iPhone users with phone usage reports. Many tech companies also let users set time limits on specific services, but users could still easily override these limits. For example, iPhone users could restrict use of app categories. Users could set a thirty-minute daily limit on use of social media apps. When time ran out the apps would look inaccessible, but they could still ignore the time limit and access them. YouTube set reminders for users to take a break. Nevertheless, YouTube let users dismiss this prompt if they watch a segment of ads. Similarly, Instagram created a feature for users to set an alert after a selected time period and turned to parents to set a daily reminder for kids.

Apple and Google created new settings to make their phones less alluring. They incorporated social "do not disturb" and "staying focused" modes on iPhone and Android phones. They let users change settings to block notifications or to turn their screens gray. Snapchat took yet another route by targeting concerns about social networks affecting kids' well-being. When a Snapchat user would type in certain words – such as "anxiety" – they would be whisked to self-help materials. Options included "Headspace Mini," which provided Snapchat users with meditations and mindfulness practices.

All these features had one thing in common: they enhanced the illusion of control. TikTok created a video series that targeted control head on. It was titled: "You are in Control." The designers explained the goal is to let users control how much time they spend online. But in a way, Google's Envelope is the most revealing. Google's Digital Well-Being department produced a paper phone that wraps around a real phone. A user could dial or even see the time but not do much else. The idea, according to Google's team, was to "try to last as long as possible before opening the envelope and getting your phone back." This was akin to wrapping a cigarette pack in an envelope, knowing it is there if needed, but not in clear sight. Google's envelope is, in essence, a test in self-control. Digital well-being features may look distinct. But, in many ways, they are not so different. They place the onus on the user to change settings and to resist temptation. One user aptly described the conundrum: "[It] makes breaking my addiction to the cellphone much easier. Although I still need a strong will of my own."[29] None of the features changes the default settings to limit time or to reduce the glowing allure of the device. Nor do they target the most addictive features of the products. Snapchat developed Headspace Mini, but kept its addictive Snapstreaks design intact. Instagram created an alert feature, but did not alter its infinite scroll. Unsurprisingly, despite initial excitement, users ultimately reported disenchantment with these features:[30]

> I've tried enabling some of Android's Digital Wellbeing features to interrupt the more self-defeating behaviors but they haven't worked ... I have tried app limits, but my lizard brain just overrides them ... I've tried setting my phone to greyscale starting around 9pm, taking the advice of psychologists who say that by sapping the color from our oversaturated phone displays, the brain is less likely to want to engage in mindless, repetitive behaviors ... but it hasn't really stopped my scrolling – it's just sapped the fun out of it.[31]

Unsurprisingly, the technological digital well-being features did not achieve more than self-help books and websites. Digital well-being strategies failed to make a dent in the spiral of increasing screen time, even before the eruption of COVID-19. They did not accomplish more because they did not target the heart of addictive design, nor were they meant to. Their purposes were to deflect criticism and pressure from the technology industry and to bolster the myth of the autonomous user. Digital well-being measures served only to strengthen the illusion of control and obscure the identity of the real choice-maker – the technology industry.

Part II
WHO ARE THE CHOICE-MAKERS?

4 CLOUDS OF SMOKE

Addiction to cigarettes governed my father's life and death. He smoked heavily and eventually became sick with emphysema. My father could have avoided his painful final years hooked to an oxygen tank by quitting smoking when he was diagnosed. But he chose otherwise. We desperately tried to resist his decision by taking his cigarettes away. He reacted with uncharacteristic anger, exercising every means at his disposal to get his cigarette pack back. We eventually gave up.

Some years later, I arrived with my family at a friends' house for dinner. Their 11-year-old son was playing with his parents' iPad, but when we came in, his parents demanded that he hand it over and join the other kids outside. His reaction brought me back to my parents' house at the time my father was diagnosed with emphysema: the boy's anger; his regression back to toddler-style wailing to demand the device; and his incessant exercise of every manipulation tool in his power throughout a long evening to regain control of the iPad. I was observing his parents' despair and remembered our own as we watched my father regain control of his cigarettes.

What Do Cigarettes Have to Do with It?

I hear this a lot: "We used to light up a cigarette when we were bored or uncomfortable, now we take out our phones." "Isn't this better?" And "how can you even compare the two?" And yes, I admit, the differences are stark. Nicotine gives a pleasure boost. But the cost is high. Smoking greatly increases the chance of serious disease. Technology, on the other hand, comes with many positive associations. Access to vast information, abundant entertainment, convenience, and easy communication are just a few benefits. Even my mother, in her 80s, who rejects with disdain the idea of social networks and shies away from any online research or shopping, still enjoys typing out her books on her laptop, sending long flowery emails, and yes, even texting.

Technology is a mixed bag, while smoking is a known hazard. Despite these differences, the tobacco wars bear striking relevance to the conflict over technology overuse. The fight against smoking was the major public health battle of the twentieth century and carries important lessons for the future of our use of technology.

The tobacco wars began in earnest in the 1950s. The numbers reveal the outcome. In 2017, 14 percent of adults aged 18 or older smoked. To compare, in 2005, 20.9 percent of adults smoked and, going back half a century, in 1949, 44–47 percent of American adults were smokers.[1] Smoking by youth under 18 has also significantly declined, despite the increase in the use of e-cigarettes.[2] Putting numbers aside, the way we live our lives has changed. Our restaurants, cinemas, and airplanes are no longer enveloped in clouds of smoke. And death and disease resulting from smoking have significantly declined.[3]

While no success is a complete success, and some Americans still smoke, this is a story about organized social action and transformation. Still, we often fail to appreciate that the road was extremely long and treacherous. Progression was not linear, but replete with twists and turns. There was no magic potion, no single legal mechanism that accomplished change. It was the combination of direct and indirect laws, litigation, and the work of many people at the local, state, and federal levels that achieved transformation. We view tobacco as vile, but still the process of controlling its use dragged over half a century. Technology's complex status guarantees that fighting to contain technology overuse will be a difficult task. The history of cigarettes can shed light on handling these obstacles.

The struggle to regulate cigarettes also reveals a deeply ingrained cultural belief: the American emphasis on personal choice and responsibility. Each person has the right to make his own choices.

As a result, each is responsible for the consequences of these decisions. The tobacco industry successfully used the personal choice and responsibility slogan for decades. Cigarette makers argued that they should not pay for the harm to smokers because smokers chose to smoke.[4] As discussed in Chapter 3, the tech industry is already promoting the personal choice and self-responsibility argument by advancing the illusion of control through its digital well-being tools. Simultaneously, users feel responsible and often guilty for constantly swiping and checking; while experts offer self-help methods to monitor and limit excessive use. The personal responsibility theme impeded progress on the tobacco front and is already doing the same on the technology overuse front.

Finally, the second-hand smoke movement carries important parallels for technology use. Evidence about the harm of second-hand smoke was a game changer in the tobacco wars. For many of us, inhaling clouds of smoke was an integral part of growing up. I recall proudly coming to sit by my father, three times a year, to show him my report card. He would typically grasp the report card in one hand while holding his cigarette in the other. He and I would sit together, head-to-head, examining my grades, shrouded in cigarette smoke.

Times have no doubt changed. Kids today barely recognize ashtrays. Smokers exit their homes in the bitter cold to smoke outside rather than expose their children to second-hand smoke. Indoors, adults no longer clutch on to cigarettes. Instead, they grab their phones. Kids approaching their parents to share a school assignment or to recount their day often fail to compete with the glowing devices. Overuse, like second-hand smoke, affects not just users; it affects those who surround them. As described in Chapter 2, relationships with those physically present are transformed. And for kids, it goes even beyond the depletion of physical relationships. Parents are models for kids. Excessive use by parents increases the likelihood that their children will eventually overuse their devices.

The Tobacco Science Wars

The technology overuse science wars are on. Science wars often involve corporate-caused harm and injury. The stakes are high. Each side barricades itself with scientific studies. Each party disparages the studies supporting the other's position. They abundantly toss around the term "junk science." Science wars are fierce. Personal lies, career ambitions, corporate interests, and murky scientific findings are the ingredients of lengthy battles. National and international agencies' findings can settle these debates or at least tilt them toward one side. Yet, they often take years, even decades, to reach consensus. Examples are plentiful, ranging from global warming to food additives. But the scientific debate involving smoking stands out because, with the benefit of hindsight, the harm from smoking seems undebatable.

Smoking became popular in the 1920s. As many Americans became smokers, few concerns were raised. An editorial from the highly regarded *Scientific American* published in 1936 stated: "Most smokers – probably all smokers – are doubtless harmed to some extent, usually not great, by smoking." It then elaborated: "cigarettes are 'a packet of rest' that quiets the nerves," and that "the average intelligent smoker knows when he is smoking too much because he does not feel well . . . and eases off, almost unconsciously."[5]

Smoking soon became widespread. By the mid-twentieth century nearly half of American adults smoked. The incidence of lung cancer cases also grew exponentially. Researchers started exploring the causes of lung cancer. In the 1950s, the first major scientific studies revealed that most lung cancer patients are smokers and tend to be heavy smokers.[6] The media spread these findings beyond medical circles. In 1952, *The Reader's Digest*, the nation's largest-circulation magazine, published an article titled "Cancer by the Carton."[7]

The tobacco industry reacted fast, but its responses were somewhat contradictory. They first turned to promoting a new product: the filtered cigarette. In the words of one company's ad: "THIS IS IT. L & M Filters Are Just What the Doctor Ordered!" The industry's campaign advertised that the filter removed nicotine and tar. The cigarette makers' reaction to the health scare was extremely successful. By the end of the 1950s, more than half of smokers smoked filtered cigarettes. But the smokers did not know about the industry's trade-off. The tobacco companies compensated for the taste robbed by filters by using stronger tobacco that yielded as much tar and nicotine as the old unfiltered brands.[8]

By 1960, the annual death toll from lung cancer surpassed 35,000. Prestigious institutions, including the American Cancer Society, the National Institute, and the National Heart Institute, published large studies about the ravages of smoking on the human body. The tobacco industry, confronting mounting damaging evidence, turned to a new production line: scientific knowledge. It founded its own research institutions: The Tobacco Industry Research Committee (TIRC) and the Tobacco Institute. These institutes funded research about tobacco-related health issues. They also dispersed scientific information to physicians and the public that backed the industry's business agenda.[9]

One report published by the TIRC in 1960 was titled, "Causation Theory of Smoking Unproved." The report contended that there is no significant evidence that shows causation between smoking and lung cancer or other ailments. This report also acted to trivialize and denigrate any other report revealing the damage from smoking. A typical exchange took place when the American Cancer Association published a large study about the value of quitting smoking. The report disclosed that quitters improved their life expectancy compared to those who continued to smoke. In response, the spokesman of the tobacco industry stated that it would be: "tragic if an overpublicized allegation that lacks scientific support were to divert and impede public or private support of sound research in such an important field of health."[10]

As the 1960s proceeded, study after study exposed the harms of smoking. The tobacco industry countered with denials, denigration, and contradicting studies. Those fighting to curtail smoking eagerly awaited an official proclamation on the hazards of smoking. In the United States, the Surgeon General finally acted in 1964. US Surgeon General Luther Terry announced in a much-anticipated press conference: "No reasonable person should dispute that cigarette smoking is a serious health hazard."[11]

The Tools of Awareness

The Surgeon General's announcement did not abruptly end the science wars. The tobacco industry insisted on a "continuing controversy" regarding the scientific findings. But the Surgeon General's report opened the door to a new era. The tobacco wars no longer centered on debating whether a problem existed, but on how to solve it.[12] Solutions focused on the tools of awareness: labeling and advertising. Limiting advertising would curtail the tobacco companies' ability to promote their product, while labels on cigarette packs and advertising about the harms of smoking would act by convincing smokers to quit. The parties shifted their energies to politics and regulation. As a result, appearances were often misleading. Important laws regulating information about smoking were, in fact, hidden victories for the tobacco industry. One example was the Federal Cigarette Labeling and Advertising Act, which Congress enacted in 1965.[13] This law required cigarette companies to post a label on cigarette packs stating: "smoking may be hazardous to your health." At first blush, this was an important achievement for the anti-smoking camp. But this law, heavily lobbied for by the tobacco industry, came in lieu of much stronger action. Following the Surgeon General's report, the Federal Trade Commission (FTC) had proposed regulations requiring cigarette companies to attach labels stating, "Caution: cigarette smoking is dangerous to health and may cause death from cancer and other diseases." The Federal Cigarette Labeling and Advertising Act, despite its impressive name, diluted the warning. It replaced "is dangerous" with "may be hazardous," and the word "cancer" did not appear anywhere on the label.[14]

Curbs on cigarette advertising, surprisingly, also reflected the tobacco industry's strategic preferences. In 1969, the Federal Communications Commission (FCC) announced a ban on all broadcast cigarette advertising.[15] The main impact was the end of television and radio smoking commercials. The last Marlboro Man commercial aired at 11:58pm on December 31, 1970. The ban went into effect on January 1, 1971.[16]

On its face, this appeared as a huge victory for anti-smoking activists. But the tobacco industry actually preferred an end to all television and radio tobacco commercials over the previous arrangement. Before the ban went into effect, the FCC implemented "The Fairness Doctrine." Fairness meant making room for all points of view. The FCC required television and radio broadcasters to air anti-smoking commercials right next to commercials for cigarettes. Tobacco executives preferred to give up television and radio commercials altogether, rather than watch the Marlboro Man galloping into the sunset followed by an American Cancer Society commercial featuring the devastating effects of lung cancer caused by smoking.[17]

Although the tobacco industry succeeded in manipulating the tools of awareness, change was taking place. The messages did alter public sentiments toward smoking. In the four years following the Surgeon General's report, the percentage of adult Americans who smoked fell from 47 to 42 percent.[18]

Litigation: Promoting Awareness and Nudging the Manufacturer

In tort litigation, plaintiffs sue to get damages for an injury. Tobacco litigation is famously known for thousands of smokers getting together to sue cigarette manufacturers for the diseases they developed because of smoking. Tort litigation, like other types of court battles, is not just about winning and losing in court. Litigation can end in victory or defeat, but often it ends in a settlement.

Damages are a common outcome, but not the only one. A manufacturer may need to change the ways it designs or sells its product to avoid future injury to customers and the risk of more litigation. It may change the design of a dangerous product or limit its sale to vulnerable groups, like kids. Some results involve promoting awareness; the manufacturer may begin warning about the potential risks of its product. Even the very existence of litigation and the media's attention promote awareness of the issue.[19]

The Master Agreement of 1996 is a complex settlement agreement with the tobacco companies, which followed decades of litigation. The tobacco companies agreed to pay $206 billion over a twenty-five-year period. But beyond the payment of damages, the Agreement prioritized promoting awareness of the hazards of smoking. It required changing future messages about tobacco by restricting advertising and promotion. Especially with an eye toward protecting youth, it prohibited advertising in youth venues and specifically prohibited the famous cartoon character "Joe Camel" and the idealized cowboy figure "The Marlboro Man."[20]

The tobacco litigation took place over decades, beginning in the 1950s. The long process of litigation and its resulting political feat – the Master Agreement – are important because they strengthened awareness and contributed significantly to reducing smoking among adults and youth. Beyond that, though, it illustrates the rise and fall of the theme of personal choice and responsibility. It was only when the personal responsibility argument lost its strength in the tobacco wars that the tables started turning.

Frank Lartigue started smoking when he was 9 years old. He smoked at least two packs a day, lighting one cigarette from another and smoking each down to small butts. In 1954, Frank was hospitalized with cancer of the larynx. Doctors removed his right vocal cord and part of his left vocal cord. Later that year, doctors diagnosed him with lung cancer. He died in 1955 at the age of 65. His wife sued Reynolds Tobacco Company and Liggett and Myers Tobacco Company, the firms that manufactured the cigarettes that Frank had smoked. The lawsuit failed, as did all tobacco lawsuits of that generation. It failed because courts refused to shift responsibility from the smokers to the tobacco companies.[21]

Frank Lartigue's case was part of the first wave of tobacco litigation, which took place in the late 1950s and the 1960s. Smokers and their families argued that cigarette makers were negligent because they failed to warn smokers of the health dangers of smoking cigarettes. Courts refused to accept this. Instead, they accepted the tobacco industry's defense that the risks of cigarette smoking were not known to them until the 1950s. By doing this, the courts implicitly put the responsibility on the smokers. In Frank Latrigue's case, the court was even quite explicit about where responsibility lay. It analogized smokers' troubles to a man who buys whiskey, drinks too much of it, and gets liver trouble as a result.[22]

Nathan Horton was a plaintiff in the second wave of tobacco litigation, which took place in the 1980s and 1990s. Horton was born in 1936 Mississippi and started smoking as a teen in the 1950s. In the mid-1980s, doctors diagnosed Horton with emphysema and lung cancer. Horton decided to go ahead and sue the tobacco companies, but he did not fare much better than Frank Lartigue, two decades earlier.

During the trial, Horton admitted that even as a child he had known about the hazards of cigarette smoking. Doctors and others had warned him consistently about the connection between smoking and disease. He and his friends regularly referred to cigarettes as "coffin sticks" and "cancer sticks." Horton also reported that since 1966 he had seen the warnings on cigarette packets. He acknowledged hearing about the Surgeon General's Report linking smoking and lung cancer.[23]

Throughout the 1980s and 1990s, tobacco companies continued to prevail because courts viewed smokers as personally responsible for their decision to smoke. Courts believed smokers, like Horton, were negligent because they knew about the risks and still chose to smoke. They concluded that even if the cigarette companies were negligent in their actions, so were the smokers. Smokers contributed their own negligence to the mix. Courts also determined that smokers assumed the risks associated with smoking. They knew that smoking could cause disease and assumed the risk when they decided to smoke. Smokers' contributory negligence and assumption of risk barred them from receiving damages, even if courts did not view them as solely responsible.[24]

It was only in the mid-1990s, with the third wave of tobacco litigation, that the balance tilted against the tobacco industry. A change in litigation practices – the rise of class actions – imposed a large threat on tobacco companies. Hundreds of thousands of plaintiffs came together to sue, raising the threat of massive punitive damages.[25] But, simultaneously, another important change took place: the breakdown of the industry's most powerful defense – the personal choice and responsibility argument.

Information leaked out of the tobacco companies' fortress, just as years later whistleblower reports would reveal inside information from Silicon Valley. This information revealed that the tobacco industry had known for decades that nicotine was addictive and had manipulated it to maximize consumption by smokers. The General Counsel of the tobacco companies stated plainly in one of the leaked memos: "We are in the business, then, of selling nicotine, an addictive drug."[26]

The debate became thornier for the tobacco industry. It was one thing to argue personal responsibility based on knowledge about the health risks of cigarettes. But it was another to claim that the addiction to nicotine was publicly known. And if cigarettes are addictive, it was also harder to argue that smokers were responsible for getting sick because they could freely choose to quit smoking.[27] As the information trickled into the courtrooms, one plaintiff's lawyer formulated the following argument: "You addicted me, and you knew it was addicting, and now you say it is my fault."[28] In 1996, a jury, for the first time, decided that the industry's responsibility exceeded the smoker's and awarded $750,000 to the plaintiff for medical and related expenses resulting from lung cancer.[29]

The demise of the personal responsibility defense was also part of an intentional litigation strategy. Smokers and their families were no longer alone in suing the tobacco industry. Attorneys General, acting for the states, joined the plaintiffs' ranks. These state officials claimed damages for the expenses paid through their health systems for smoking-related diseases. As plaintiffs, states were very different from smokers. They represented the non-smoking general public that bore the health costs of smoking. Tobacco companies could no longer convincingly resort to the personal responsibility argument, because they could not argue that the general public was personally responsible for the actions of smokers. It was, then, the breakdown of the great defense and fear of limitless liability that finally drew the cigarette companies to the settlement table.[30]

Second-Hand Smoke and the Demise of Personal Responsibility

My family had one uncontested idol. It was Humphrey Bogart, known as Rick in the movie *Casablanca*. Rick romantically held a cigarette as he said: "Play it again, Sam." Sam played the song Rick had listened to with his one and only true love in Paris before the war had erupted, and they'd had to part. We watched this movie again, and again, and again. My father, a poet, did not view smoking as a vice or even a harmless occupation. He idolized it. To him, it was an indispensable part of a romantic way of living. But then the world changed on him.

I moved to New York in 1998. My father loved New York and came to visit me frequently. In 2002, New York banned smoking in restaurants and bars to protect non-smokers from second-hand smoke.[31] At the time, Israel and most European cities did not prohibit smoking in dining venues. The New York ban outraged my father. "This is fascist," he proclaimed. He still came. But flying became an ordeal for him. All international airlines banned smoking on the eleven-hour flight between Tel Aviv and New York.[32] My father was angry about the long smokeless flights. He was fuming when he had to step out of a restaurant to smoke outside. Repeatedly, he announced that New York without its smoke-filled jazz bars had lost its spirit. His last visit was in 2010. Eventually, he refused to come. "Move back to Israel," he said. My father was relentlessly unforgiving. He felt attacked for what he believed was his right to live the romantic life embodied by Bogart.

Today, we recognize that second-hand smoke inflicts damage on non-smokers. According to the Centers for Disease Control and Prevention (CDC), since 1964, exposure to second-hand smoke has caused health problems that led to the death of approximately 2,500,000 non-smokers. Second-hand smoke causes heart disease and lung cancer among adults. It also impacts children's health by increasing incidence of Sudden Infant Death Syndrome (SIDS), respiratory infections, and asthma attacks.[33] The information about the risks of second-hand smoke started trickling out in the 1980s and contributed to the demise of the personal responsibility narrative. Second-hand smoke information came out just as cigarette companies had bolstered their personal responsibility argument by pointing to the labeling on cigarette packs. They argued that since every cigarette pack then contained warnings, and every smoker had full information to make his or her own decision, smokers were making an informed choice to smoke, for which they were responsible.[34]

The public was quickly convinced that smoking harms non-smokers. A 1987 CDC survey revealed that 75 percent of respondents believed that second-hand smoke was harmful to non-smokers, and 70 percent said they were annoyed by other people's smoke.[35] In 1993, the Environmental Protection Agency (EPA) classified second-hand smoke as "lethal to man." It also labeled it as "a serious and substantial public health risk" responsible for cancers and heart disease and implicated in kids' illnesses, such as pneumonia, bronchitis, and asthma.[36] This information about second-hand smoke rattled tobacco companies' argument that smoking was a personal choice in which each person could balance, for himself, the risk of smoking with the pleasure of smoking. With bystanders as victims, this argument no longer held water.[37]

The second-hand smoke movement not only undermined the tobacco industry's prime argument. It also limited the use of tobacco products. It did so not by limiting access to the purchase of cigarettes. Instead, it restricted the freedom to actively smoke. Change occurred rapidly, beginning in the 1980s. First privately, as businesses and airlines segregated smokers into smoking sections and then banned smoking altogether.[38] In 1988, the US government restricted smoking on flights. By 1995, forty-one states had restricted smoking in government work sites, twenty-six had limited it in private work sites, and thirty-two had banned it in restaurants. Forty-five states restricted smoking in a variety of other locations, such as day-care centers, shopping malls, grocery stores, enclosed arenas, vehicles of public transportation, and hospitals.[39]

As the regulations increased, smoking became deviant conduct. While in 1970 nearly half the adult population smoked, by 1995 only 25 percent of adults were smokers and growing segments of the public viewed smoking as pathological.[40] Smokers found that wherever they went, smoking was frowned upon. One long-term smoker expressed his frustration with the change, explaining that what used to be a badge of "long-term grace under pressure" became "a process of humiliation."[41]

The tobacco industry tried to protect its customers and its business by making smoking an individual rights issue. The industry framed the issue in terms of discrimination: "It is dangerous when you try to paint our members as social pariahs and to make 60 to 80 million smoking Americans second class citizens. We already sit in the back of the plane and the bus."[42] Lobbied by tobacco companies, some states even passed smokers' rights laws. The cigarette manufacturers hoped that this legislation would overrule municipal laws prohibiting smoking in public places. But, unlike my father, most smokers refused to join the fight.[43] The smokers' rights movement was a non-starter.

Barring Access to Minors

Before moving to New York as a grown-up, I had moved there for one year in 1982. In 1982, New York was my land of endless consumption. In Israel, we had one television channel. But in New York, viewing options were boundless. I discovered the joy of flicking between channels. I also relished the abundance of New York delis with their wide collections of candy bars. But my biggest love turned out to be coffee-flavored Häagen-Dazs ice cream. Every evening, I ventured out to the deli to buy ice cream, which I planned on eating while watching endless re-runs of *The Love Boat*. On my way out, I would usually hear my father call: "Get me two packs of Rothmans," and my mother would add, "And a pack of Kent Lights."

I remember crossing Broadway near Lincoln Center, heading to the neighborhood deli. I was 13 years old, but I was small with long blond braids; I looked no more than 11. After picking up my ice cream, I would approach the salesperson, requesting two packs of Rothmans and one pack of Kent Lights. I paid about $1 for each pack of cigarettes and about $2 for my pint of coffee Häagen-Dazs ice cream. This was typical of the times. Although New York had had a law on the books since 1883 prohibiting selling cigarettes to minors, kids had no trouble purchasing tobacco products in New York or elsewhere.[44]

Fast forward to New York today. A kid entering a deli to purchase cigarettes is unlikely to emerge with a pack in hand. Signs declaring "Under 21 no tobacco, we card" hang in stores and are strictly implemented.[45] Across America, it is much harder for kids to buy cigarettes these days because of a federal law enacted in 1992. Although, throughout the twentieth century, states had laws prohibiting the sale of cigarettes to minors, these laws often remained unenforced. The Synar Amendment changed this. It not only required all states to prohibit the sale of cigarettes to minors under the age of 18, but it also made sure that states enforced this restriction. The Synar Amendment tied the receipt of federal substance abuse benefits to the implementation of these laws.[46]

Restricting access to a product is an extreme measure. It is reminiscent of the days of alcohol prohibition. It also contradicts the tenet of personal choice and responsibility. But protecting children from harm is also a popular theme in American culture and politics. We view minors as too young to make rational decisions for themselves. We also know that the impact of bad habits picked up early in life is often hard to reverse. Studies show the majority of smokers started as teens.[47]

Legislators focused on prohibiting sales to minors to reduce access to cigarettes and to decrease the likelihood that teens would take up smoking in the first place.[48] The cultural dogma of freedom of choice and responsibility is weaker as it applies to kids. This made restricting tobacco access for minors politically feasible.

Prohibiting sales to minors directly limits access. But access can also be limited indirectly by imposing taxes. When I bought cigarettes for my parents in 1982, a cigarette pack cost about $1. The cost of a pack of cigarettes in New York today is $13. Adjusting only for inflation, the current price should be $2.65. The price increase is the result of taxation. From 1980 to 1998, most states raised their excise taxes significantly and cigarette taxes are still rising.[49] Imagine a smoker residing in New York who consumes one packet a day. Smoking becomes an expensive habit, with a monthly expenditure of $390. Many heavy smokers consume two packs a day. For them, smoking costs $780 a month and $9,360 annually. To put this in context, the average yearly income per person in New York is $39,326.[50]

Tobacco companies tried to manipulate prices to balance tax increases. Addicted consumers continued to purchase cigarettes despite rising prices. But studies showed that heightened taxes have significantly impacted cigarette consumption. A 10 percent increase in cigarette prices decreased overall cigarette consumption between 2.5 and 5 percent. Rising prices over time reduced the number of smokers and overall number of cigarettes smoked. The young are particularly vulnerable to price increases. Taxation then becomes an indirect barrier to access. Research has shown that high prices reduce the likelihood that teens will become smokers in the first place.[51]

Lessons from the Tobacco Wars

The cigarette wars are still ongoing. E-cigarettes became popular, concerningly among kids. But the warriors of the tobacco wars won many important battles against traditional cigarettes. The resilience of the tobacco industry highlighted important cultural narratives and also gave birth to creative solutions. Important lessons going forward include:

- The science wars may be long and could be dirty, yet are inevitable.
- The dogma of personal choice and responsibility plays a central role in addiction debates. But even this powerful cultural theme can and has broken down. It happened:
  - when there was evidence of covert corporate intent to addict;
  - when there was harm to innocent bystanders;
  - when minors were involved.
- Promoting awareness can be done directly through labeling and advertising, but these tools may be inadequate by themselves. The promotion of awareness takes place also indirectly through litigation.
- Prohibiting access or impeding it by imposing taxes can work effectively for minors.

5 THE FOOD WARS

In 1998, I worked in a law firm in midtown Manhattan. I spent too many long days and nights at my desk, unsurprisingly gaining weight. I wanted to diet, but it turned out to be a bigger challenge than I had expected. Until then, I had lived most of my life in Israel. The Israeli diet is very different from the American diet. I grew up regularly eating vegetable salads with light dressings. My American friends are often amazed when they realize my family and I still eat vegetables for breakfast. I recall, then, my disappointment as I tried out many lunch places around my office. These lunch joints offered mainly sandwiches. When I spotted a dish that resembled a salad it usually floated in mayonnaise.

Twenty years later, I lived in Murray Hill, not far from midtown Manhattan. On days when I worked at home and decided not to fix my own lunch, I went – just as I had two decades before – to explore the lunch offerings of midtown Manhattan. Things have certainly changed. Every block seemed to boast at least one "make your own salad" establishment offering dozens of fresh ingredients. The walls featured large menus listing calories. Lines were very long. Forty to fifty people often stood waiting patiently. New York is the city of passing fads, but this transition toward healthier and fresher foods appears permanent and goes beyond restaurants. Supermarkets are now stocked with fresh produce, often highlighting local products. This change is both a cause and a result of the food wars.

What Are the Food Wars?

The food wars are mostly a twenty-first-century phenomenon, and they are essentially fought on two fronts. The first is the fight against obesity. Obesity can have severe consequences, including cardiovascular diseases, high cholesterol, type 2 diabetes, sleep apnea, stroke, and depression.[1] Annual healthcare cost estimates range from $149 billion to $260 billion per year.[2] These costs account for almost 21 percent of US medical spending.[3] Obesity rates have risen dramatically since the 1960s.[4] They increased from 15 percent in 1976–80 to 34 percent in 2007–08 among adults.[5] Obesity among children and adolescents increased from around 5 percent in 1980 to around 16.9 percent in 2008.[6]

On February 9, 2010, former First Lady Michelle Obama announced a campaign to fight childhood obesity. She launched the campaign, saying: "The truth is, our kids didn't do this to themselves. Our kids didn't choose to make food products with tons of fat and sugar and supersize portions, and then to have those foods marketed to them wherever they turn."[7] Michelle Obama's campaign titled "Let's Move" attracted significant attention to the topic of obesity and its causes.

The food wars have one overarching objective: to prevent the food industry from selling products that entice people to eat more at the expense of a healthy diet.[8] The fight against obesity focuses on limiting the intake of foods that are high in calories or in sugar and replacing them with healthier foods. This battle often targets junk food and sodas. But in another related battle, the public is increasingly demanding healthier food. People prefer organic food and food that is locally grown. Europeans are opposing genetically modified food. And in the United States, consumers are increasingly objecting to artificial additives. They also demand that if a product is labeled as "natural," it will, indeed, be naturally made.[9]

The food wars are very relevant to the technology overuse debate. In important ways, food is much more similar to technology than to cigarettes. Food is good and bad mixed together. We need food to subsist. Some food products are harmful when consumed excessively, but not so when consumed in moderation. First Amendment challenges raising freedom of speech violations were successful at preventing attempts to regulate food because of this mixed status. But these legal battles pressured food manufacturers to redesign their products and labels. The story of food differs in an important way from that of cigarettes. Freedom of speech rights did not significantly obstruct cigarette regulation because the harms of smoking dominated the debate. But technology, like food, is a hybrid creature. First Amendment challenges and redesign are likely to be integral parts of any efforts to curtail technology overuse.

Freedom of Speech as a Shield

The food industry frequently raised First Amendment arguments to fight restrictions on labeling and advertising its products. While I was researching the food wars, I shared my findings with friends, and they often became perplexed. "But, isn't the First Amendment about freedom of speech?" they asked. "What do food ingredients on juice containers have to do with freedom of speech?" It was indeed surprising to my non-lawyer friends that First Amendment protection applies to food.[10] They were quite perplexed that the Constitution protects labeling and advertising of food products and not just our political views.

The food wars did not give birth to First Amendment claims to challenge labeling and advertising restrictions. In fact, the tobacco industry tried them before. In 2009, cigarette companies argued that a law that required very specific warnings on cigarette packages and mandated they comprise 50 percent of the packet violated their freedom of speech.[11] Food manufacturers, though, brought these freedom of speech claims to the center of the stage. We are currently in the midst of the food wars. First Amendment claims sometimes succeed and at other times fail. Their evolution is hard to predict because law can be decades in the making and then still continue to evolve. What we can expect, though, is a repeat of the same type of First Amendment claims in the technology overuse debate. Technology companies have already started making freedom of speech arguments similar to those of the food manufacturers.

Food companies brought up First Amendment claims on different fronts. The City of San Francisco took on the fight against obesity and enacted a law requiring warnings on sodas and sugary drinks. It read: "Warning – Drinking beverages with added sugar(s) contribute to obesity, diabetes, and tooth decay. This is a message from the City and County of San Francisco." The American Beverage Association (ABA), fearing this law would start a trend across the country, challenged it immediately in court. It argued that the San Francisco law violated the First Amendment, and it won.[12]

We usually think that freedom of speech is about our rights to freely express ideas or views. This is true. But these rights go further. Freedom of speech rights also protect us from coercion. The government cannot just force us to express ideas or views.[13] This is where the First Amendment and San Francisco's labeling law coalesced. Coca-Cola, Pepsi, Gatorade, and other drink manufacturers clearly had no desire to highlight a connection between their products, weight, and diabetes. In fact, just like the tobacco industry before them, drink manufacturers worked hard to fund research to disprove any such connection.[14]

Does this mean that the government can never compel any warnings? Of course not. There are warnings all around us. But marketing messages are commercial speech. This ties the government's hands. It can only compel the disclosure of "purely factual and uncontroversial information."[15] This distinction is crucial because it requires identifying what is a fact and what is an opinion. It also requires deciding what information is uncontroversial. It basically puts truth at the center of the food wars' First Amendment debate.

Truth unfortunately is often not conveniently objective. It is particularly hard to distill while the science wars are ongoing. Corporate interests and money heighten the fights over what the truth is. In this case, the parties had to address whether drinks with added sugar contribute to obesity and diabetes. Indeed, many studies show they do.[16] Other studies sponsored by the Food and Beverage Industry, though, were five times more likely to find no positive association between sugary drinks and obesity.[17] But the fight about truth is not just about conflicting studies. It is also about subtle untruths and manipulation. The American Beverage Association announced that the Association: "is concerned about the obesity issue in America and is proudly doing its best to help improve health and wellness."[18] Professor

Marion Nestle showed how the ABA reframed the issues in her book, *Soda Politics: Taking on Big Soda and Winning.* She listed the ABA's assertions and added her own comments:

- Sodas can be part of healthful diets [Yes, but only in small amounts]
- Other Foods and beverages also contribute calories. [They do, but sodas contribute one-third of the sugar consumed in the United States and with other sugary drinks contribute half. Their calories are empty, and they are well established to promote poor health.]
- Physical activity is more important. [Activity is important, but it takes considerable effort to balance excessive calorie intake.][19]

The ABA prevailed in its court battle against the City of San Francisco beverages warning. The court did not find that the information about the link between sugary drinks, obesity, and diabetes was "factual and uncontroversial." It viewed the information as San Francisco's subjective one-sided view about sugar-sweetened beverages.[20]

Legal fights involving food and speech have intensified, and we see their aftermath all around us. Calories on menus is one arena. Once, I was waiting with a colleague in an airport for a delayed flight heading home from a conference, and food options were limited. My colleague opted for McDonald's, but I wanted a salad. We both stared at the menu board, amazed to see that his Big Mac contained 540 calories, about the same as my Southwest Buttermilk Crispy Chicken salad, which contained 520 calories. We now have menus with calories in chain restaurants all over the country. But New York City was a pioneer when it required menus to list calories in 2008. At the time, the New York State Restaurant Association raised a First Amendment challenge protesting compelled speech, but it lost.[21]

Freedom of speech claims have appeared in other food-related litigation. In Vermont, a law required labels to identify if a food product was genetically modified.[22] Meanwhile, across the country in California, consumers sued Post, the cereal maker known for its best-selling Honey Bunches of Oats. These consumers argued that Post used misleading terms on its cereals like "nutritious," "wholesome," "healthy," "less processed," "good for your family," "good for your health," and "balanced" without disclosing that the added sugar in the cereal could have negative health impacts.[23] In these, and a growing number of other cases, food manufacturers raised freedom of speech claims emphasizing their rights to express their opinions.[24]

First Amendment food-related litigation frequently involves requirements to disclose information and claims of compelled speech. But some resemble instead our regular understanding of free speech claims. These are arguments that claim a law prohibits speech (as opposed to forcing it). The Vermont "genetically modified food" case is an example of a traditional freedom of speech claim. The law prohibited producers from labeling genetically modified food as "natural." Food manufacturers argued that this is an illegal restriction on what they may say because the label "natural" is not misleading for genetically modified food. They won their First Amendment claim and managed to invalidate the law. The court agreed that there is no consensus that genetically modified food is not natural.[25]

The Resilient Personal Responsibility Defense

Another strand of lawsuits against food and beverage manufacturers focused on junk food and obesity. In 2002, a group of New York teenagers and their parents sued McDonald's. Ashley Pelman was 14 years old, 4 feet and 10 inches tall, and weighed 170 pounds. Jazlyn Bradley was 19 years old, 5 feet and 6 inches tall, and weighed 270 pounds. Ashley and Jazlyn ate – every school day – for breakfast, lunch, and snacks – mostly McDonald's Happy Meals, McMuffins, and Big Macs. They claimed that eating McDonald's food on a regular basis made them obese and afflicted with diabetes, coronary disease, high blood pressure, and high cholesterol.[26]

The New York Court strongly rejected the teenagers' arguments. It explained that since consumers commonly know how unhealthy McDonald's food is and still choose to eat it, they cannot then turn and blame McDonald's for failing to warn them.[27] The Court's opinion resonated with the lingo of personal responsibility.[28] The judge wrote quite bluntly: "If a person knows or should have known that eating copious orders of supersized McDonald's product is unhealthy and may result in weight gain ... it is not the place of the law to protect them from their own excesses. Nobody is forced to eat at McDonald's ... nobody is forced to supersize their meal or choose less healthy options on the menu."[29] It continued to tie personal responsibility to free choice by explaining that, as long as a consumer exercises free choice with appropriate knowledge, the food manufacturer will not be legally responsible.[30]

McDonald's won this lawsuit, but it sounded an alarm in McDonald's corporate headquarters. The company feared that thousands of "McLawsuits" would follow and worked frantically to incorporate the personal responsibility shield into federal law. Its lobbyists promoted a bill called the "Personal Responsibility Food Consumption Act," also known as the "Cheeseburger Bill," which would shield companies like McDonald's, Burger King, and KFC. It stated that food manufacturers and vendors could not be held responsible for obesity, heart disease, or other health-related issues caused by the consumption of food. The bill plainly explained it would prohibit these lawsuits because: "fostering a culture of acceptance of personal responsibility is one of the most important ways to promote a healthier society ... [these] lawsuits are not only legally frivolous and economically damaging, but also harmful to a healthy America."[31] The bill was never enacted as a federal law, but half the states now have "Cheeseburger Laws," also called "Commonsense Consumption Acts," to prevent these kinds of lawsuits.[32]

The food industry clearly followed in the footsteps of the tobacco industry. Food corporations repeatedly asserted the right to individual choice and the importance of individual responsibility for one's own actions. They used individual choice and personal responsibility arguments as defenses in litigation and to lobby for laws that would protect them from legal liability. But they also went further. By promoting the idea of a nanny state, they made this part of a very public debate.

The Nanny State as the New Villain

In 2012, Mayor Bloomberg of New York City prohibited restaurants from serving sugary drinks of over 16 ounces. His goal was to address growing obesity among New York residents. As Bloomberg explained it: "The nice thing about the soda thing is it's really just a suggestion. So, if you want to buy 32 ounces, you just have to carry it back to your seat in two cups. And maybe that would convince you to only take one, but if you want two you can do it. I think government's job ... is to give you advice, not to force you [to] do things."[33]

A storm ensued. The soft-drink industry mounted a campaign capturing national attention. Eventually those fighting the restriction won. New York restaurants can still serve drinks of any size.[34] The media asked: "What's next? Limits on the width of a pizza slice, size of hamburger, or amount of cream cheese on your bagel?"[35] The attacks on Mayor Bloomberg became personal. He was nicknamed "Nanny Bloomberg." The *New York Post* featured him dressed as Mary Poppins.[36] Other opposers promoted an ad with Bloomberg in a dowdy dress and a neck scarf with the title "The Nanny: You Only Thought You Lived in the Land of the Free."[37]

Bloomberg's "Portion Cap," as it was officially called, was a strategy to limit access to sugary drinks. It did not, for example, prohibit drinking Coke altogether. It just made it more difficult to drink a lot of Coke when dining out. Limiting access is not just about restricting access. It also promotes awareness by getting attention. Bloomberg's initiative failed, but the issue itself – the impact of sugary drinks on obesity and health – got significant publicity.

The beverage industry led the fight against the Bloomberg initiative. Soda companies emphasized that personal choice is a fundamental American freedom. They argued that parents know best what their kids should eat or drink.[38] But the beverage industry did not operate alone. The media and the public joined the attack. Prohibition or limitation on access conflict with deeply held American beliefs about personal autonomy and responsibility.[39] Academics discuss "paternalism" and "the slippery slope."[40] The public talks about "the nanny state" and asks what the next step might be – would the government force us to eat broccoli? The idea is the same. How much can the government force someone to do (or not do) something it considers good (or bad) for them? Can the government do this even if this individual choice does not affect other people? Nannies do that all the time. They tell kids when to go to sleep, what to eat, and how much TV to watch. But can we "nanny" adults? And if we engage in "nanny-ism" – for example, by controlling certain drugs like opioids and limiting public access to them – when does it go too far?[41]

The government employs different methods to stir people toward what it believes will benefit them. Some methods, like providing information, are light-handed, leaving room for more individual choice. Other methods, though, are harsher, making certain choices impossible.[42] The Bloomberg Portion Cap initiative irked so many because it foreclosed certain options for consuming highly sweetened beverages.

The Bloomberg initiative also scared people. They worried that it was only the first step. This in essence is the slippery slope legal argument, which is a form of legal anxiety. We look at a court decision or a law and may think that this specific result by itself is not so bad. But we are still worried. We are concerned about the future because this decision could open the door to much worse results. We worry that we have stepped onto the slippery slope.

Back to Bloomberg's Portion Cap. Perhaps ordering Sprite in two smaller orders instead of one large drink is a small interference with our autonomy. But the public concern was where would we slip to? Would the next law prohibit selling sugary drinks in restaurants entirely? The repeated use of the nanny image manifested the public's anxiety over what would happen next. Would we become increasingly like children who can no longer exert power over our daily decisions? Nanny Bloomberg's image is likely to loom large going forward in any debate about restricting technology overuse.

Local Innovation and the Powers from Above

As a child, I spent many summer days by the pool with my mother and brother. I recall drinking one or two Cokes with my lunch daily. I did hear that if you took a tooth and placed it in a glass of Coke it would melt. This story alluded to some risk that comes with consuming Coke. But I, like other 1970s kids, ignored it. At some point, though, things changed, and Coke became the villain of the healthy childhood. Today, Coke and other sodas are no longer a menu choice for health-conscious parents. Younger kids going out for dinner with their families can choose apple juice, cranberry juice, or lemonade as a treat. Coke, 7-UP, or Sprite are usually not permitted.

Bloomberg was not a lone ranger combating sugar-sweetened beverages (SSB). Many health advocates focused on SSB because research linked them to obesity and type 2 diabetes. Studies have shown that SSB are very high in calories and are often consumed in large amounts.[43] Faced with these studies, governments looked for measures to decrease the over-consumption of these drinks. By imposing taxes and making SSB more expensive, they acted to discourage excessive consumption.

Many studies have now shown that taxes on SSB effectively reduced the amounts of SSB consumed.[44] A study conducted three years after the city of Berkeley enacted a penny-per-ounce tax on SSB showed a 52 percent reduction of SSB consumption among Berkley's low-income residents.[45] Studies do show that soda taxes have a greater impact on low-income families. Researchers also debate whether a reduction in SSB consumption affects overall obesity rates in light of the availability of other high-calorie options. But, overall, the data indicates that taxes on SSB can play an important role in a comprehensive plan to combat obesity.[46]

Governments around the globe have imposed national SSB taxes. But, in the United States, using taxes to limit SSB consumption proved trickier. We often expect Congress to execute legal change. But increasingly, legal change has come from the bottom up. It is growing locally. This is the state of soda taxes in the United States. There are no federal or state laws that impose soda taxes. There are, though, quite a few municipalities that collect these taxes, including San Francisco, Berkeley, Seattle, and Philadelphia.[47] The beverage industry reacts quickly to quash any local law, fearing a growing national epidemic. It views every soda tax, regardless of the size of the locality, as an existential threat. In Richmond, a retired cardiologist serving as a board member spent $25,293 to promote his tax proposal. The beverage industry spent over $2 million to prevent that proposal from going through.[48]

Fighting local initiatives on each local turf is one strategy, but not the most efficient one. A more effective way is blocking soda taxes in many localities through one broader action. This is done by taking advantage of our legal hierarchy. The legal term for this is preemption.

Preemption is a bit like the card game "War," which I used to play with my grandmother. We each had a stack of cards and, in every round, we each pulled one out. Whoever got the higher card won that round. I would pull a prince of hearts and she would pull a seven of diamonds. I would win that round and take both cards. Preemption implements the same general principle: the higher law supersedes the lower law. A state law can strike out a local law, and a federal law can strike out a state law.[49]

The beverage industry's fight against soda taxes implemented the principles of the game of War. But it not only pulled the cards; it also created them. Corporations poured masses of money into lobbying at both the federal and the state levels.[50] Arizona and Michigan have passed laws prohibiting cities and towns from imposing taxes on SSB.[51] Other states are following suit. Notably, California, where several municipalities imposed soda taxes, enacted a law in 2018 that in effect said "no more." Under the innocuous wording of prohibiting taxes on groceries for twelve years, it put a halt to any additional soda taxes.[52]

The Health Food Enigma: Awareness and Redesign

Frosties was my favorite childhood cereal. But by the time my oldest child was born in 2002, I knew that flakes covered with sugar were not a nutritious breakfast for a growing boy. So, instead, I fed him his favorite cereal: Honey Nut Cheerios. I was confident that I was giving my son a healthy breakfast. After all, the packaging of the cereal box stated that it was made with "100% whole grain oats," "contain[ed] no artificial flavors or colors," and could even "help lower your cholesterol." Eventually I learned that I may have made some misguided choices.

In the last two decades, the public has increasingly demanded healthier food. Food manufacturers have reacted by labeling their products to emphasize the "natural," "healthy," and "organic" qualities of their products. But families making significant efforts to feed their children healthy food were later furious to find out that, in fact, many of these products were not as wholesome as they believed. Disappointed customers got together to petition, and even sue, producers of items as diverse as shampoo, juice, and ice cream. Consumers sued General Mills, which makes my son's favorite cereal, because – while it emphasized certain healthy ingredients – its products were still saturated with sugar.[53]

Ben Cohen and Jerry Greenfield founded Ben and Jerry's in the 1970s. They started out taking a $5 correspondence course in ice-cream-making from Penn State University. They then opened their first ice cream shop in a renovated gas station in Vermont. Things have changed dramatically since then. Ben & Jerry's is no longer a tiny local Vermont business. It has become a nationally known ice cream brand. And, in 2000, the international conglomerate Unilever purchased them. Still, through the years, Ben and Jerry's has consistently promoted their ice cream as wholesome, made with natural ingredients, and produced through practices that respect the planet and its inhabitants.[54]

Despite Ben & Jerry's health and environmental agenda, or perhaps because of it, the company is constantly battling legal challenges involving the wholesomeness of its products. In one action, the Center for Science in the Public Interest (CSPI), a consumer advocacy group, threatened legal action unless Ben & Jerry's removed the term "All Natural" from its ice creams and frozen yogurts. CSPI wrote that "All Natural" is misleading because the products contain many non-natural ingredients. They published a long list of ingredients that included alkalized cocoa, anhydrous dextrose, and corn syrup.[55] Ben and Jerry's reaction illustrates how litigation, or even the threat of legal action, can create change. The company decided to remove the term "All Natural" from their products.[56] Consumers eating a Ben and Jerry's ice cream today are less likely to mistakenly believe they are eating a natural, wholesome product. Consumers can now make a more informed decision.

A flurry of lawsuits and legal petitions changed packaging in supermarkets across America. Ben and Jerry's removed the term "natural" not only to avoid costly litigation, but also to avoid harmful publicity by making the controversy go away. The litigation revolving around healthy, natural, and organic claims prompted companies to engage in self-regulation. Food companies learned lessons from the trials of tobacco companies. They decided to take preemptive action, by deleting these descriptors from their products, to avoid the costs of litigation and harmful publicity.[57] Today, parents no longer hand their screaming toddlers a pack of "Natural Goldfish." They dispense a bag which features only "Goldfish"; the manufacturer removed "natural." Similarly, "Natural Naked Juice" became just "Naked Juice." Many other food producers made similar changes.

Some food companies took an additional step. They redesigned their products. Consumers sued Snapple for labeling its sweetened tea containing high fructose syrup as "all natural." In 2009, Snapple reacted by changing the high fructose syrup in its tea to sugar.[58] Kraft also opted for redesign by changing the famous yellow-orange color of its Mac and Cheese. Kraft reacted to a petition signed by 270,000 parents. The petition had demanded that Kraft remove artificial colors 5 and 6, which some studies showed were linked to hyperactivity, skin conditions, and cancer. Kraft replaced the artificial dyes with spices, increased whole grains, and lowered sodium and fat. It started selling the new product without much ado. The media reported that, 50 million boxes later, no one had noticed the difference.[59]

Despite these changes, the food wars are ongoing and far from resolved. Food producers want to maximize profit. They rely on longer shelf life and modern agricultural methods to do so. It is then no surprise that the food industry continues to use additives, preservatives, pesticides, and animals raised in harsh factory conditions. In 2017, the media exposed that Kraft's transformed macaroni and cheese product actually contains high concentrations of harmful chemicals that can cause male hormone disruption.[60] And, in 2018, the Organic Consumers Association (OCA) sued Ben and Jerry's for falsely advertising that their ice cream is made by "happy cows" raised in caring dairies. OCA claimed Ben and Jerry's, just like other food corporations, use cows raised in standard factory-style, mass-production dairy operations.[61] The struggles are ongoing, but some progress has been made, and, importantly, public awareness has been increasing.

Consumer action has played another important role – it mobilized the Food and Drug Administration (FDA). The FDA sets the rules for food labeling and permitted ingredients. Unfortunately, the FDA is often slow to act. Despite all the controversy around what "natural" means, it has yet to define the term. Does "natural" mean no artificial or synthetic ingredients, or does it also mean organic and not genetically modified? Still, in some cases, consumer legal action persuaded the FDA to finally act. This happened with the evaporated cane juice lawsuits.

Evaporated cane juice is really a form of sugar. But suppose you are a diligent consumer seeking healthy products, picking up Greek yogurt for your family. Aren't you more likely to buy a product with evaporated cane juice on the label rather than sugar? Evaporated cane juice suggests juice, which sounds healthier than sugar. The lawsuits targeted many of the "good guys" of the food industry who used "evaporated cane juice" on their products' labels. Customers sued Chobani, the manufacturer of Greek yogurt, and many others, including Whole Foods and Trader Joe's.[62] In 2009, the FDA did issue a draft guideline about listing "evaporated cane juice" on labels. But then nothing happened. Many lawsuits and massive public confusion eventually persuaded the FDA to issue final guidance. In 2016, the FDA pronounced that the term "evaporated cane juice" is misleading, and food manufacturers should use the term "sugar" instead.[63]

Don't Tell Us What to Do! We Know!

The food industry's primary focus on self-regulation involved advertising to children. Commercials for unhealthy foods like sodas, fast food, and cereals particularly influence children. For years, companies took advantage of this and spent billions of dollars marketing to minors. Many adults still remember some of these commercials they viewed as children. In the 1980s, a Pepsi commercial called "Michael Jackson's Pepsi Generation" mesmerized a generation of kids. It featured fashionably dressed kids dancing in the streets to the tune of Michael Jackson's song "Billie Jean." The kids, of course, held Pepsi cans and then amazingly bumped into Michael Jackson himself.

The rise of obesity at the beginning of the twenty-first century changed the standards for food advertising to kids worldwide. For example, in 2007, the United Kingdom prohibited airing TV commercials of foods that are considered unhealthy aimed at children under the age of 16.[64] Joining the international trend, the US government published draft standards that restricted advertising of unhealthy food for kids. These draft standards were only voluntary, but the food industry rose against this regulatory threat. It wanted to retain control and avoid the fate of its international counterparts.[65]

In 2006, eighteen major food companies joined to create the Children's Food and Beverage Advertising Initiative (CFBAI). These companies included the heavyweights of the industry, including McDonald's, Kraft, Campbell's Soup, Kellogg's, Burger King, Nestle, General Mills, and Coca-Cola. The organization developed a uniform criterion of what food can be advertised to kids under the age of 12. These criteria set limits on calories, saturated fat, sodium, and sugar and imposed minimal quantities for important food groups like vegetables. In addition, each company developed its own pledge. Burger King, for example, pledged not to advertise its products at all to children under the age of 6. Under the CFBAI rules, if Burger King went ahead and violated its own promise by advertising to toddlers, the organization could remove it from the initiative and notify government regulatory authorities.[66]

No doubt, the CFBAI members sought to fend off regulation by showing that it was unnecessary. By regulating themselves they could gain control over advertising restrictions. They viewed government regulation, even if initially voluntary and loose, as still dangerous. It could open the door to additional, and more demanding, government oversight down the line. But food companies had an additional motivation. They were newly operating in a transformed consumer environment, in which large segments of the public were seeking healthy food. Public relations were paramount to them as they were to the tobacco companies before them. Food manufacturers wanted to change their public image from promoters of junk food to health warriors. Coca-Cola, one of CFBAI's members, announced in 2013 its "Coming Together" initiative against obesity. Coca-Cola's promotions declared "Beating obesity will take all of us ... [A]s the world's leading beverage company, we can play an important role by creating awareness around choice, helping consumers make the most informed decisions for themselves and their families, and by inspiring people everywhere to find the fun in movement." And although they shifted the blame for obesity to a lack of movement, Coca-Cola still promised to market responsibly and not advertise to children under the age of 12.[67]

Self-regulation has an important advantage. It ducks the First Amendment hurdle. When organizations voluntarily restrict their advertising, there is no freedom of speech problem. If the industry had not opted for self-regulation, and the government had enacted its advertising standards, the industry had a fair chance of defeating them in a First Amendment action. Tobacco manufacturers actually won a similar battle. They invalidated a Massachusetts law that banned tobacco ads within 1,000 feet of schools and playgrounds because it violated the First Amendment. This happened in 2001, when the dangers of smoking to youth had been well known for years.[68]

Even though self-regulation overcomes the First Amendment obstacle, an important question still remains: was self-regulation successful or did the food industry manipulate it to serve its own goals? Studies show that in some ways self-regulation made a difference, but in others it still has a way to go. It is quite clear that the members of the CFBAI, the big players in the junk food industry, have kept their individual pledges. They do not advertise to kids under 12 food products that do not meet CFBAI's nutrition standards, and some have even refrained from advertising to kids at all (depending on their pledge).

There is significant debate about whether self-regulation of advertising is overall successful. Are advertisers promoting healthier food to kids? Some studies show an overall improvement in the nutritional value of products advertised to kids. They also point to a decline in the number of food ads during kids' programming. But studies also show that kids are still exposed to a significant amount of low nutrition advertising. Basically, opponents of self-regulation argue that despite self-regulation, food companies are still not advertising "healthy" food to kids.[69]

Why are we getting such mixed results? For one thing, restrictions on advertising apply to kids' media, but kids often watch programming meant for adults. Food companies can still freely advertise low nutrition food there. A second reason is that, although the major manufacturers of "junk food" are members of the CFBAI, many other food companies are not. These companies can advertise their products to kids of all ages with no restrictions. On top of that, since CFBAI set its standards, the methods of advertising have changed. Kids today are less likely to watch traditional TV commercials. In fact, they are less likely to watch TV. Instead, they consume information on the Internet. Adjusting to this new reality, food companies pay YouTube influencers to promote their products to kids online. And, although some studies indicate that advertisers are not exposing kids to unhealthy foods, this point is far from settled. The definition of "healthy" is still a point of much debate.[70] Most importantly, still, results are mixed because the restriction is a narrow self-regulation measure. It is against the interests of the implementor – the food industry – to accomplish real change.

Minors: The Soft Spot

Obesity plagues both adults and children. But the food industry restricted only its children-aimed advertising. A similar phenomenon occurred with tobacco. Laws prohibited only minors, not adults, from buying cigarettes. Generally, we are less concerned about limiting children's ability to choose. We restrict children's choices to shield them from rash immature decisions, and governments use schools to implement policies restricting children's choices. This made fighting childhood obesity easier compared to adult obesity.[71]

Laws tackled the childhood obesity problem from different angles, starting with vending machines that usually dispense non-nutritious snacks. These are everywhere, and we could not imagine restricting them in cinemas, airports, or other public places. But since 2014, the federal government started to implement nutrition standards for all foods sold in schools, including through vending machines.[72] In a completely different approach, authorities compelled schools to measure students' body-mass index and send the reports to parents.[73] States also required schools to increase students' physical activity time.[74] To compare, efforts to influence adult behavior included offering employees reduced health insurance premiums for joining wellness programs. But employees would have likely revolted against a mandatory requirement to spend forty-five minutes a day doing crossjacks and push-ups.[75]

Lessons from the Food Wars

The food wars are still ongoing. The war against obesity is far from won.[76] Regardless, the food wars highlight important strategies that are likely to emerge in any struggle to curtail technology overuse.

- Consumer action matters. Threats of costly litigation and bad publicity induce companies to change labels to provide better information and sometimes redesign their products. Even failed legal action created pressure for change.
- Food, like technology, is a mixed bag of benefits and risks. Companies selling products that are not inherently harmful have an important tool at their disposal: the First Amendment. Technology companies, like the food industry, are likely to successfully raise freedom of speech claims to fend off regulation of their products.
- Self-regulation to restrict advertising to children accomplished mixed results. Although self-regulation removes the First Amendment obstacle, it failed to accomplish significant change because that was against the financial interests of the implementors – the food industry.
- The "Nanny State" is a powerful cultural icon. It reflects the enduring strength of American attachment to personal choice and personal responsibility and is likely to come up against efforts to contain overuse.
- Legal change is increasingly emerging locally from cities and small towns. Corporations fight back by lobbying to supersede local laws by enacting state or federal laws that trump them. As we will see in Chapter 6, technology companies are already using preemption to fight local laws and fend off privacy regulations.
- Each strategy to fight obesity and improve food products made some headway, but there is no one magic cure. Food is a complicated topic. So is technology. Any effort to balance the good and the evil requires many small steps to achieve a larger mission.
- Minors are the Achilles heel. There is more flexibility where kids are involved. This is where the personal responsibility and choice argument breaks and social change begins to emerge.

6 THE PRIVACY PHOENIX

Harvesting Humans

Industries rely heavily on resources. Resource scarcity and price fluctuations can significantly affect business outcomes. Traditional industries rely on tangible materials. The automobile industry, for example, uses iron, aluminum, glass, and other physical resources. In recent years, we have seen a shift toward increased use of intangible resources, like patents or information.[1] The Internet economy is not the first to rely on intangible resources, but it does one thing differently. It keeps these resources at the back of the stage – in the shadows.

The Internet economy relies on twin crucial resources. The first resource is time – our attention.[2] This creates the overuse problem discussed throughout this book. The second resource is users' personal data. Internet companies' reliance on personal data produces the privacy problem. Data is as vital as time to the Internet economy's business model. Services are often free for users, but users' personal data is sold to advertisers who generate ads that effectively target consumers based on the collected data. Personal information for advertising is most effective when users maximize their time online and increase their exposure to the ads. Internet companies obscure their use of data and time because, unlike the automobile manufacturers, they do not mine their resources underground. Instead, they harvest them from their customers and their customers' social networks. They do so without their customers' real consent or comprehension of the harvesting process.

We now know that Internet companies entice us to overuse our time, but the Internet privacy problem is an older one. Of course, age is relative. Internet privacy is still a twenty-first-century problem. Since the turn of the century, a growing group of law professors and privacy watchdog organizations, like the Electronic Privacy Information Center (EPIC), have relentlessly fought to protect online privacy.[3] For years, efforts to curb the collection and sale of personal information on the Internet encountered little success. But these days, change is in the air.

Studying the evolution of online privacy is crucial to resolving the overuse problem. The issues are so closely related. Not only is the same business model at stake, but the same main characters – the Internet titans – are fighting the war. As the privacy battles are intensifying, the parties are forming important strategies. Some strategies take after the tobacco and food wars, and some are unique to Silicon Valley culture. Despite the uncertainty of outcome and timing, the privacy battles can already shed important light on future action to curb overuse.

Facebook's Corporate Narcissism

Online companies and privacy advocates have been at odds for years. Facebook, the social network and targeted advertising empire that presides over billions of users, played a central role in this clash. But Facebook's trajectory is not unique. Its resistance tells a much bigger story about technology companies and their opposition to privacy regulation.

The collection of personal data has always been at the heart and soul of the Internet economy. We do not pay fees, whether we use a Gmail account or watch a YouTube video. But, indirectly, we pay a price. The giants of the Internet, like Facebook and Google, use and sell our personal information to advertisers to target ads at those of us most likely to consume the products. For example, pregnant women who have not yet shared their news with loved ones sometimes realize the Internet "knows" about their pregnancy. They begin seeing ads for baby gear and maternity clothes long before their pregnancy starts to show.

Early on, technology companies fiercely resisted any regulation to protect the privacy of users' information. Limits on data collection could collapse or seriously restrict their entire revenue model. Still, unlike cigarette and food manufacturers who acted solely to maximize profit, this is not just a story about maximizing revenues, but also a tale about corporate narcissism.

Facebook emerged as a corporate narcissist, but it did not do so in a void. Our adoration of technology and faith in its ability to promote progress and create a better society gave birth to a generation of tech corporate narcissists. The early settlers of the Internet, who later became the giants we know today, had utopian views of the Internet. For years they viewed themselves as warriors creating, enhancing, and working to preserve this utopian world. And our desire to believe them empowered them to propagate this message, even as their actions contradicted it.

For years, Mark Zuckerberg, Facebook's founder and CEO, believed that he was acting for an almost sacred goal. His goal was to connect billions of users. Zuckerberg was not a lone believer sitting in Facebook's corporate ivory tower. A senior Facebook officer wrote in a 2016 memo: "We connect people. Period. This is why all the work we do ... is justified."[4] And indeed, Facebook's network accounts for 2.9 billion monthly active users.[5] This is more than a quarter of the world's population. But Meta, Facebook's parent company, connects more than just Facebook users. Meta owns Instagram, which has surpassed 2 billion monthly users.[6] Meta also owns WhatsApp, the most popular online messenger, which has over 2 billion active users worldwide.[7]

Roger McNamee, an early investor in Facebook and a mentor to Mark Zuckerberg, published a 2019 book titled: *Zucked: Waking up to the Facebook Catastrophe.* McNamee described how deeply this phenomenon, which I call "corporate narcissism," dominated Facebook's leadership: "To them, connecting 2.2 billion people is so obviously a good thing, and continued growth so important, that they cannot imagine that the problems that have resulted could be in any way linked to their designs or business."[8]

Facebook's form of narcissism is not a product of its success. This utopian faith emerged as the Internet became popular, among Internet start-ups, large companies, and scholars alike. In 2000, I was an aspiring scholar writing my doctorate dissertation about online life at NYU School of Law. Some years later, as a professor, I joined a growing group of legal scholars writing about law and the Internet. Early on, many had concerns about legal regulation of the Internet.

They trusted the Internet's ability to connect the world, produce large collaborative projects, bring education to the masses, and enhance democracy.[9]

Many legal academics lean toward the left of the political spectrum, and they are often suspicious of corporations. But in this case, things were different. In these early days of the Internet, many academics celebrated Silicon Valley. I recall scholars particularly supporting Google, which espoused the motto "Don't be Evil" and led projects like Google Books and Google Books Library Project to scan books and make them accessible online.[10] The pillars of the new Internet economy clearly believed they were the good guys. Unfortunately, they also managed to convince many others.

Facebook was not the only corporate narcissist on the block. But it was a strong representative of its genre. For me, Facebook was part of my personal history and love-hate relationship with the Internet. I have been using it since 2007 as my social network of choice. This is where I experience my own "Privacy Paradox." The Privacy Paradox is a common phenomenon. We believe that we care about privacy, but then our online actions demonstrate the opposite.[11] We post, search, and share thoughtlessly too often, divulging our personal information. I write and teach about privacy law and direct an Institute for Privacy Protection, and I still find Facebook irresistible. I work on this book in twenty-minute increments with no online distractions during these periods. But when my timer rings for the end of a writing session, I too often go on Facebook.

I originally joined Facebook to keep in touch with colleagues in my field. But during my early days on Facebook, something strange happened. One weekend, I bought tickets on Fandango for my 6-year-old son to watch the movie *Kung Fu Panda*. The next day, as I dropped him off at school, a friend – one of the other moms – asked me, "How was Kung Fu Panda?" I was taken aback since I had never mentioned to her that I was going to watch the film. She explained that she saw on her Facebook Newsfeed that "Gaia bought Kung Fu Panda tickets on Fandango."

It turned out to be "Beacon," Facebook's innovation, which shared the information about my Kung Fu Panda tickets. Facebook used Beacon to enhance its advertising. Beacon sent Facebook data from external websites, like Fandango or Yelp. Facebook explained that

Beacon let users share their experiences with friends. But Facebook's main motivation was that a friend's choice advertised a service or product more effectively than a generic ad.[12] For example, my friend's interest in the *Kung Fu Panda* movie increased when she saw that I had purchased tickets for my son, who was her child's classmate.

Beacon did not fly well. I was not the only one uncomfortable about it. Many Facebook users worried that something they did anywhere on the Internet could suddenly appear without warning on their friends' newsfeeds. Reactions followed. The MoveOn Organization, a civic action group, organized user petitions demanding that Facebook not publish their activity unless they specifically consented. Facebook users even filed a class action lawsuit.[13] In reaction, on December 5, 2007, Mark Zuckerberg published a public response to the Beacon crisis. Zuckerberg's reaction illustrates all the elements of Facebook's successful strategy to push back on attempts to protect Facebook users' privacy.

Zuckerberg started out with a heartfelt apology:

> About a month ago, we released a new feature called Beacon to try to help people share information with their friends about things they do on the web. We've made a lot of mistakes building this feature, but we've made even more with how we've handled them. We simply did a bad job with this release, and I apologize for it. While I am disappointed with our mistakes, we appreciate all the feedback we have received from our users.

He then highlighted Facebook's utopian vision: connecting people by sharing information about their actions all over the Internet.

> When we first thought of Beacon, our goal was to build a simple product to let people share information across sites with their friends . . .

Zuckerberg then moved on to emphasize Facebook's commitment to privacy and letting people control their personal information:

> Facebook has succeeded so far in part because it gives people control over what and how they share information . . .

And finally, Zuckerberg announced a change to the feature that had caused the uproar:

Last week we changed Beacon to be an opt-in system, and today we're releasing a privacy control to turn off Beacon completely. You can find it here. If you select that you don't want to share some of Beacon actions or if you turn off Beacon, then Facebook won't store those actions even when partners send them to Facebook.[14]

In some ways, Facebook's strategy resembles tactics that the tobacco and food industries had used. Cigarette companies and food manufacturers paid homage to health. Recall the tobacco industry promoting filtered cigarettes as the healthy solution. Facebook's lip service to privacy is reminiscent of these attempts. In addition, the food, and the tobacco industries, when pressured, often reacted with highly publicized "fixes." For example, Ben and Jerry's removed the term "natural" from their ice creams. Their goal was to quiet public controversy and criticism and avoid legal action. Here, Facebook announced that it would fix Beacon by making it an option only for users who selected it.

Although Facebook executed well-proven strategies, it also employed tactics that were unique to itself and to other Silicon Valley companies. Facebook always apologized and promised to do better. These heartfelt apologies worked. They worked at least partly because Facebook accompanied them with its utopian vision, which portrayed it as the good guy. Apologies always came with a touch of corporate narcissism reminding the public that Facebook's goal is to connect the world. Facebook's mission statement stated it plainly: "Give people the power to build community and bring the world closer together."[15] Meta, Facebook's parent company, continues to claim that its "products empower more than 3 billion people around the world to share ideas, offer support and make a difference."[16]

Facebook is not the only company to have aspirational wording in its mission statement. Coca-Cola, for example, declares that its mission is to "craft the brands and choice of drinks that people love, to refresh them in body & spirit."[17] But other companies, like Coca-Cola, also emphasize that their goal is to create value – to make money for their shareholders. Facebook's mission statement is unique, not only in its exclusive focus on its utopian goal, but also in the way the company communicates its mission throughout its operations. It is not just a slogan, but it drives the entire company's vibe. "Connecting the world" is imparted consistently to the public and internally. As Mark Zuckerberg described it in a public announcement, "I started Facebook to connect my college. I always thought one day someone would connect the whole world, but I never thought it would be us ... we cared so much about this idea – that all people want to connect. So we just kept pushing forward, day by day ..."[18]

Apologize, give homage to privacy, promise to fix, and – above all – believe and remind everyone that you are the good guys, working to better the world. This strategy worked for the giants of the Internet, like Facebook and Google, because they burst through an open door. We admire innovation and progress. We believe they improve human welfare. When the Internet became mainstream just before the turn of the century, we marveled at it. Some called it "the greatest innovation catalyst of our age." Many believed that an open, decentralized Internet – not governed by any laws – would maximize its potential for innovation.[19] We wanted to accept their apologies, to believe these were just genuine errors and that all was well.

The Veil Is Lifted

Facebook's strategy worked long after Beacon and through Facebook's IPO in 2012. As the years went by, Facebook continued to create tools for advertisers to leverage knowledge of users' activities on other websites to target them on Facebook. Occasionally, a damaging disclosure came out. Facebook repeatedly apologized, recommitted to privacy and to its vision, and promised to make a fix. Facebook promised to fix, but whether it actually did is unknown. Regulators or the public could not inspect Facebook's algorithm and use of data. Facebook, Google, and the other Internet mega players continued to use individuals' personal information practically uninterrupted, at least in the United States.

Facebook's strategy worked until it didn't. It worked for longer than it should have because we wanted to believe that technology is inherently good. In 2015, the media revealed that Cambridge Analytica, a company working for Senator Ted Cruz, had used psychological data harvested from tens of millions of people's Facebook accounts without their consent.[20] Facebook withstood the initial storm using its usual strategy. But then the scandals kept escalating. In March 2018, reports revealed that Cambridge Analytica had used Facebook user information to aid the Trump campaign and to tilt the presidential election results.[21] Facebook once again resorted to its regular formula. It published full-page ads featuring a personal letter from Mark Zuckerberg in the *New York Times*, *Wall Street Journal*, *Washington Post*, and six British papers. Zuckerberg wrote: "We have a responsibility to protect your information. If we can't we don't deserve it ... This was a breach of trust and I'm sorry we didn't do more at the time. We are taking steps to make sure this doesn't happen again."[22] But the heartfelt apology and homage to privacy no longer worked.

The scandals and the bad news just kept piling up. The media reported that Russia had used Facebook accounts to purchase Facebook ads, target users, and manipulate the US elections. As a result, Zuckerberg testified before a hostile and suspicious Congress.[23] Another story revealed that, contrary to its promises, Facebook had sent millions of marketing messages to phone numbers that users provided as part of the two-factor authentication security feature.[24] Then it turned out that, over the years, Facebook had granted device makers, such as Apple, Amazon, and Blackberry, access to the data of the device user's Facebook friends.[25] Again, awareness was key to change. Once the public and the media reluctantly realized that Facebook was not "the good guy," Pandora's box was opened.

Intensive legal action followed public reports of Facebook's misuse of users' data. The FTC, the government's privacy watchdog, imposed a $5 billion fine on Facebook. This was the first time the FTC had applied a relatively heavy-handed approach to privacy violators. To compare, in 2012, the FTC imposed a fine of only $22 million on Google.[26] State attorneys general, representing a host of states, joined in suing Facebook for privacy violations.[27] Recall that state attorneys general also played an important role in the 1990s tobacco litigation that produced the Master Agreement – the comprehensive settlement with the cigarette companies. But particularly threatening, and telling, was the significant increase in the number of class action lawsuits against Facebook.

Class actions are especially foreboding for Facebook and any corporation. The large number of plaintiffs attracts negative media attention and creates a risk of a large financial liability. The number of class actions against Facebook rose exponentially from 2018. Users brought dozens of class actions seeking damages for the Cambridge Analytica data violations.[28] But, beyond that, users began to challenge many aspects of Facebook's operations. Users sued, charging that Messenger – Facebook's text messaging application – scrapes call and text log information from their phones to incorporate into its user profiles for advertising purposes.[29] Facebook users also sued, accusing Facebook of tracking their geographical locations without their consent and profiting from the information by selling it to advertisers.[30] Facebook settled another lawsuit for $90 million, where users accused it of tracking their Internet activity even after they had logged out of Facebook.[31] Users clearly had become aware that Facebook's business model relied on harvesting their data. A 2018 survey showed a 66 percent decline in trust in Facebook as a result of the Cambridge Analytica revelations.[32] Later surveys showed that the trend of distrust in the company persisted.[33] But even beyond that, something else has changed.

The public revelations and legal actions shook up Facebook's leadership. Facebook could no longer declare that no regulation was needed. In some ways, it is now in the same place that the tobacco companies stood in, over half a century ago. First, Facebook realized that arguing against limiting the collection and use of personal information had become futile. Second, it also understood that it may be better to support a federal law and then lobby to weaken it than to fight it altogether. This change of sentiment was clearly echoed in Mark Zuckerberg's testimony before Congress in 2018. Zuckerberg said: "My position is not that there should be no regulation." He then added: "I think the real question, as the internet becomes more important in people's lives, is what is the right regulation, not whether there should be or not."[34]

Creating the Myth of Self-Control

Facebook's story is not unique. Facebook is part of an Internet culture that believed it could do no wrong. Harvard Law Professor Lawrence Lessig famously wrote in his 1999 book *Codes and Other*

Laws of Cyberspace that "code is law." Lessig meant that Internet users, large and small, govern the Internet through coding. It was an idea of a naturally evolving non-coercive form of governance.[35] This was the trend in the early days of the Internet. And although some legal regulation eventually occurred, a hands-off approach prevailed through the Obama era.

Many believed that Internet companies could regulate themselves. So did the government. Why? Mostly it boils down to, once again, wanting them to be the good guys who can do it. But there is more to it. Some thought the Internet was a unique technology that should be treated differently from any technology that came before it.[36] There are also some deeply ingrained convictions about law and technology that played a role here. Law cannot keep up with technology.[37] Law cannot successfully regulate technology because it quickly becomes obsolete.[38] Government intervention suffocates innovation.[39] Let the market control because regulators cannot understand technology sufficiently well.[40]

We thought then that the Internet was special. We also held, and perhaps still hold, certain beliefs about whether law can regulate new technologies. But there was something else going on that helped companies avert regulation. Companies collected, used, and sold our personal information with no transparency. Compare this to when we eat junk food day after day. We end up gaining weight and may suffer worse health consequences, like diabetes. We realize, whether we want to or not, that we are eating unhealthy, high-calorie food. But, with our personal information, for years, we rarely got glimpses of how companies used our data and what the consequences were. We found it easier to ignore and believe all is well.

I taught my first class as a law professor in 2004, during the early days of the Internet. It was a privacy class held in the evening, with thirteen students in the class. I was quite nervous. Some of the students were older than me. They knew I was brand new. I was also unsure why the students had selected my class. Were they interested in the then-backwater topic of privacy? I suspected many had chosen that class because it fit their work schedules. As the semester progressed, I taught them about different privacy topics. They found some of the topics more familiar, like the right to be free from illegal searches by the government. But when we got to online privacy, I sensed resistance and bewilderment. I recall asking "Does anyone know what cookies are?" Few students raised their hands. My students mostly did not acknowledge that collection of personal information online presented risks. In 2004, the Internet was not a problem; it was a boon.

Over the years, my privacy classes filled with many students. I now no longer labor to explain that the online collection and use of personal information is a problem. My students know this. They have witnessed the privacy scandals, intensifying media scrutiny, and ensuing litigation. They find the topic intriguing, but they are also in that classroom for practical reasons. They foresee that the area of privacy law holds much promise for their future careers as lawyers. Privacy regulation originating outside the United States and in cities, towns, and individual states across America is, unexpectedly, pressuring online companies to change their data practices.

Winds from the Old World

For Europeans privacy is a human right. When you lose privacy, you lose dignity. In the United States, privacy is not held on a pedestal. Instead, it is measured in terms of harm. Privacy protection is granted usually only when there is a quantifiable economic harm; that is, money is lost.[41] But the picture is more complex than preferences about privacy itself. Freedom of speech in the United States is as central as privacy is in Europe. We saw in Chapter 5 that food manufacturers successfully used freedom of speech protections to avoid disclosing information about food ingredients. Legislators and courts frequently evaluate whether freedom of speech protections should trump public health, privacy, and social solidarity.[42] For years, we paid the price for those that we gained in protecting speech.

Given these preferences, it is not surprising that two very different privacy regimes developed in Europe and in the United States. Europe offers its residents comprehensive privacy protection of their personal information, including online information, while US laws provide much weaker privacy protections, which for years rarely applied to online information. The differences were so striking it was sometimes hard to grasp. I used to illustrate this to my students when we reached the topic of "The Right to Be Forgotten." What options do you have when an unflattering or, even worse, a damaging item about you is posted online? Will it follow you for the rest of your life?

I would instruct my students to go on the European Google website and see what European residents can request Google to remove from its search results. The answer was quite a lot. Europeans can request the removal of information that is inadequate, irrelevant, or excessive. However, Google will not remove information if there is a public interest in it – if the information is about a politician, for example. I would then instruct my students to go to the US Google removal page to explore what options they have as US residents. They would quickly see, to their surprise, that in the United States, Google would remove search results only if they were child sexual abuse imagery or were illegal – most commonly copyright violations. Privacy was not mentioned.

These two privacy regimes coexisted for a while. It was not a harmonious coexistence because information has no geographic borders. But each legal regime implemented its approach to privacy protection without destabilizing the other. Then in 2016 things changed. The European Union adopted a privacy law called the General Data Protection Regulation (GDPR). This law strengthened privacy protections within Europe. It imposed potentially huge fines for violations. And, importantly, it has a long arm. It applies European privacy laws to non-European organizations that offer goods and services to EU residents or that monitor their behavior there.[43] This law promised to have a huge impact, and not only on the Facebooks and Googles of the world. Using personal information, online and offline, is an integral part of doing business in the twenty-first century. US companies as diverse as McDonald's, The Gap, CitiGroup, and Johnson & Johnson needed to change their privacy practices to comply with European laws. For example, a US company is no longer able to freely collect data on European residents who visit its website; the company now needs to acquire explicit consent.

Everyone braced for the law to come into effect in 2018. Many companies frantically sought answers and prepared. I sat on a panel of experts in an event held for pharmaceutical companies at a New York law firm. One question kept coming up: how can we have different privacy protections for European information than for US information? Indeed, this was when European law started transforming US privacy law from the outside. Many US companies had to change their privacy practices to comply with the strictest law – the European one. It was just too complicated to provide no protections for some information while protecting other data.[44]

Unlike food and cigarettes, data and online platforms are not local. Data about users is collected and transferred globally. Social networks and online games, like Instagram or Fortnite, are also not local. Users converge on these platforms from all corners of the world. We saw that outside influence affected data collection practices in the United States. The same could be true for design that affects the time we spend online. Foreign laws are more likely to impact the redesign of social networks and games to contain overuse, than they could affect the nutritional value of the hamburger we eat.

Change from the Bottom up

By 2018, the US media had become a privacy watchdog. Reports regularly exposed new privacy scandals. These revelations emerged while the new assertive European law forced US companies to rethink their privacy practices. It was at that time that the state of California made a bold move. California enacted a law called the California Consumer Privacy Act (CCPA), which looks like a close family member of the European law. This law gave Californian residents many rights that no US residents had enjoyed before. For example, under the California law, a California resident who shops on Amazon can prohibit Amazon from selling her personal information to anyone else. She can require Amazon to let her know what information it has about her. She can even do the most magical act of all: request Amazon to remove information about her from its database. California's law is a game changer in US privacy law. For the first time in the United States, a law significantly limits the actions of companies that collect and use personal information, and it does so in the name of privacy. Not only that, but this also signals a change beyond California. Other states are following suit with similar laws.[45]

California's move may be the boldest yet, but states are not the only new privacy activists. Cities and towns have joined in as well. Recall how municipalities spearheaded innovative moves to fight obesity, like imposing soda taxes. Once again, innovation is coming from the bottom up. Municipalities are stepping in where the federal government has not acted. Many cities and towns have made privacy a priority. They regulate drones that fly and take pictures of private homes. They limit police use of surveillance technology. Municipalities also make sure that the local personal data they collect on individuals is protected.[46]

Of particular importance is municipalities' turn to regulating private companies' collection and sale of personal information. San Francisco has done it through its Privacy First Initiative. It uses its bargaining power in assigning city contracts to promote privacy standards. For example, a yellow bus company contracting with the City of San Francisco to bus students to school needs to disclose to the City their data practices, which covers data on students and employees, and to secure this data.[47] New York attempted to pass a bill which would ban cellphone companies and mobile apps from selling customer location data to marketers and businesses.[48]

There are no guarantees. Some municipal laws will remain in force and influence privacy practices. Other proposed municipal laws will fail. Regardless, there is a clear feeling that change is happening. The giants of the Internet sense it and have altered strategy. Recall the cigarette companies preferring to support a prohibition on cigarette commercials to avoid a greater evil. They favored no cigarette commercials over sharing the screen with the American Cancer Society's smoking hazards campaign. Opting for the lesser evil is happening again.

The Internet giants – Google, Facebook, Twitter, Amazon, and many others – no longer argue against regulation. They have turned to lobbying for a new federal privacy law. Like their predecessors, the cigarette and food industries, the Internet giants are pinning their hopes on preemption. They are hoping for a federal law with diluted privacy protections, which will supersede the emerging network of state and local laws. A federal law will simplify compliance. Adjusting data practices to one law is much easier than adjusting it to multiple laws. But most importantly, their goal is to end up with a law that is less restrictive of their business practices than the European or California laws.[49]

Lessons from the Privacy Battleground

Collecting and selling personal data has finally emerged as a major social problem. While the GDPR and CCPA are important steps, technologies including algorithms, facial imaging, and – to be sure – future innovations, mean the privacy wars are far from over. Even under regulations, corporations often play privacy theater, going through the motions of privacy protection, but in practice offering diluted protection.[50] Still, although the struggles over data and privacy are only now entering the center of the stage and are not resolved, they provide insight for the road that lies ahead to curtail overuse.

- Awareness of privacy harms was key for change to:
  - challenge the tech giants' "good guys" image; and
  - combat the lack of transparency of companies' data practices.
- Technology companies use their predecessor industries' traditional public relations strategies, specifically, by paying homage to privacy and proposing short-term fixes.
- European law changed US companies' data practices because online data is not confined by geographical borders.
- Municipalities and states have emerged as pioneers in enacting privacy-protecting laws. In response, the tech industry has turned to federal preemption to supersede and dilute these laws.

7 LESSONS FROM BATTLING TITANS

Technology overuse is a novel problem. For the first time in history, electronic communications have replaced a significant part of real-life face-to-face interactions. The harms are also unique. But battles between corporations and activists seeking to protect the public from harmful products have happened before. And when they did, the stakes were often high, and the fight prolonged. This past gives us a window into the future. We can extract from the battles of the past, the choices and obstacles likely to confront a movement to curtail technology overuse.

The First Amendment Mountain

The First Amendment is one legal concept that the public, not just lawyers, is familiar with. Beyond political disagreements, even some proponents of free speech protections believe courts have extended its protections too far.[1] We saw, for example, how freedom of speech protections expanded to food labels.

To understand how we got here, we need, first, to identify what the First Amendment protects. The First Amendment protects "speech," but what does that really mean? Some things are intuitively speech. Take a *New York Times* editorial article criticizing President Biden's handling of the economy. This is clearly speech, and we expect the First Amendment to protect it. But twenty-five years ago, the Supreme Court started down a different path. These days, the legal definition of protected speech does not always match common intuitions.[2]

Law can influence ordinary life in unexpected ways. A First Amendment Supreme Court case can even influence how kids celebrate their birthdays. I recall a weekend afternoon in 2017, when we attended a birthday party hosted by family friends for both adults and kids. The kids could play outside, but a group of them (mostly boys aged 10–13) chose to congregate around the Xbox playing *Star Wars Battlefront 2*. In the game, the kids could control figures from the Star Wars film as they shot and killed their enemies. I observed the shooting and killing as I passed by.

How did the Supreme Court affect this birthday party? In 2011, the Supreme Court decided that violent video games are speech that deserves First Amendment protection. Justice Antonin Scalia explained that, like books, plays, and movies, video games communicate ideas and social messages. The Court refused to categorize violent games as low-value speech that does not deserve protection. What did this mean in practice? It meant that states cannot restrict kids' access to violent video games because the games are protected under the First Amendment.[3] The First Amendment serves as a strong shield, preventing parents from successfully suing game manufacturers for harmful effects of gaming on kids.[4]

As we have already seen, many design features encourage overuse. When I posted a Facebook post with my picture in a coffee shop announcing the beginning of my sabbatical dedicated to writing this book, and my post attracted many more likes and comments than usual, of course I kept checking the app to see how many more I had received. Are "likes" protected speech? Are the red alert buttons on our apps or the "infinite scroll" and "pulling down" features of our Instagram and Twitter feeds protected speech? We do not know yet. Some legal scholars believe they should not be so.[5] But as laws and courts continuously expand First Amendment protection – signaling that data is protected speech and social networks have special status – fighting device manufacturers and social networks' First Amendment defenses is likely to be an uphill battle.[6]

Tackling the Personal Responsibility Argument

The personal responsibility argument has already entered the overuse debate. Game-makers were the first to directly bring up the personal responsibility defense. They raised it to fight against the WHO's definition of Internet gaming as a disorder, and in legal battles surrounding loot boxes (an addictive feature, commonly integrated into video games). Game-makers argued that the users had chosen to play these games and that they and/or their parents were responsible for any ensuing harm. Tech companies raised the personal responsibility argument indirectly when they developed their digital well-being tools. These tools, like Apple's Screen Time, aimed to assist users in taking responsibility for limiting their time online. And similarly, psychologists seeking to solve the overuse problem highlighted personal responsibility by emphasizing the importance of self-help measures, like creating phone-free zones in the house.

We saw that cigarette and food manufacturers raised individual choice and personal responsibility arguments to ward off government regulation of their products. In recent years, the specter of the nanny state – famously portrayed by Nanny Bloomberg – popularized the icon of the individual who makes her own choices and bears responsibility for the outcomes. But this icon has vulnerabilities. These are the places where social responsibility prevails and communal efforts to contain overuse can succeed:

> *Intention to addict*: Corporations, arguing that consumers are responsible for the harm caused to them by their products, found that this strategy can backfire. Revelations that corporations acted intentionally and covertly to addict their customers undermined the personal responsibility argument. Recall, for example, when information leaked out that the tobacco industry knew but kept secret the addictive qualities of nicotine. The personal responsibility argument broke down when it turned out smokers were not making autonomous choices and could not be held accountable. The technology industry is likely to face a similar obstacle to any personal responsibility argument. Silicon Valley whistleblowers have already stepped out and revealed how Big Tech stealthily designs its gadgets to keep us hooked.

Impact on Innocent Bystanders: Cigarette companies regularly raised personal responsibility arguments as a defense in courts. They pointed out that smokers knew what they were getting into. The tobacco industry won all litigation until the 1990s, when things changed. Medical journals publishing findings about the impact on innocent bystanders contributed to this shift. The information about second-hand smoke transformed the litigation trajectory. Similarly, overuse impacts not only heavy tech users. Researchers have found that children suffer second-hand harm when adults model technology overuse. Children who watch their parents spend many hours on their screens are more likely to become heavy users themselves when they grow up and get their own devices.[7] The second-hand harms are not limited to very young children. Adults and teens who are light technology users can also suffer second-hand harms from technology overuse. When a spouse spends many hours on her phone, the well-being of her significant other is diminished as their relationship is affected.[8] A teen who would like to avoid social media feels compelled to join because most of her friends communicate through Instagram. Reluctantly, she is then exposed to the harm of overuse.

Making Choices for Kids: Making choices for kids is okay. For adults less so. Prohibiting cigarette sales to minors is acceptable. But forbidding adults from smoking is unlikely to fly. Schools' weighing kids, requiring physical activities, or limiting vending machine purchases are accepted. Again, we feel differently applying these measures to adults. Intervening to protect children, then, is where the personal responsibility argument breaks. Here, parenting or "nannying" prevails. Many parents these days are intensively engaged in their kids' lives and lobby socially for causes that promote their children's welfare.[9] Unsurprisingly, we already see parent groups lobbying for decreased use of technology for kids. A group of parents, for example, formed the organization "Wait Until 8th," where parents can come together to commit to not giving their kids cellphones until eighth grade.[10] Parents are already lobbying and litigating through class actions, and they are likely to continue to spearhead the movement to curtail overuse.[11]

Regulating the Middlemen: People squirm when laws directly intervene in everyday regular choices. Smokers revolted when laws prohibited them from smoking in restaurants. But laws that require manufacturers to change their product design are different. They are not in direct conflict with individual choice. Take, for example, a law mandating large labels on cigarette boxes stating "Smoking kills" or a law requiring schools to serve fresh fruit and vegetables at lunch. People view laws that target design to be less restrictive than those targeting use. The former leave more options open. It also matters who is targeted. Laws regulating users seem more infantilizing, as opposed to laws influencing users indirectly by focusing on the middlemen. Looking back at technology overuse, laws regulating device and social network design would not be in a direct conflict with ideas of personal responsibility. In contrast, imagine a law requiring that all cellphones need to be checked in at the entrance to a cinema. This kind of law prohibiting and strictly enforcing use of cellphones in certain areas would be far less popular because it conflicts with our ideas of individual choice.

The self-choice and personal responsibility argument, then, is strong but not infallible. It can break down, and it does. Evidence that companies intended to addict; proof of harm to innocent bystanders; interventions targeted at protecting kids; and interventions targeting design changes through the middlemen all make it less likely that fears of the nanny state will prevail.

Legitimizing Interventions

There is no one magic solution. History has shown us that activists have taken multiple roads simultaneously to produce results. Legal strategies take different forms, and some are less "interventionist" than others. Some tactics are subtle: what we call "nudges."[12] Providing information through labeling and advertising, such as requiring labels to report trans-fat levels, is a nudge. On the other hand, imposing a soda tax that creates a price barrier to buying Coca-Cola is more interventionist. Laws prohibiting smoking by minors or smoking in public spaces are even tougher interventions.[13] Combining legal strategies is vital not only to address different aspects of the overuse problem, but also because interventionist tools are more likely to evoke significant public opposition.

Some strategies are more interventionist, nannying, or in academic terms "paternalistic." The image of Nanny Bloomberg still looms large. Those opposing interventionist rules believe they undermine autonomy. They view these laws as the government telling people what would be best for them, instead of allowing them to make their own choices.[14] Imagine a nanny taking an iPad from a kid, telling him he spent enough time playing and now needs to take a shower and have dinner. This seems okay. But then think of his mother coming home from work, scrolling through Instagram pictures on her iPad. Would it be okay if the nanny took mom's iPad, letting her know that she has spent forty-five minutes on it, and it is time to have dinner with the kids? Probably not. How about a law that requires online game-makers to technologically limit the amount of time per day a person can play an online game? Opposers would argue that this is an infantilization of adults and an impermissible interference with adult autonomous decision-making.[15]

Still, we do have laws that constrain our decision-making. Some of these laws are strongly interventionist, banning activities that can cause significant harm.[16] For example, the government illegalized cocaine even for adults, because of the severity of its harms. Preventing injury legitimizes interventionist rules. Preventing harm to innocent bystanders provides even stronger legitimacy. Lawmakers justified prohibiting smoking in public places on the basis of the need to protect non-smokers from the harms of second-hand smoke.

Chapter 2 described the harms of technology overuse: the detrimental impact on children's development and mental health; the effects on adults in terms of addiction, social bonds, and well-being. We also saw that technology overuse causes indirect harm. It affects children of over-users who, through modeling, suffer the impact of second-hand use. And it affects quality of life for light users as their relationships with partners, families, and friends are impoverished and transformed.

Despite the direct and second-hand harms, we can expect opposition to more interventionist legal strategies aimed at containing overuse. Still, why are we here in the first place? We got here because technology hijacked our ability to make reflective choices as to how we spend our time. We need legal action to restore this autonomy. It turns out that justifying legal interventions is easier when the goal is to correct a loss of autonomy. An intervention to contain overuse would restore our ability to make thoughtful decisions instead of diminish it.[17] Currently, we spend endless hours on our screens. This is not a conscious, deliberate, autonomous decision. The designs of our devices and apps determine this result. These legal interventions would not infantilize us; to the contrary, they would reinstate us as the captains of our ships.

The Role of Awareness

During the first sessions of my outreach program in 2017, many parents I spoke to had not yet realized that a technology overuse problem existed. The parents who did notice it usually thought something was wrong with their children or their family. They did not recognize that this was a social problem that affected all of us. Starting out then, I truly believed that with more programs like mine, media coverage, warning labels, and other disclosure methods, the problem would be solved. I thought that people just didn't realize how much time they spent on screens, and once they did, and got reminders of the risks, they would reduce their time online. In fact, I so staunchly believed awareness would solve the problem that I originally used the words "The Power of Awareness" in the title of my book.

Years later, I still believe awareness of the problem, and of the harms, is a necessary step to resolving the technology overuse problem. But now I know awareness is insufficient by itself. The law can regulate the tools of awareness like labels, advertising, and ratings. But, again, these tools are not enough. Eating a Big Mac, even when you know of the risks of obesity, is more enticing than ordering a salad. Quitting smoking is extremely difficult even when you recognize smoking can kill you. And even when we know we are better off reducing our screen time, refraining from constantly picking up our phone to check messages and notifications is challenging.

Relying on spreading information as the only strategy is also risky. How can informing people be risky? Because if you know something is dangerous and still choose to do it, aren't you responsible for the consequences? This is exactly what happened during the tobacco litigation. Smokers faced a new challenge when cigarette pack labels clearly indicated the risks of smoking. The tobacco industry could then successfully argue that smokers alone are responsible for the ravages of smoking because they knew the risks and kept smoking. Even today, lung cancer patients are treated differently than other cancer patients because people assume they smoked and brought the disease upon themselves. So, although disseminating information through labeling and advertising is crucial, it is rarely enough.

The Risks of Self-Regulation

Industries, facing accusations that their products are harmful, usually go through a cycle. They initially ignore the problem. They then move to denial when allegations intensify and become a public relations problem. Eventually, the industry actively enters the science wars by refuting scientific studies and producing its own. But, at a certain point, they need to incorporate a different strategy: acknowledging the problem and offering a targeted solution. Cigarette companies offered the filtered cigarette as a healthy option and technology companies offered privacy settings to give users choices. Facebook even opened pop-up privacy cafés to offer users assistance in checking their privacy settings.[18]

After recognizing the problem and proposing a specific solution, the next step is often the industry lobbying for self-regulation. The industry shifts from asserting "all is fine" to admitting a major problem, but then insisting it can solve it without outside interference. Recall, for example, how the giants of the food industry pledged to restrict advertising of unhealthy food to children under the age of 12. The technology industry repeatedly asserted it could regulate itself. And throughout President Obama's administration, it successfully fended off government regulation.[19]

Industry self-regulation looks like an attractive solution for overuse. It is enticing because it bypasses the First Amendment obstacle and fends off nanny state objections. The First Amendment would not be an issue because litigants can only raise freedom of speech claims to challenge government action. If there is no law mandating change, then there is no government action to challenge. Similarly, if companies choose to make changes, there is no "nanny" problem. All seems good.

Unfortunately, history has proven that self-regulation left unchecked is precarious. Industries have regularly abused self-regulation to avoid getting to the heart of the matter.

The technology industry adeptly endorses the "Do It Ourselves" method. Once tech-addiction became a hot topic, the technology industry, as discussed in Chapter 3, opted for the digital wellbeing route. Apple, for example, came up with Screen Time. Still, it did not make limited time the default setting that a user needs to turn off. Instead, it kept unrestricted time as the default setting a user needs to change to restrict herself.

Apple's design of parental controls to manage kids' time on devices reveals a lot about the hazards of self-regulation. My twins, born in 2007, entered tweendom at a time when parents started recognizing the risks of overuse. I was determined to limit their screen as much as socially feasible. I installed a time-limit app on their phone restricting their use of certain apps, like games or YouTube. I also used Apple's parental controls to restrict their use of their Mac computers. We maintained a reasonable tech-life balance for a family living in New York City in 2019. But, in December 2019, when school closed for the holidays and we were packing to leave town, our tech-life equilibrium destabilized.

My son let me know that he had updated his Mac's operating system, and that the parental controls no longer worked. I tried to quickly reset them the usual way but failed. I realized that Apple no longer had a setting called Parental Controls. This meant I needed to invest much more time in finding a way to reinstate the status quo. We left New York to go to Israel. In Israel, I realized that, without parental controls, my son's computer time extended significantly. I tried fixing it quickly again. He even tried to help me, but to no avail. It eventually took hours of searching online and watching videos to implement the new system. His time on his Mac was restricted once again, but less effectively than before. The password changed from a complicated multi-symbol password to an easy to detect four-digit passcode. When he needed extra time for his homework, I had to add time repeatedly for each app instead of the whole computer. The new system irritated both of us. Apple had taken the passive-aggressive move of acknowledging the overuse problem and providing a solution. But, at the same time, it had made the solution so cumbersome and inaccessible that many parents were likely to understandably give up in the process.

The Science Wars

Industries vehemently deny that their products cause harm. Scientists seeking to prove a product is harmful need to show it is that particular product that creates the injury, and not multiple other possible causes. The labor intensity of good scientific research, combined with industry resistance, creates prolonged science wars. In retrospect, we know that cigarette smoking causes undeniable harm. But even these science wars dragged on for decades. The intensity of the tobacco science wars is even more perplexing considering the extraordinary death toll of smoking. While the first major scientific studies came out in the 1950s, the tobacco industry's denial, contradiction, and self-subsidized studies effectively delayed an end to the science wars. It was only in 1964 that the Surgeon General announced that smoking is a major health hazard.

Historically, science wars have moved forward when reputable scientific establishments (like the American Cancer Association) or leading medical journals (like the *New England Journal of Medicine*) endorsed a stand. But the wars have subsided only once governmental bodies assessed the relevant evidence and made pronouncements. The science wars of overuse are still raging, but evidence is accruing. Findings are pointing to increased urgency, especially where children are concerned. Some organizations like the World Health Organization, the American Psychiatric Association, and the American Pediatric Association have addressed some aspects of the problem, but their recommendations are narrow. The science wars will continue and make it harder to implement law and policy without comprehensive recommendations by governmental or professional organizations.

Takeaway Points

The battles of the past provide guidance for action to contain addictive technologies by pointing to likely obstacles and potential solutions:

- Advocates fighting to contain overuse will likely face significant First Amendment challenges.
- Technology companies already raise the personal responsibility argument, but it faces substantial obstacles because
  - of emerging evidence of intention to addict;
  - of impact on bystanders;
  - of children's enhanced vulnerability; and
  - activists could target redesign by manufacturers instead of focusing on changing user behavior.
- There is no magic potion. Legal tools of all shapes and forms are needed. Labeling and advertising to spread awareness are not enough.
- Opting for self-regulation evades the First Amendment and personal responsibility obstacles, but technology companies left to self-regulate, without constant legal pressure, are likely to manipulate designs to maintain overuse.
- While evidence of the harms of overuse is accumulating, the science wars are still on. A governmental agency taking an official stand will promote closure, which is critical for legal action.

Part III
FIGHTING FOR CHOICE

8 THE ART OF REDESIGN

There Is No Time Machine

Our connectivity is here to stay. Our phones, computers, and tablets will remain until replaced by the communication tools of the future. We are unlikely to return to an era of limited connectivity. And neither should we. When considering the good, the bad, and the ugly of connectivity, the good stands out. Learning about the misfortunes of others, whether across the globe or even in our own city. Connecting to help ourselves, friends, and strangers. We will never know, but would definitely hope, that an Internet in 1939 would have prevented the horrors of the Holocaust that followed.

Redesign should not reverse progress. Its goal should be to give us the opportunity to pause and reflect on our choices. Right now, we too often act as automatons: surfing, clicking, checking, and posting. We are at the mercy of what Woodrow Hartzog, in his book *Privacy's Blueprint: The Battle to Control the Design of New Technologies*, calls "abusive design."

Hartzog identifies "abusive design" as a design that lawmakers should target. An abusive design, he writes, "unreasonably frustrates our ability to make autonomous decisions and puts us at greater risk of harm or makes us regret our decisions."[1] Currently, we do not evaluate how we want to be connected. Neither do we reflect on our moment-to-moment decisions as we use our devices and social networks, although most of us regret the amount of time we aimlessly spend online. Some of us suffer the greater harms of addiction, attention problems, and even anxiety and depression.

Hartzog calls for lawmakers to push for redesign to protect individuals' ability to act autonomously. "Design is power," he writes, "because people react to design in predictable ways . . . Design is powerful because we as people are more easily manipulated than we'd like to think. We often fail to act in our own self-interest. We like to think of ourselves as rational and autonomous actors, but the fact is that we are not."[2] He explains that lawmakers should look at the way that systems are designed to exploit our predictable biases and interfere with our decision-making processes against our interests.[3]

We do not have to do away with our technologies, but we can redesign them to make them less abusive and addictive. Freud's analogy of the horse and his rider is instrumental here. While our instinctive desire – the horse – is to stay on our screens, we should focus on becoming the rider "who has to hold in check the superior strength of the horse."[4] We can do so by collectively pushing for redesign of both our technologies and the physical spaces in which we use them.

A Redesign Success Story: Trans-Fat

The tale of trans-fat is a strikingly successful redesign story. It is about food, not technology, but the struggles and strategic moves are all too relevant. Although trans-fat reached notoriety only in the twenty-first century, it was, in fact, invented at the beginning of the twentieth century. In 1902, the scientist Wilhelm Norman discovered that adding hydrogen to vegetable oil would make the vegetable oil solid, creating trans-fat.[5] Why did this invention gain so much traction? Because it gave foods longer shelf life. Food would not expire, so stores would not need to replace unsold stock. Consumers could also keep food products longer at home without compromising taste and freshness. Restaurants no longer needed to repeatedly change the oil they used for frying. Trans-fat was, in a way, a "miracle" ingredient. It worked for a very wide range of products: from cookies, tortilla chips, and French fries to donuts, creamers, and margarine.

Today, over two decades into the twenty-first century, we know trans-fat is bad for us. But this was not always the case. As late as the

1980s, the National Heart Savers Association pressured food manufacturers to replace saturated fats with trans-fats because they believed that trans-fat was the healthier option.[6] Fortunately, not everyone supported this move. One of those who didn't was a university professor named Fred Kummerow.

In the 1950s, Kummerow, then a young professor, convinced a local hospital in Illinois to let him study the arteries of people who had died of heart disease. Kummerow discovered to his ultimate surprise that the arteries contained high levels of trans-fat. Struck by this discovery, Kummerow moved on to test his developing hypothesis on rats. He showed that when he fed rats trans-fat, the lab rats developed a hardening and narrowing of arteries that commonly causes heart attacks. Not only that, but when he stopped feeding the rats with trans-fat, the arteries went back to normal. Kummerow published his report in 1957 in the prestigious journal *Science*, but his work was dismissed. Saturated fats remained the villain and trans-fat the safe option.[7]

Kummerow did not rest and continued conducting studies pointing to the harmful effects of trans-fat throughout his life.[8] Eventually, others joined Kummerow, and the evidence villainizing trans-fat piled up. Studies showed that trans-fat caused a wide range of health problems, including increasing the risk for heart disease, stroke, and type 2 diabetes, and raising cholesterol levels.[9] In 2006, professors from the Harvard School of Public Health published an article in the influential *New England Journal of Medicine* claiming that trans-fat causes between 72,000 and 228,000 deaths a year.[10] By the twenty-first century, scientists did not fight the war against trans-fat by themselves. Public advocacy groups and lawyers leading class actions filed multiple lawsuits against food manufacturers and restaurant chains using trans-fat, including Kraft (the producer of Oreo cookies), Burger King, KFC, and McDonald's.[11]

In 2006, faced with an avalanche of medical evidence and strong public advocacy, the FDA required all food manufacturers to clearly label how much trans-fat was in their products.[12] Local authorities then went a step further: they banned the use of trans-fat. In 2006, New York City was the first city in the country to require restaurants, cafeterias, and schools to eliminate trans-fat. And in

2010, California was the first state to ban trans-fat in restaurants and baked goods.[13]

The results were quite remarkable. In 2012, a Centers for Disease Control and Prevention (CDC) study designed to measure the impact of the labeling regulation found that blood levels of trans-fats in the US population had decreased by 58 percent.[14] What happened? Clearly, consumers were paying attention and some avoided products with high levels of trans-fat. In 1995, only 32 percent of Americans surveyed had heard about trans-fat and only 11 percent knew of its harmful effects.[15] By 2008, though, 91 percent of Americans surveyed had heard about trans-fat and 79 percent thought trans-fat was not healthful.[16] But consumers' choices explain only part of the change.

Manufacturers paid close attention as well. They reformulated their products to decrease or eliminate trans-fat. Manufacturers realized that a label stating "0 trans-fat" would increase sales, improve their public image, and avoid legal liability. As a result, the grocery food products scene has changed with many products appearing on the market with lower or no trans-fat. This, in turn, made it easier for consumers to select products with less trans-fat.[17] The overall result was an important boon for public health as individuals consumed far less trans-fat than before the labeling regulation went into effect.

The food scene changed, and the ground was then ripe for the FDA's next step. In June 2015, the FDA went further and announced an outright ban on trans-fat.[18] Kummerow was then a 100-year-old professor and still actively running his lab at the University of Illinois. He was able to see his life's work completed before dying two years later at the age of 102.[19] The trans-fat story shows that redesign is possible. The food industry resisted the change for as long as it could, but, despite all the economic advantages of using trans-fat, pressure on all fronts eventually forced the industry to redesign products and eliminate the use of trans-fat.

Tech Redesign and Windows of Opportunity

Technology is usually designed behind closed doors. We rarely get insight as to what transpired in the creation process of popular networks or games like Snapchat or Fortnite. We do not know who participates in the process. Are these executives, psychologists, or only programmers?[20] We just take design for granted. Once in a while, though, startling information leaks out, and then we pay attention. This happened when Cambridge Analytica accessed the private information of more than 50 million Facebook users and used it to influence the 2016 election results. But, usually, we pay little attention to technology. It merges into the background of our lives. It is invisible.[21] Still, it controls how we act.[22] Invisibility means that we do not notice it. It also means that we view it as unchangeable. Still, the design process of a game, a social network, or a smartphone can be ongoing.[23]

The story of the bicycle illustrates all of this. The bicycle as we know it today has two wheels of equal size and is used for transportation. But, in its early days, the bicycle went through many design permutations. One dominant form emerged around the 1870s. It had two wheels of unequal size. The front wheel was ten times larger than the back wheel. Unsurprisingly, it was extremely difficult to ride. Its purpose was not transportation. It was a macho sport vehicle; mostly young men rode it. Eventually, one conception of the bicycle prevailed – the bicycle as a transportation vehicle. The bicycle stabilized to the form we know today, and now the design of the bicycle is unlikely to change.[24] It has become invisible.

Many technologies faced initial opposition. We banned the use of human cloning because we found its very use troubling. More often we disagree on how and when a technology should be used. We grapple with artificial intelligence: what role should it play? Should it autonomously screen job applicants? How should it be used? How can we make it more transparent? While the process may take time, once we determine how technologies are used, they often become invisible, just like the bicycle did. Our use of screens, however, took a different trajectory. It slipped in unnoticed. In a way, it was almost invisible from the outset.

Our screens, social networks, and online games have been with us for a while now. We did not really pay attention as our lives transformed and we spent more and more time on our screens. Some – especially parents – began noticing the technologies and their impacts on children. But, for most people, invisibility prevailed. Then the Coronavirus pandemic changed this. Screens and virtual communications played such a central role during the pandemic that we became vividly aware of them and how they affect our lives. We could finally see them clearly. We saw the good and how they preserved some semblance of normal life. But we could also appreciate what they cannot provide us with in terms of human connection. Parents clearly perceived their dangerous allure for kids who spent alarmingly increasing amounts of their waking hours online. It is in moments like this, when technologies are visible, that the time is ripe for redesign.

Redesign Principles for Choice

Principle One: Default Settings for Restricted Use

Our default settings are preprogrammed to induce overuse. They set no limit on how much time we can spend on our phones. Neither do they restrict how long we can use specific apps, like Facebook, YouTube, or games like Candy Crush. Netflix's autoplay – streaming the next episode before we can click pause – is a default setting which makes it more likely we will watch another and another and another episode. Binge watching is not accidental; it is facilitated by design. Similarly, our phones' default settings send us alerts of incoming messages unless we intentionally change the settings to turn them off.

Preprogramming for overuse is not a functional necessity. Technology companies preprogramed these default settings to maximize their revenues. But how could it be different? Consider if default settings were instead preprogrammed to limit use. For example, default settings for phones could allow two hours for total phone time, half an hour for social networks, and half an hour for game playing. This does not mean that the preprogrammed settings would be set in stone. A user could still increase or decrease the time allotted to any category. They could change their general settings or do it on a daily basis. But they would still be starting from a different baseline.

Why do default settings matter if we can change them anyway? They make a difference because studies show that default settings can powerfully nudge users in a certain direction. Default settings are effective because we simply cannot pay attention to everything. As a result, we often choose mindlessly. Cass Sunstein calls it the "yeah, whatever" approach. Changing a default setting requires us to actively make a choice, and we often don't bother. A second reason that default settings matter is that we often perceive them as recommendations for the best options. We are less likely to increase our screen time if we believe that restricted time is recommended.[25]

Default rules have huge potential, but they can also fail to accomplish their goals. Laws or market pressure can impose default options, but changing consumers' choices is less likely to succeed when the companies presenting the options to consumers oppose the dictated default choices. Tech companies fall into this category. They do not want a default option that limits time spent. Their business model relies on the opposite default – maximizing user time. A business can greatly weaken the effectiveness of a default option that goes against its business model. It can make it easier, and even alluring, to opt out. Imagine a user selecting a default option that limits time on social networks to one hour a day. Device makers and social networks that oppose this default could send notifications to the user, even during her off time, alerting her to Facebook activity. The user is now more likely to want to opt out of the default and increase her time on social networks. Default options are also less likely to work when consumers are conflicted about their choice. The allures of constant connectivity are so strong that users are likely to have weakened resolutions. Privacy is a potent example. Consumers stress its importance, but then take no steps to protect themselves because online convenience is so enticing. All of this does not mean that default rules could not work. It does mean, though, that effective default options will require careful thought coupled with other sources of legal pressure.[26]

Principle 2: Eliminating Manipulative Features

The technology industry uses many design features to extend our time online. Redesigning for choice requires prohibiting any abusive design that contains clearly manipulative features. Many designs are manipulative, but the most suspect are those that target our deepest psychological vulnerabilities and those that serve no purpose but to keep the user online or draw her back to the same online platform.

Snapstreaks is a striking example of a feature that exists solely to ensure that users constantly return to the app. As described in

Chapter 3, users need to send each other snapstreaks every twenty-four hours to keep their ranking on Snapchat. The streaks' content is irrelevant, but kids keep returning to Snapchat to avoid losing their streak with a friend and having to start anew.

Another ubiquitous, highly suspect feature is the infinite scroll. It is the web design that automatically uploads more content as we scroll down. We never need to click on the next page or upload more. Infinite scroll is everywhere. On Facebook, Instagram, Twitter, and Snapchat. Aza Raskin, the inventor of the infinite scroll, said he regrets this invention and what it has done to us.[27] The infinite scroll takes away our natural stopping cues. Its goal is just to have us linger on for longer.

Other features are clearly manipulative because they purposefully target our psychological vulnerabilities. Loot boxes in online games are a prime example. Loot boxes contain items that can be used in the game, like weapons or powers that can enhance the player's character. Sometimes players can just find the loot boxes, but in some games they can also pay in game currency to purchase them. Importantly, the player does not know in advance what is contained in the loot box. Loot boxes implement the same random reward model applied by slot machines. Sometimes a player gets the reward and sometimes he does not, so he keeps going.

Principle 3: Developing Alternative Online Business Models and Devices

Our devices are now set to maximize connectivity. But a truly competitive market would offer mainstream alternative devices configured for restricted use. Picture a popular phone for middle-school kids that incorporates some smartphone functions like Google Maps, but does not provide access to social networks and games. Similarly, business models can vary for social networks and other online platforms. A subscription fee model could replace the model relying on time and data as revenue resources. Competition could thrive if businesses compete to offer low addiction ratings to parents shopping for suitable online games for their children.

In Israel, a mainstream option of an alternative phone model has existed for years. "The Kosher Phone" is the go-to phone for the ultra-orthodox population. It debuted in the early 2000s, when the cellphone instigated a crisis in that community by creating a gateway to secular thought, culture, and media, as well as sexual content. In 2004, the rabbinical leadership formed the Rabbi Committee for Communication to advocate for the manufacture of a "Kosher Phone." The Rabbi Committee hired an attorney to negotiate with the cellular phone companies. Simultaneously, the rabbinical leadership urged their constituency not to use smartphones, ultimately applying some rather heavy-handed measures. The rabbi leadership prohibited orthodox schools from accepting students whose parents did not use Kosher Phones. They also exerted pressure on orthodox newspapers not to advertise smartphones.

This combination of tactics created immense market pressure on Israel's cellular phone companies. The cellphone companies, rather than lose the business of a large segment of the Israeli population, retreated. The result was the Kosher Phone. The classic Kosher Phone had only one function – voice calls. It did not have the usual functions of a smartphone, such as Internet-browsing, camera, games, and texting. Eventually, additional versions of the Kosher Phone emerged. For example, one model allowed access to certain rabbi-approved apps, but not to Internet browsing.[28] And as the Kosher Phone has continued to evolve, it has highlighted ways in which market demand can lead to redesign.

Designing alternative models that will gain widespread adoption is a process of trial and error. One of the phone models already on the market illustrates this. It is "The Light Phone," created by two innovators: Joe Hollier and Kaiwei Tang. Hollier and Tang met in a Google incubator in New York City, while working on new software apps. But as Kaiwei Tang explained, they quickly concluded that "the last thing … the world needed was another app … These products didn't respect the user or their time." Instead, they decided to focus on making people more connected, but not in a digital way.

Hollier and Tang decided to build the anti-smartphone. They wanted to design a phone that would be used as little as possible by being disconnected from the Internet. In 2017, they created the "Light Phone." They designed the Light Phone as a secondary phone that gives the user the option of leaving the smartphone behind. A user of the first Light Phone could take a walk in nature, step away from Facebook and work emails, navigate her own way without Google Maps, but would still know that her kids could reach her by phone if needed. It turned out, though, that for many people the first Light Phone was too light. Social networks were easy to dispense with, but certain other functions of the smartphone seemed less dispensable.

Hollier and Tang then proceeded to design Light Phone 2. Light Phone 2 caters to a broader market. It targets people who want a secondary phone and others who want to replace the traditional smartphone altogether. Light Phone 2 makes calls and sends and receives texts, but it also has an alarm, a hotspot, a calculator, a simple music player, a podcast tool, and directions. Hollier and Tang are considering adding more tools, but the line is drawn at not adding social media, Internet browsing, emails, news, or ads.[29] Developing alternative devices may require some exploration and involve trial and error. Still, devices that maximize connectivity need not be the only mainstream options.

Designing Physical Spaces for Choice

Everywhere we go, we use our phones. We sit on a bench in the park or wait in line, and we pop out our phones. When we have dinner with a friend in a restaurant, we place our phones on the table. If the friend needs to answer a call, text, or email during our outing, we instinctively pick up on our own phone in the meantime. It is not just socially acceptable, but even expected. We do not consider it polite to stare at someone when they speak on the phone or text. These are now our social norms.

But what if this is not exactly what we want? People often say they are unhappy with how much they and those around them use their phones. Can we challenge these norms by restricting or discouraging phone use in different locations? It is hard to change people's habits when these reflect what they actually want to do. But what if they actually want to act differently? In that case, pushing toward change has a higher likelihood of success.[30]

Redesigning technologies is not the only option. Redesigning the way our physical spaces look and limiting device use in certain places is crucial as well. Redesign can involve changing entire neighborhoods. In suburbs, people live in homes separated from stores, restaurants, and workplaces. Walking is often not an option and cars are a necessity of life. When smartphones and social networks became popular, they increased the built-in seclusion of suburban life. Many suburbs' residents, especially kids who cannot drive, now spend large amounts of time in their bedrooms on their phones.

Critics of suburban life pointed out decades ago that it contributes to social isolation. Since the 1980s, a movement called "New Urbanism" challenged the idea of suburban life. This movement called for creating mixed neighborhoods where people live, shop, go to school, and work in the same place. These would be neighborhoods where people can walk instead of spending time secluded in cars. The New Urbanists admitted that physical design cannot solve everything, but they urged that it could promote social connectedness.[31] These ideas are more relevant today than ever before. Consider Lindsay, a 15-year-old living in a vital urban center, walking home from school with her friends, stopping at a coffee shop or a park. Now, compare her with 15-year-old Lillian, who lives in a suburb. Lillian's mom picks her up from school and, once Lillian arrives home, she can only interact with her friends through texting or social networks. Since she now has a way to interact remotely, Lillian is less likely to initiate more logistically complicated in-person get-togethers.

Redesigning neighborhoods is one option, but these are longer-term projects. Designing smaller physical spaces can happen much more quickly. Some years ago, I was flying with my family on our annual trip to visit relatives in Israel. Our flight to Israel left late at night from Newark Airport. Once we got through security, we looked for a restaurant to have dinner. To my amazement (and my kids' delight), every restaurant in the terminal had an iPad installed on its tables. Our table for four diners had four iPads, one for each of us. We had to place our order through the iPad instead of speaking to a waiter. My kids then started playing games on the iPads. The presence of the iPads, with their glowing possibilities, silenced our conversation that evening. I later learned that a company called OTG transformed all New York City's airports by installing thousands of iPads. New York's airports are now designed to induce overuse. Travelers have no choice but to dine with iPads separating them from their travel companions.

iPads on restaurant tables are not yet a staple in every airport, but the use of tablets (and since the pandemic QR Codes) to economize and reduce wait-staff costs or attract customers may expand this trend even beyond airports to restaurants and cafés. One goal of redesign is to discourage design trends that make it practically impossible for people to interact with one another instead of screens. Disincentivizing restaurant and café owners from adopting designs, like placing tablets on every table, could accomplish this goal. But redesign of physical spaces is not just about the physical structure.

Redesign of physical spaces is also about repurposing uses. We are now accustomed to no smoking spaces. Still, in the late 1980s, when local authorities and businesses announced the first smoke-free zones, smokers were outraged. Even the public at large was incredulous.[32] Similarly, today, when all the buzz is about building smart cities and maximizing connectivity, technology-free zones may seem implausible. The question is: are they really?

Technology-free zones can enhance work, studying, and even leisure. We believe that spending some time in a park produces a refreshing break. But then we often sit down on a bench, scrolling on our phones. Are we still getting the benefits of a revitalizing break? A study showed that we don't. The researchers gave study participants a cognitive test, instructing them to remember number sequences. After the test, one group of participants went to a barren place and the other group went to a park for fifteen minutes. Half of each group took their laptops. The researchers instructed them to do whatever they wanted on their laptops. They could watch videos on YouTube, read the news, or check personal mail. The participants then re-took the cognitive test. Only one post-break group scored significantly higher: those who sat in a park without their laptops. The group who sat in the park with their laptops did not benefit from the break at all.[33]

We find it hard to resist our devices. But there are many options for how businesses or local authorities can help us to reduce this struggle. These include prohibiting device use, requiring payment for connection, limiting permitted connection time, not providing Wi-Fi connection, and blocking cell reception. A park or a confined area of the park could prohibit use of electronic devices. Cafés or communal workspaces could also announce "no electronic device" zones or even offer incentives not to use them. For nearly a decade, I worked on my laptop at the same café next to my house. I liked it because it had a large communal table where I could place all my work materials. One morning when I arrived, I saw a sign on the table: "Put your devices away, and your dessert is on us." The owners noticed that the café's clients tended to spend more time on their phones than talking to one another, and they tried to change this.

Smartphones have completely changed how it feels to be on vacation. They have made it easier in some ways. We get lost less often by using a maps app and we can re-do our plans on the spot. But we can no longer really escape. We can see our work email at all times. We are constantly busy documenting and posting on social networks. We see a beautiful statue or our kids playing joyfully in the hotel's pool and we immediately capture the moment. Recording the moments has become more significant than living them.

The tourism industry has reacted in varying ways. Some locations have offered a new option: a digital-free vacation resort, sometimes coupled with a meditation retreat. Others tried to induce their guests to unhook, while recognizing their different preferences and needs. The Wyndham Grand Hotel chain implemented phone-free zones in pools. An executive at one of the chain's hotels reported that "87% of poolside guests were on their phones and not in the water over the weekend." They did not choose to ban cellphones, but – similar to my café – gave incentives. They offered different rewards to guests who used lock boxes to lock away their phones. These rewards included special off-menu items, exclusive pool floats or books, a chance to win enough reward points for a five-day vacation, and even a 5 percent discount on their stay.[34]

Creative approaches can change the way travelers use technology. When hotels started offering no smoking rooms, it was a novelty. Hotels could let guests who want to get away choose no-Internet or even no-cell-reception rooms. Some museums already prohibit picture-taking for different reasons, including art preservation, copyright protection, and museum store profits.[35] But tourist attractions, like churches or castles, could prohibit picture-taking to help visitors focus on experiencing their environment. Tourists could still purchase digital or printed pictures as they leave to preserve or share their memories. But they would then be present in the moment.

Finally, schools are a natural place for no-phone zones. Kids are more vulnerable to the impact of overuse, and we often protect kids by restricting their choices. France banned cellphones in all schools in 2018. In the United States, restrictions on phone use are imposed by local authorities or the schools themselves. Those explain that phones impact focus and test scores, as well as impede social interactions among kids. In some schools, the ban is comprehensive and includes even lunch time to encourage kids to engage with one another face to face.[36]

Takeaway Points

- We can redesign "abusive designs." Abusive designs are designs that impede our ability to make autonomous choices and manipulate us to act against our self-interest.
- We have windows of opportunity when we can create change through redesign. They occur when we can clearly see a technology and its impact on our lives. The Coronavirus pandemic created this window of opportunity by highlighting the cost of vastly increased screen time.
- Redesign to reduce technology overuse should include the following principles:
  - preprogramming default settings that encourage limited use;
  - eliminating manipulative features that purposefully target our psychological vulnerabilities, or those that serve no purpose but to make us linger on a certain app or keep returning to it;
  - designing alternative devices for restricted use and alternative business models for websites and apps;
  - redesigning and repurposing physical spaces to contain overuse. Relevant spaces range from whole neighborhoods to schools, hotels, parks, cafés, and airports.

9 THE TOOLS OF AWARENESS

Venturing Out

In 2017, I began giving lectures to parents about technology overuse through my school outreach program. I explained that this is not just about kids playing video games all night, but that it is about all of us. We are all over-users. We all love our technologies too much. We all use them much more than we intend. I talked about the costs to ourselves, our families, and our relationships. I discussed self-help measures because I knew parents wanted a solution. But I was honest about the difficulty of limiting kids' use of smartphones, social networks, and games. I then opened the floor for discussion, hoping parents could give one another ideas that had worked in their community. During the first year, what followed astounded me. As one parent after another spoke, revealing their struggles, the other parents turned around to one another. "You too?" was the resounding reaction. Followed by reactions such as, "My daughter said I was the only parent prohibiting her from using Snapchat!" There was a sense of surprise, but also a sense of relief that they were all together in this.

These moments made me realize the importance of awareness of technology overuse. Later, in private conversations, parents recounted watching their 10-year-old child playing Minecraft all day on the weekend. They told me how he would then throw a tantrum as they tried to place limits. They were ashamed because they thought the challenge they faced was unique. They worried about their children. They blamed themselves. Hearing my talk and the other parents sharing similar experiences lifted the isolation, burden, and shame.

These talks helped take the skeletons out of the closets. In the months that followed, I saw change taking place within these communities. In one school in Manhattan, parents and administration collaborated to address overuse. They changed cellphone and social media guidelines, including prohibiting use of cellular phones in school at all times – even recess. The school also issued recommendations to parents as to best practices for smartphone use at home.

I saw how addressing groups and raising awareness could create new avenues for promoting change. But I realized this was small-scale change. Overuse was molding the habits of a whole generation of kids, and adults were not immune either. We often failed to recognize how our life has changed and is still changing. Promoting awareness needed to happen on a broader scale.

Truth from the Trenches of Silicon Valley

Something then changed in Silicon Valley. The very same people who spend their days and dedicate their careers to developing our technologies became cautious. They worried about the impact on their kids. The media reported surprising concern among both the giants of the tech industry and employees of the pillar companies of the web economy, like Google, Amazon, and Facebook.

Bill Gates, the founder of Microsoft, revealed that he did not give his kids smartphones until they were 14. Steve Jobs, who built the Apple empire, admitted that he prohibited his children from using the iPad. Reports exposed a popular unexpected school choice for kids of tech employees – the Waldorf schools. The Waldorf schools drastically limit the role of technology in kids' education and upbringing. These schools do not incorporate technology into teaching until eighth grade. They embrace a philosophy that computers inhibit creative thinking, movement, human interaction, and attention span. Waldorf schools have a retro look. If you take a tour, you will not see smartboards and iPads. Instead, you will observe classrooms stocked with blackboards, colorful chalk, and wooden desks filled with workbooks and pencils.

The unexpected parenting trend in Silicon Valley is not limited to school choice. It also involves younger children. Parents are taking drastic measures to prevent preschool-aged kids from exposure to screens – even indirectly. They prohibit their nannies from using screens near the kids. Beyond just prohibiting television or iPad access, some tech industry parents forbid nannies from using their own smartphones while caring for the kids for any purpose other than communicating with the parents.[1]

News reports about Silicon Valley's parenting choices came at the same time as revelations from Silicon Valley whistleblowers. The most prominent "defector" is probably Tristan Harris. In November 2016, *The Atlantic* featured a story about Harris, a former senior Google employee, titled: *The Binge Breaker: Tristan Harris Believes Silicon Valley Is Addicting Us to Our Phones. He's Determined to Make It Stop.* The story recounted 32-year-old Harris's journey through Silicon Valley.[2]

Tristan Harris studied computer science at Stanford, where he joined psychologist B. J. Fogg's lab. Fogg's lab is known for instructing many tech entrepreneurs on how to influence users' behavior through software design. Despite his roots and his subsequent work to develop products aimed at hooking users, Harris became a skeptic. A Google employee, it seemed at first that Harris was on track to transform Google from within. Google appointed him to the position of "Product Philosopher." But, eventually, Harris left Google to take a different approach. He now works to influence Silicon Valley from the outside by exposing what he learned as an insider. Using the media, TED talks, the "Social Dilemma" documentary, and his Time Well Spent website, Harris relentlessly exposes the ways our technologies are designed to addict us and explains how they could be designed instead to limit use.[3]

The media stories emanating from Silicon Valley were pivotal. Harris was just the first in a series of whistleblowers. They raised red flags about our screens and digital communications. Skepticism emanating from the temple of technology carries significance. These reports provided a wake-up call that the technologies themselves, not necessarily the users, are responsible for overuse. But wake-up calls are only the first step. Developing awareness, spreading it broadly, and maintaining it over time requires more concerted action. The law, unbeknown to many of us, operates – directly and indirectly, and sometimes quite invisibly – to promote awareness.

Raising Awareness through Law

We usually think about the law as a set of prohibitions, for example, criminal law: forbidding murder, theft, or assault. We also think of law when we sign agreements: when we enter a rental agreement for an apartment or open a bank account and sign and initial many pages of standard contracts. On tax filing day, we remember our legal duty to pay taxes and report our financial activities to the government. But the law does not only set the rules of the game. It has another important role; it also sends messages. It can make us aware of dangers. It can let us know what actions are prohibited and what acts are desirable.[4]

We see these messages all around us, but we often do not connect them to the law – at least not automatically. We see them on product labels. Cigarette packs have labels which read: "Smoking Causes Lung Cancer." McDonald's menus inform us that a Big Mac contains 563 calories. Commercials intend to deliver messages. Pharmaceutical commercials do not just promote drugs, but also warn of potential side effects. Similarly, media ratings provide another notification system. Ratings are intended to alert viewers, especially parents, to the nature of media content. The movie *The Avengers* was rated PG-13, alerting parents that the violence and certain crude language in the film may be inappropriate for kids under 13. All these messages are legally designed information systems intended not to dictate an outcome, but to stir us – or gently nudge us – in a certain direction.[5] These messages can even indirectly pressure companies to redesign their products. We saw in Chapter 8 that, once the law required companies to include levels of trans-fat on their labels, not only did consumers prefer to purchase products without trans-fat, but also food manufacturers eliminated trans-fat from their products to cater to the public's new preference.

Delivering Warnings

Some legally mandated public messages have become success stories. People listened and made better choices. But some messages failed to accomplish their purposes. Why are some messages heard while others are ignored? It mostly depends on complexity.[6] Some laws are simply unrealistic. They require companies to disclose so much information that customers never even attempt to read the fine print.[7]

A few years ago, I bought an apartment. There are many laws that require disclosing information in real estate transactions. During the closing, the attorneys handed me multiple disclosure forms from the bank and the sellers. I had been teaching Property Law for fourteen years. I could, if I decided to, read and understand these forms. But I did not make the slightest attempt to do so. I just signed document after document as expeditiously as I could. I never processed the information because the burden was too high. I made the choice most people do to ignore the overwhelming amount of information provided.

We are less likely to hear complex messages, but not all messages need to be complicated. Messages can attempt to grab attention, make people skeptical, and make them aware that a problem exists. A message can be valuable even if it does not give complete information. Some decisions, like deciding which mortgage to get, require more information. But learning that an activity is unhealthy can be enough to make users aware of the risk and eager to learn more without providing many details.[8]

To be heard, messages need to be simple and accessible. Large bold letters, bright colors, and graphics transmit messages effectively. For messages to be successful, less is often more, and blunt is better. Warnings on cigarette packs started making a real impact when their design changed to include large bold font covering most of the pack with unforgiving messages like: "Smoking kills."[9] Consumers found nutritional labels easier to interpret when traffic light signals were used. Under this system, McDonald's nutritional information for a large fries would be marked red under fat content, indicating "stop," instead of only stating that there are 23 grams of fat. A pack of spinach would display a label marked green under fat content, indicating "go," instead of stating o grams of fat. Similarly, skull and crossbones warning signs on labels work better than text to indicate danger.[10]

Timing also matters. People are more likely to use information if they receive it when it is relevant for them while making a decision. When I go with my kids to get pizza for lunch in New York City (where pizza options are plentiful), we may change our dining decision if we see a B food safety grade displayed at the entrance of the restaurant. But we would be less likely to change our mind if we saw the B grade after we had already sat down and started ordering.[11] The requirement for food establishments to prominently display their safety grade increases the likelihood that people will consider it when deciding whether to dine there.

Advertising

Sometimes we clearly see the law in action, but other times the law's involvement is completely or partially hidden from us. Warning labels and ratings are two examples of the semi-invisible hand of the law. Advertising is another. The comprehensive decades-long media campaign against cigarettes vividly illustrates the ways in which law has subtly molded public messages about smoking.[12] It started with accumulating the funds – the first requirement for any large-scale advertising campaign. Both federal and state governments dedicated funding to these campaigns. But it was the tobacco companies who reluctantly paid the bulk of the bill to support anti-smoking campaigns. Tobacco companies facing massive lawsuits acquiesced to funding these campaigns as part of a historical settlement deal.[13] The anti-smoking campaigns included ads emphasizing the adverse health effects of smoking, messages portraying the tobacco industry as deceptive and manipulative, and messages focusing on second-hand smoke and the changing social norms around smoking.

Some campaigns were particularly effective. One of those was called "Tips from Former Smokers." The Centers for Disease Control and Prevention (CDC) started the campaign in 2012 with an investment of $54 million. This campaign was unique in that it did not spare its viewers. It intentionally did not filter the harsh reality of the impact of smoking. The campaign showed the ravages of smoking at its worst: the cancer, the amputations, the paralysis, and much more. Unlike other campaigns, this campaign was not about pointing fingers at the culprits – the cigarette companies. Instead, it emphasized the everyday hell of the people paying the price, each in his or her own way.

One story was about Brandon. Brandon lost two limbs to Buerger's Disease, a condition linked to smoking. In his video, Brandon described his morning routine, which included allowing extra time to put on his prosthetic legs and shaving carefully in order not to cut the stoma (the opening made in his throat to facilitate breathing). Another story was about Suzy, a former smoker, who had been paralyzed following a stroke. She described how her 23-year-old son helps her bathe and go to the bathroom. Then came a portrait of Terrie, who was inflicted with throat and oral cancer. The video showed her putting in her teeth, putting on her wig, and adjusting her hands-free device as she got ready for another day.[14] These campaigns were overall very successful. Follow-up studies showed that hundreds of thousands of Americans quit smoking as a result of the "Tips from Former Smokers" campaign.[15]

The "Tips from Former Smokers" campaign was upfront about delivering the message, but campaigns can also take subtler forms. One form is the prohibition of certain advertising. When we don't receive particular messages our related conduct may change. Again, the history of the fight against cigarettes provides a striking example. A 1969 federal law prohibited tobacco companies from advertising on the major communication channels of the time – radio and television.[16] By the 1970s, television viewers watched a mix of commercials advertising products including Lowenbrau beer, Tootsie Pops, and, of course, Coca-Cola. But commercials enticing viewers to smoke were no longer in the mix.[17]

The moratorium on cigarette advertising to all audiences was unique in its breadth, but restrictions on advertising to children are more common. In the United Kingdom, laws prohibit advertising junk food to kids.[18] Under these rules, for example, the British Advertising Standards Authority (ASA) banned Cadbury's use of a storybook titled "The Tale of the Great Easter Bunny" on its website, which featured kids hunting for eggs.[19] In the United States, while there is no overall prohibition, regulators use targeted restrictions on enticing kids to eat unhealthy foods. One is known as the "Happy Meal Ban." For years, fast food chains like McDonald's attracted kids and their parents by offering a toy with a kids' meal. San Francisco, as part of its war against obesity, decided to prohibit Happy Meals. San Francisco no longer allows its restaurants to offer toys with meals unless these meals meet very specific nutritional standards. Qualifying meals may not exceed 600 calories or contain more than half a gram of trans-fat. They also need to include a certain quota of fruits and vegetables.[20]

Sending Overuse Alerts in a Digital World

Messages about overuse do not need to disclose sophisticated information. They need to raise awareness of the problem of overuse. They must persistently remind people of it. For some people, these messages will provide a relief by explaining the physical, psychological, and social impacts they were already feeling. Others may want to seek more information about the impact on themselves or their children.

Sending clear and simple messages is key. Delivering messages at the point of decision-making can also promote effectiveness. Rating systems can do both. We are very familiar with movie ratings. Parents often check if a movie is rated G, PG, or R before taking a young child to watch it in a cinema. Quite a few also refer to ratings for video games, although these are less well-known than movie ratings. Following public and legal pressure, video game-makers adopted a voluntary rating system that rates games according to age.

Age ratings can be helpful. When my daughter was 7, she asked me to download a game for her on my iPad. I did it without paying much attention. The next day I heard her talking about the walk she took with her boyfriend Nick on the beach. Very surprised, I asked her who Nick was. She explained, "He is my boyfriend in the game you downloaded for me yesterday – Hollywood University." I quickly looked up the game and saw that it was rated Teen (13+). I did not need to explore any further to decide to retrieve the iPad and delete the game.

The problem is that age ratings convey only partial information. For years, experts and parents criticized video game ratings because they are age-based rather than content-based. Parents want to know how much violence or sexual content is in a game. They find strictly age-based ratings less helpful because there is disagreement about what is appropriate for a 10-year-old.[21] Now, though, when I click on "Hollywood University Rising Stars" on Apple's app store, I can see Apple's rating of 12+. While age rating is still key, if I click on the age rating, I can see additional information Apple has added about sexual content, violence, substance, and profanity. The description for sexual content is: "Infrequent/Mild Mature/Suggestive Theme." There is no category for addictiveness.

Parents today actually worry more about kids spending too much time on online games than about the specific content like sex or violence.[22] In 2020, for example, 350 million people were registered on Fortnite.[23] Some, a small minority of Fortnite players, become addicted and end up in rehab. But most players just overuse. Fortnite is clearly alluring. The vast majority of players play a lot. About a third of Fortnite players play six to ten hours a week; 17.3 percent play eleven to fifteen hours a week; 13 percent play sixteen to twenty hours a week, and 5 percent play more than twenty-one hours a week.[24] The makers of Fortnite do not market it as an educational game. But the designers of Minecraft, another popular video game, successfully marketed their game to parents as an educational tool, claiming it enhances creativity, problem-solving, self-direction, and collaboration. Parents then eagerly introduced the game to their children, only for some to realize later that asking the kids to take a break from playing Minecraft provoked extreme, often before-unseen, expressions of anger.[25] When parents contemplate and understand the potential harm, ratings are likely to be a helpful tool in managing children's interaction with technology.[26]

Ratings can convey information about the risk of addiction using the successful traffic lights method. Imagine a rating in an app store or next to a download web game button indicating red for highly addictive risk, yellow for moderate risk, and green for low risk. Ratings can be based on the type of design features in the games. As discussed in Chapter 3, game designers use features like loot boxes and intermittent rewards to hook users to games. Ratings should display at the time a parent decides whether to download a game for a child, making the information particularly relevant.

Rating systems can also inform adults downloading their own games, but mostly they are an effective way to warn parents getting games for children. Ratings are less useful for social networks or for smartphone use because deciding not to use becomes much harder when enough people are using them that critical mass is reached or surpassed.[27] Consider Instagram, whose user base grew from 90 million users in 2013 to 2 billion users by 2021.[28] In 2018, 72 percent of teens used Instagram and 60 percent used Snapchat, while TikTok has become the leading social network for younger teens.[29] It is very difficult today for a teen to avoid joining at least one, if not all, of these networks.

Delivering messages about overuse of social networks, smartphones, and online games to adults (and even older kids) requires different messaging. Now, imagine, a warning or a pop-up displaying whenever you go on a website to download a game like Fortnite or Minecraft. Consider a notice advising that: "Playing this game could lead to harmful excessive use," or a message highlighting the time lost: "You have spent three hours on Fortnite, in this time you could have read 120 book pages." Like warnings about cigarettes, unhealthy food, and alcohol, messages should be blunt to get attention. Some warnings could highlight the worst potential outcomes, such as addiction, anxiety, and depression.

Warnings about excessive use can appear daily when picking up the phone in the morning or accessing a game or a social network for the first time that day. Pop-up warnings can also show up periodically when a device, game, or social network is used for a long time. Imagine a Fortnite user logging into his game at 10am on a Saturday morning and receiving the following warning: "Excessive play may be harmful." At 1pm, another pop-up appears: "You have been playing for three hours; off-screen activity is recommended." Tech companies already offer diluted versions of these pop-ups. For example, Instagram offers a "take a break" feature. But it is not the default setting; instead, the user needs to turn it on. It also does not contain language that warns of the potential harm. Tech companies, like food and tobacco companies, will not send effective messages, unless laws require them to do so.

What about advertising? Consider a restriction on advertising addictive digital products to young kids – the system would restrict Fortnite, for example, from advertising in venues that cater to younger children. My 7-year-old daughter learned about Hollywood University from a video ad playing on an online game that was suitable for her age. Prohibiting advertising inappropriate or highly addictive products where the target audience is young kids could have prevented that incident.

In the past, restricting advertising for kids focused mainly on traditional media, like TV commercials. But tech companies advertising is often non-traditional. Tech companies advertise their products on Internet websites, including on social media. Increasingly, companies have begun promoting their products by paying influencers on websites like YouTube or Instagram.

Effective influencers are people like 29-year-old Richard Tyler Blevins, better known as Ninja. Ninja has 24 million followers just on YouTube. He rose to fame by playing Fortnite Battle Royale on his social media account. Companies now pay Ninja large sums to promote other games to his followers.[30] Influencers are for today's kids what TV commercials were for kids growing up in the 1980s. Furthermore, they are semi-celebrities, and kids identify with them and with the products they endorse. The FTC reacted and is increasingly regulating influencers as marketers.[31] Prohibiting influencers from marketing addictive products and requiring them to warn about the risks of excessive play or use would need to be part of any plan to raise awareness through advertising.

Influencers are critical for delivering messages to younger audiences. Some influencers may actually voluntarily promote overuse messaging, whether for pay or to advance their own agendas. Influencers have, in fact, already taken this approach. "Yes Theory" is a YouTube channel of four men in their 20s promoting the idea that life is best lived outside your comfort zone. They put themselves in difficult, mentally challenging situations, for their 7 million followers to watch. One of their challenges was thirty days without social media. They went beyond undertaking the challenge and inspiring others to do the same; they also highlighted the harms of overuse.

Takeaway Points

- Laws can raise awareness of the risks of overuse by delivering messages through labeling, advertising, and rating systems.
- To be effective, messages need to be short and clear (even blunt), use graphics, and be delivered at decision-making time.

- Effective ways to deliver messages in a digital world:
  - a traffic light rating system for addictiveness of online games;
  - intermittent digital warnings about the harm of overuse of games, social networks, or phones based on excessive time spent by user;
  - restricting advertising of addictive digital products to children;
  - applying advertising restrictions to social network influencers, as well as taking advantage of their ability to promote an overuse agenda.

10 THE GROUND IS BURNING

From Hope to Urgency

Most parents came to hear my talks because they were desperate. They wanted to know what to do to re-engage with their kids. Without fail, when I switched to my slide that listed the self-help methods, parents took out their phones to take pictures of that slide. I suggested using apps limiting time on devices. I talked about creating device-free times and zones during mealtimes or certain hours before bed. I talked about the importance of modeling. When parents spend a lot of time on their phones, so will children once they get them. I spoke at length and offered a list of strategies. I wanted badly to offer hope. But by 2019, I felt discouraged. I was no longer a believer. I still felt these methods could make a difference, especially when the children were on board. But I realized that self-help could only solve a small part of the problem.

I did not want to disappoint the parents. As a mother, I understood exactly the bind they were in. But I needed to speak the truth. And so, my lectures started changing. I still talked about strategies to use at home. But I emphasized more and more that we are fighting a difficult war against designs choreographed to addict us. I emphasized that we need to do more legally and lobby as parents to pressure technology companies to change their designs. And then, very soon thereafter, came the pandemic.

Children spent all day on their screens. The parents, who in 2019 were discouraged, became powerless. They needed to work; they needed to keep their kids entertained at home with little social interaction. Limiting screen time became a luxury few could afford.[1] And on top of that came school time. During the pandemic, screens replaced hours of paper and pencil. Kids sat through many days and hours of virtual school. Virtual school consisted of both live classroom interactions and independent assignments. Still, regardless of the format, schoolwork took place on screens. Even students attending school in person spent their class time on personal computers to synchronize the classroom with peers studying remotely. And both at home and in school, through their personal computers, kids got access to the Internet during class time. The allures of gaming and social media messaging infiltrated their classroom time.

No matter how you measured it, kids' screen time skyrocketed during the pandemic. One survey showed that the percentage of kids of all ages spending more than four hours daily nearly doubled. This was true even for the younger kids: 26 percent of 0–4-year-olds and 44 percent of 5–10-year-olds now spent more than four hours on their devices.[2] Another study found that 12- to 13-year-old children's screen time went up from 3.8 hours before the pandemic to 7.7 hours during the pandemic.[3]

Teachers tried their best to provide their students with normal school days, but they struggled as well. Even before the pandemic, educators frequently referred to "student engagement." But the challenge of virtual school pressured teachers to incorporate new means to engage students. Some teachers desperate to keep their students' attention during long, remote teaching days integrated tech's most addictive products into the curriculum: social networks and games. While before the pandemic, students used popular online games and social networks outside of school, they now infiltrated the classroom.[4]

Teachers incorporated games like Roblox, Minecraft, and even Fortnite into their lessons. The "bad guys" of the technology industry, some of the gaming companies known for hooking kids to screens through dopamine loops, seized the opportunity to develop their "educational" offerings. Some established flourishing educational departments collaborating with teachers and schools. The Roblox education department website announced: "Roblox is more than an online entertainment platform, it's an educational tool where the opportunities for creativity and imagination are limitless." It offered free webinars for educators to learn how to incorporate Roblox into their classes.[5] Similarly, Minecraft's education department offered: "Join the Minecraft Teacher Academy to take free courses and become a Minecraft-certified teacher."[6] Increasingly, educators turned also to social networks to engage students. TikTok emerged as a particularly popular platform for teachers. Teachers used TikTok videos to educate children as young as kindergarteners.[7] On TikTok, they crafted bite-size micro lessons or assignments and connect with students, commonly using hashtags like #teachersOfTikTok.[8]

As the pandemic school year progressed into 2021, the realities of screens in schools dawned on me personally. One friend reported that her son goes to school in person, but the kids use computers all day in the classroom, many playing games and paying little attention to the teacher. Another friend told me proudly that her daughter was preparing a podcast by interviewing experts about Colonial America. The following week she was less enthusiastic. The teacher posted the podcasts on a YouTube channel. The kids are competing for likes and her daughter is insisting on getting her own YouTube channel. From another mom, I heard that her son is studying history through a Roblox game mode called "Assassin's Creed: Odyssey," which is set in Ancient Greece. Since then, whenever she asks him to get off Roblox, he insists it is homework.

Screen immersion carried another cost. My kids stayed home to study in virtual school, while I left the house a couple of mornings a week to teach my law students in person. When I returned home, I usually found my own middle-schoolers where I left them that morning: right in front of their computers. They rejected my coaxing to go outside, saying they were too tired or that they had to finish homework on their computers. They did seem exhausted. Like many other parents, I felt powerless to forcefully cut screen time and mandate outside excursions.

During the spring of 2021, about a year into the pandemic, I was plowing through the medical and psychological research on how screen time affects children. My goal was to incorporate into this book a complete picture of what was already an extensive field of research. I was also personally motivated. There was little I could do to change the trajectory of my kids' days during the pandemic, but I was concerned that much of this will remain the status quo going forward. Like many parents, I struggled to work at home while accommodating different virtual school schedules, endless home-cooked meals, and constant interruptions. It was during these chaotic days in our Manhattan apartment that my research turned to the new brain scan studies, some published just before or during the pandemic.

Traditional psychology studies already pointed to a strong connection between excessive screen time and cognitive development when a new breed of studies entered the arena. Neuroscientists conducting brain imaging studies examined the impact of screen time on kids' developing brain structure. Brain structure changes significantly not just through early childhood, but also through the second decade of life. Typically, gray matter decreases, and white matter increases with enduring impacts on cognition. Brain structure is affected not only by genetics, but also by environmental effects. The brain imaging studies increasingly relied on a uniquely extensive database. The data came from the Adolescent Brain Cognitive Development Study (The ABCD Study), a ten-year longitudinal study launched in 2015 of over 11,000 9- to 10-year-old kids. The ABCD study examines the impact of environmental factors, including screen time, on children's brains, by scanning their brains every two years for a ten-year period.[9]

A group of researchers at the Cincinnati Children's Hospital Medical Center and University of Cincinnati conducted a leading study in the field, which was published in *JAMA Pediatrics* in 2020. The researchers used brain imaging techniques to examine the organization and myelination of white matter tracts in the brains of 3- to 5-year-old children. They focused on white matter tracts because these influence nerve cells' abilities to transmit information faster, in turn enabling more complex brain processes that underlie cognitive functioning. White matter tracts are also highly sensitive to environmental factors. The researchers focused on areas of the brain related to developing reading and writing skills as kids get older. When they correlated children's white matter organization with their exposure to screens, they found that the white matter tracts of children with high screen exposure were not as structurally organized as those of the children with lower screen exposure. Furthermore, greater screen exposure was related not only to less organized white matter, but also to lower cognitive assessment scores.[10] And while this study focused on smaller children, other studies using brain imaging to scan the brains of kids aged 8 to 18 reached similar conclusions.[11]

While neuroscientists are still exploring the impact of screen time on children's developing brains, the brain imaging studies signaled that, by 2021, we have reached a new stage in the science wars about screen time. That spring, I contacted Tzipi Horowitz-Kraus, one of the researchers on the Cincinnati University team, which conducted the *JAMA Pediatrics* study and other major research in the field. Tzipi divides her time between research in the United States and her faculty position in the Technion University in Israel. We both Zoomed from home, weaving our conversation as our children appeared in the background. Tzipi was in Israel, her three children just ended school, while mine, in New York, sat for breakfast before settling down for virtual school.

Tzipi's interest in children's learning evolved early on. Growing up, she witnessed her brothers struggle as their teachers cast them off as lazy, while, in fact, they suffered from dyslexia and ADHD. Years later, studying biology and specializing in cognitive neuroscience, she focused on how environmental factors affect biological biomarkers in our brains. Tzipi started her work on screens studying kids with dyslexia. She then moved on to conduct brain imaging studies of the impact of environmental effects, like reading time and screen exposure, on the reading abilities of special needs children, as well as general education children.

I asked Tzipi the question, which lingered in my mind, ever since I read the brain imaging studies: "What does it mean that we see these structural changes in the brains? Are they reversible?" Tzipi explained that no one knows for sure. We do know that our brain has plasticity. It is malleable and can change reacting to experience. Still, we do not know what it would take to reverse screen exposure for kids after their brains have changed. Can we create an environment without screens or with fewer screens that will reverse what happened? How long would it take?

Dr. Dimitri Christakis, the lead author of the APA's screen time guidelines, summarized where we are: "In many ways, the concern that investigators like I have is that we're sort of in the midst of a natural kind of uncontrolled experiment on the next generation of children."[12] But can we afford to run this experiment? Can we afford to let screen time escalate because it is easier? Can we just leave our kids in front of their screens in their rooms and in the classroom just knowing what we already know?

Abuse and Neglect

We intuitively know what child abuse is. But what is emotional neglect? Emotional neglect occurs when a parent does not provide the child's basic needs, including when the parent is detached, interacts with a child only when necessary, or provides the child with insufficient warmth, nurturing, or praise. There are plenty of studies documenting the harms of neglect. However, in practice, the state rarely prosecutes neglect unless it is combined with exposure to physical abuse.[13] Still, laws are not just about enforcement. Abuse and neglect laws, like other laws that prohibit behaving in a certain way, convey our moral condemnation of these behaviors.[14] Rules prohibiting child neglect and psychological abuse are important because they send the message that children require parental caring and nurturing.

So how are kids and screens connected to child abuse and neglect? Legal enforcement of abuse and neglect applies to a specific child. But moral condemnation of the harms of these practices does not. If we detach, leave our children in front of screens, and largely give up on in-person interactions, we will neglect a whole generation of children. Unfortunately, screens are so convenient. It is easy to just let them take over. Especially since self-help largely failed and we feel powerless. Powerlessness can inadvertently lead to neglect. The dangers of neglect are always amplified when combined with abuse. This is where our children are at. We have a choice whether to fight for them or to neglect them to face abuse on their own, in classrooms and bedrooms, trapped by the tech industry's abusive designs.

Generational neglect is not a legal term. But, in recent years, youth and advocates fighting against climate change defended children rights in terms of generational neglect. They argued that: "climate change represents a shocking abdication of one generation's responsibility to the next, violating principles of intergenerational equity." They also blamed governments and corporations for "environmental abuse."[15] Greta Thunberg, the young climate activist, famously said in the 2019 UN Climate Action Summit: "This is all wrong. I shouldn't be up here. I should be back in school on the other side of the ocean. Yet you all come to us young people for hope. How dare you. You have stolen my dreams and my childhood with your empty words." In the United States, a group of children and teens sued the US government, protesting its actions affecting climate change. This litigation, which started in 2015, focuses on plaintiffs' constitutional rights and whether they even have standing – a right to sue.[16] Still, the language of generational neglect reverberates. An appellate court judge commented during the hearing: "You present compelling evidence of inaction ... It may even rise to the level of criminal neglect."[17]

As adults, we are torn about technology and kids. We believe our kids need technological skills to get ahead in life, but feel powerless to balance their use of technology. Still, just as with climate change, time is running out. Studies are piling up pointing to a significant impact on a generation of children. Effects on kids are accumulating from over a decade of smartphones, social networks, games, and then topped by a pandemic. While more is to be learned, failing to take certain collective action now could amount to irreversible neglect. Fortunately, as discussed earlier in the book, while corporations often successfully raise the self-choice and personal responsibility arguments, this strategy breaks down when it comes to kids. Society is less concerned about restricting kids' choices and often uses schools to implement these choices.

Screens in Schools

In the last decade, governments prioritized integrating technology into schools. We just lived through the era of "The more the better!" and "a laptop for every child." Education leaders saw technology as the gateway to knowledge. A magic potion that can dismantle centuries-old barriers of scarce resources and learning differences. Long policy documents prescribed replacing textbooks with e-books; teaching students through specialized online materials; using software to assess each student's progress; instructing through games and much more.[18]

Integration of technology into the classroom did happen. But it did so very gradually. Every fall since 2007, when my first child started school, I attended Back to School Nights in my kids' classrooms. During Back-to-School Nights, teachers tell parents about the curriculum and their teaching methods. My last round of pre-pandemic Back to School Nights took place in the fall of 2019. The classrooms did look different from when I started out in 2007. Teachers now used interactive smartboards, mostly to show movies and slides. Still, e-books did not replace textbooks, although some kids used Kindle. Neither did laptops replace pen and paper. Students still hand-wrote most of their assignments and used laptops only for specific assignments during the day. Teachers were divided on the use of Google Classroom. Some teachers placed all their assignments on Google Classroom and even included videos for review, while many others used it sparingly as a backup for students to verify assignments or contact the teacher with a question. Individual assessment software and games did not take over classrooms, although teachers occasionally used specific platforms like Kahoot (a learning game quizzes platform) or coding kits.

For over a decade while governments kept pushing schools to integrate technology, and educators struggled to do so, researchers studied how well it worked. They found that the answer was not straightforward and discovered some surprising and counter-intuitive findings. For example, we know that kids and young adults rely far less on printers than previous generations. Printing documents instead of reading them online actually ages a person, in the same way that owning an @aol email account does. Expectedly, then, researchers found that college students overwhelmingly preferred to read digitally. They also found that students' reading was faster and that the students believed their comprehension of the materials was better. But, surprisingly, results showed that overall comprehension was better for print over digital reading.[19]

Many studies focused on higher education. This was not a coincidence. Unlike K–12 schools, universities endorsed technology much faster and more overwhelmingly. Online learning became the hot trend (and the cash cow) for many universities. But even learning in the physical university lecture room changed. Universities, for about two decades now, accommodated laptops and provided free Internet access in classrooms. Practically all my law school students use their laptops in class. I sometimes get to see their screens when I sit at the back of the classroom to evaluate junior colleagues. Frequently, I see that the students are not taking notes, but instead are elsewhere online, whether on Instagram, playing a game, or messaging. This is the norm. But researchers found that multitasking in the classroom can negatively impact the academic performance not only of the multi-taskers themselves, but of others, by distracting the students around them in their vicinity.[20]

Policymakers strongly believed that technology in the classroom will improve learning outcomes for school kids. They also hoped that technology will be the great equalizer, closing gaps between kids of different socio-economic backgrounds. Unfortunately, research draws a less rosy picture. In 2017, the National Bureau of Economic Research executed an overview of the research and concluded that giving children a computer to learn through in school has a limited impact on their learning.[21] The Organisation for Economic Co-operation and Development (OECD) conducted a large international study published in 2015, which found that students who use computers moderately at school have somewhat better learning outcomes than students who use computers rarely. But, students who use computers very frequently at school do a lot worse in most learning outcomes. Even more concerningly, the study's results showed no appreciable improvements in students' achievements in reading, mathematics, or science in the countries that had invested heavily in technology for education. Finally, the results revealed that technology is of little help in bridging the skills divide between advantaged and disadvantaged students.[22]

What happened? As researchers conducting the brain imaging studies explained, learning requires intensive, in-person teacher–student interactions. Kids learn better from people, not from machines. A second explanation leaves more room for hope for finding a place for technology in the classroom. We have more to learn. Which technologies are effective in the classroom? How much technology is not too much? And how can teachers do a better a job of teaching with technology?[23]

Evidently, we could see the warning signs before the pandemic. More was not always better for technology in the classroom. But now more is already there. Teachers discovered the powerful allure of games and social networks to engage students. Students got used to studying on screens throughout the day, exposed to online distractions. Students and teachers alike adjusted to Google Classroom and other online platforms as their learning hubs. Screen time rocketed. The classroom equilibrium has no doubt changed. Still, many decisions need to be made in coming years. Should students continue to use laptops in school throughout the school day or some parts of it? Would online hubs like Google Classroom retain their central role or retreat into the background as a repository of class assignments? Should teachers set aside their newly discovered teaching methods to engage kids through games and social networks?

The decision about what goes on in school is not just about school: what happens in school filters into the home. If classwork takes place on screens, so does homework. When schools incorporate teaching through Minecraft or TikTok, they give these games and social networks legitimacy. They signal pedagogic approval. When Minecraft is homework, a parent trying to convince her child to stop playing is engaging in a losing battle. Homework and playtime merge and the hours pile on. Addictive technologies make it hard for users to stop. When a student gets on TikTok to review her biology lectures, she will likely stay there much longer than intended, lured by unrelated videos. When homework, games, and social networks are integrated, students face significant challenges focusing on the task on hand.

While for over a decade, technology companies controlled how we spend our time, during the pandemic they became stakeholders in our education systems. The "bad guys" of the technology industry are now invested in educational departments and collaborations with schools. We have let the fox into the chicken coop. It will not leave by itself. This makes careful decision-making about incorporating technology into the classroom more crucial than ever before.

The federal government, through guidelines and through money, pushes states hard to maximize technology integration into the classroom. In their rush to technologize the future, federal guidelines do consider equality between students, and account for students' privacy. But the impact of excessive screen time as a consideration is sorely missing.[24] We now have a window of opportunity to act intentionally and urgently to change federal and local education policy guidelines. If we do not do so, Big Tech's new hold in the classroom will determine these for us.

The devil is not in the details. It is in the framework. It is about shifting what lawyers call the burden of proof. In television shows we see prosecutors arguing to prove guilt beyond reasonable doubt. This means that the prosecutors, not the defense, need to present evidence to prove that the suspect committed the crime beyond reasonable doubt. In education, right now, agenda setters assume that learning through technology is superior. Those who disagree need to prove otherwise. But accumulating evidence points to the need to change who should convince who, in other words, who carries the burden of proof. If we do so, those who want to integrate technology into the classroom would need to prove that replacing a human teacher with a specific technology (like a game quiz to assess students or a video teaching math) would result in a superior outcome.[25]

It is also about shifting the simplistic agenda of "the more the better" to a "restricting model." This means restricting use of personal technology (laptops, open Internet access, or smartphones) unless it actually accomplishes learning objectives instead of distracting students. We know that college students have trouble concentrating in class when they can just surf off to Instagram. Can we expect a ninth grader to resist the temptation of playing a game online during a geometry class?

Although federal policy is still focused on the technology magic pill as the remedy for all the education system maladies, once again, as we saw with the food and privacy wars, change is brewing bottom up. States and even cities are restricting screen times in educational settings. It started gradually since 2010, with younger children in early education centers, first focusing on television and video and on whether content was educationally appropriate. Some years later, laws and a flurry of bills started limiting screen time of any type and targeting older school kids as well.[26]

State laws have interesting behavior trends. Like clothes, they have fashions. They tend to emerge together from neighboring states and sometimes sweep over the country. They first appear as proposed laws – as bills – and may fail to pass or take a few tries. When I study bills, I feel a bit like an anthropologist. Bills tell us a lot about where we are or want to go as a society. A Massachusetts bill offers a glimpse into what could be a better, more balanced future. The bill sends a message of urgency. It starts by referring to the brain imaging studies we investigated earlier in the chapter. It includes comprehensive steps away from the status quo:

- Ending the technology mandate across the curriculum for kids K–12, not just younger kids.
- Imposing strict screen time limits. For grades K–7, no more than four to five hours a month of screen time; and for grades 8–12, no more than two hours a day.
- Even when screen time is assigned, it needs to undergo a cost-benefit analysis. Screen time must serve educational goals, not convenience, and be weighed against the physical, psychological harms and the risk of addiction.
- No cellphones on school site.[27]

The Massachusetts bill includes a ban on cellphones in schools. Banning cellphones in schools is an emerging international and local trend. France led the way, banning phones in schools in 2018, including during lunch and recess. According to the French government, the impact of phones on social interaction necessitated this sweeping move.[28] In the United States, most efforts to ban phones in schools came locally from municipalities and most often from schools themselves.[29] Although some authorities like Ontario and New York City imposed cellphone bans and then reversed them, reports from schools that adopted the ban indicate the potential for change.[30]

In one high school, an eleventh-grade student, Serena Masciotra, admitted the initial difficulties of withdrawal. "It was hard," Masciotra said. "I was used to checking my phone and communicating with my friends instantly. Suddenly I had to wait to communicate with them, face to face, at lunch. But now? My phone is out of my mind. It's a relief. I no longer feel the constant need to stay updated."[31] Changes affected students both individually and as a community. The principal reported: "There was a huge difference in the atmosphere – in the cafeteria, the hallways, the classroom . . . It's definitely louder in the cafeteria because they are talking to each other. It's noisy, but it's fun noise. Lots of laughter."[32]

Takeaway Points

- Brain imaging scans reveal concerning differences between brain structures in areas of the brain responsible for learning and development between children exposed to excessive screen time and those who are not.
- Time is of the essence for a generation of children increasingly exposed to screens for over a decade.
- Education policy pre-pandemic pushed for incorporating technology into the classroom, although studies revealed mixed results of its effectiveness.
- During the pandemic, schools took a step further, incorporating screens and also Big Tech's most addictive products into the classroom.
- There is an urgent need to reframe education policy about integration of technology into the classroom on a case-by case basis rather than a blanket preference.

11 THE ACHILLES HEEL

As the science wars raged on, a grassroots movement emerged. Parents and regulators took action to protect children against technology overuse. It is not surprising that children came first. They bear the brunt of the harm. They are also where corporate vulnerability lies. Action began against online gaming and spread to social networks. Children are the Achilles heel of the technology industry's hold on manipulative designs to sustain an abusive business model. But, protecting children also opens the door for more. Any gain made for kids is a step toward change for all.

Loot Boxes: "The Low Hanging Fruit"

Jonathan Peniket grew up in a town on the outskirts of London. He started playing FIFA Ultimate Team, the popular soccer video game, when he was 12. In FIFA, the player's goal is to win a soccer game, and they increase their chances of doing so by creating the best team. A player first chooses a nationality for the team, then receives his players with names, pictures, and scores, appearing on virtual cards. Players can earn virtual coins to buy new virtual cards and improve their team. But it is hard work to earn them through playing, which encourages players to use real-world money to enhance the team faster. A player purchasing virtual cards does not know their contents in advance. Opening the cards comes with great virtual fanfare of sounds and colors. Players rarely receive the "gold" virtual cards of top players, which are worth large sums of real-world money.

Jonathan at first spent about £200 ($260) on virtual packs in each cycle of FIFA to keep his team competitive. Things changed when he was in his final year of high school. By then, he had a debit card, which he could use to spend more. Around that time, a friend died and then Jonathan's mother received a cancer diagnosis. Jonathan barely played a match of FIFA anymore. Instead, he spent hours opening loot boxes every day. At first, he purchased £20 of virtual cards per sitting. He kept spending more, eventually purchasing virtual cards for up to £80 per sitting – four or five times a night.

Jonathan was not addicted to FIFA. He was addicted to opening packs. The "buzz of chance," as he put it, around potentially unveiling a top player. It was a reliable rush for him, a soothing mechanism when life otherwise seemed miserable. The game never ended for Jonathan. No matter what players popped out of his packs, the game continued to release new players so his team was never complete. Eventually feeling guilty, he told his parents he thought he spent £700 on the game. They looked up his statements and found that he had spent £2,700.[1]

The virtual cards that Jonathan compulsively opened are called loot boxes. "Loot boxes" is a term that kids are very familiar with, but adults less so. They come in different shapes and forms. In FIFA they appear as virtual cards; in Fortnite as llamas containing rewards. A loot box is basically a reward system in a game that lets players use real money to purchase surprise virtual items that can, if they happen to be useful, help them progress in the game.

Loot boxes are relatively new to the game industry. In the late 1970s, my brother and I used to play a home video game system called Atari. Each game came in a cartridge. Like many kids at the time, our favorite was Pac-Man. We sat next to our childhood red round table, on which we placed the console with the inserted game cartridge, and each held on to a controller. We spent hours watching Pac-Man consume wafers while avoiding the ghosts that pursued him, so we could proceed to the next level. Atari sold its video games as a finished product. This was the game industry's business model for years.

It was only at the beginning of the twenty-first century that the game industry altered its way of doing business. It did so by selling supplemental digital products to enhance the game experience. The industry termed these "microtransactions" and "in-game purchases." Some game-makers sold only cosmetic changes, but others offered in-game advantages, like additional powers for the player's game character. Purchasing items made sense for users because players could save a lot of time by buying a virtual item, say a powerful sword, instead of earning it through playing the game. Next came loot boxes, which added an element of randomization to microtransactions. Now if a player wanted to buy a sword, he often could not purchase that sword directly like before. Instead, he would have to open one or many loot boxes until he either found the sword or gave up the search. Eventually, the game industry lined up with the dominant online business model by offering free games. Game companies nowadays frequently do not charge players to purchase the game to begin playing. Instead, they rely on significant revenues from microtransactions through loot boxes.[2]

Loot boxes are very addictive, especially for kids. They were meant to be. Designers of loot boxes implemented the same intermittent reward system discussed in Chapter 3. They modeled loot boxes to resemble slot machines in many ways. First, the outcome is random; a player gets the desired reward based on luck, not skill. Second, the probability of getting the desired item is low. This means a player needs to keep purchasing loot boxes. Third, the loot box plays music and features special animation when it is about to open to create tension. The player does not know what is inside. Only once the loot box completes these multi-steps is the reward revealed.[3] Opening a loot box gives the player a rush: the moment of anticipation followed by release. As a designer of the popular game Overwatch described it: "When the box is there, you're excited at the possibilities of what could be inside." ... Click the "Open loot box" button and the box bursts open, sending four disks into the sky. Their rarity is indicated by colored streaks to further build the suspense. "Seeing purple or gold you start to think about what specific legendary or epic [item] you've unlocked. This all happens so fast, but it was those discrete steps that we felt maximized excitement and anticipation."[4]

Loot boxes mix games with money. Their impact on kids is stronger than on adults. Kids are more likely to get addicted because they take less time than adults to build a strong reward circuit around an addictive substance or feature. Kids are more inclined to engage in risk-taking behaviors and risky decision-making than adults and, in addition, kids often lack a critical understanding of money and financial management.[5]

About 2 percent of gamers are responsible for most of the industry's profits. Game-makers call them "whales." These players make up for most gamers who do not pay or pay very little. So why still addict all these players to the game? The first reason is that a non-paying player may one day still purchase a loot box; if he stops playing, he never will. In addition, the more players the merrier on online games. For example, in some games, players join alliances to fight major battles and compare victories. It is necessary to have as many players as possible to add the social aspect. Game-makers achieve these goals by ensuring that both paying and non-paying players spend as much time as possible on the game.[6]

The picture of children gambling online raised alarms. The Internet is replete with addictive designs, but when money and gambling were added to the mix, loot boxes became the low-hanging fruit for legal intervention. Loot boxes pose needless extra risks for kids. Research shows that minors exposed to game-of-chance mechanisms are more likely to engage in pathological gaming later in life.[7] But importantly, this is not just about the fate of loot boxes. The legal action surrounding loot boxes is a microcosm for what will happen next. It illustrates the legal avenues at play and those likely to be part of a larger movement to combat overuse well beyond loot boxes.

The fight against loot boxes already includes some familiar moves. The game industry immediately raised the personal choice and personal responsibility arguments. In an FTC workshop on loot boxes, a leading legal representative of the gaming industry said:

> Microtransactions give players a choice. No one is forced to spend money in a video game that is free to play. They choose what they want to spend and when they want to spend it and how they want to spend it. Effectively, it's a try-before-you-buy model. You get to get out there and play a game. If you like the game and you want to spend money in the game, well, then do so.[8]

Other representatives of the industry placed the responsibility on parents. An official with the Entertainment Software Association (ESA) stated: "We look forward to sharing . . . the tools and information the industry already provides that keeps the control of in-game spending in parents' hands . . . Parents already have the ability to limit or prohibit in-game purchases with easy to use parental controls."[9] The president of the Entertainment Software Rating Board (ESRB) explained at the FTC workshop: "We want to make sure that parents know that when they see that in-game purchase notice . . . if they want to limit their child's ability to spend money, they know how to do it."[10]

Regulators around the world have considered whether children's online games are, in fact, gambling. Some countries, such as the Netherlands, Belgium, and Japan, have placed comprehensive – although not complete – bans on loot boxes. Belgium, for example, prohibited games in which loot boxes are purchased for real money because these constitute illegal gambling.[11] The Netherlands banned loot boxes that have resale value in the real world, and prohibited the use of addictive loot boxes' design features, like the audio-visual effects that accompany box opening.[12] In response, some game-makers redesigned their products for these markets, while others ceased selling their products there.[13] Many other countries are considering following suit, including Spain and the United Kingdom.[14]

Not all regulators chose a blanket ban that affects adults as well as children. Some countries – including Australia and China – explored restricting access by kids alone instead of banning loot boxes for all. They examined different ways of only preventing minors from having access to loot boxes, including ratings for loot boxes games (such as 18+) or requiring an ID to purchase video games with loot boxes.[15] China took a different approach by imposing a spending limit of $28–57 per month on loot boxes, depending on the age of the child.[16]

In addition to banning access to loot boxes, there is another option: increasing transparency. Focusing on transparency helps increase public awareness. Ratings indicating that a game containing loot boxes is inappropriate for minors provide more transparency. These ratings can either assist in implementing a ban on loot boxes for children or replace a ban as a softer measure to raise awareness. Ratings are not the only way to provide transparency for loot boxes.

China, for example, opted for transparency by requiring that all game developers reveal the odds of winning any virtual item in a loot box.[17]

In the United States, a flurry of action surrounds loot boxes. The dust has not settled yet. But as we saw before through the tobacco and privacy wars, all roads are taken simultaneously. Both Congress and state legislatures proposed laws to regulate loot boxes. Options oscillated between prohibiting use of loot boxes in games used by minors,[18] and including labels, such as: "Warning: This game contains a gambling-like mechanism that may promote the development of a gaming disorder that increases the risk of harmful mental or physical health effects, and may expose the user to significant financial risk."[19]

Parents made courtrooms their battlefields. They filed class actions against game-makers of popular games containing loot boxes, including Fortnite, FIFA, and Overwatch. Parents argued that kids spending money on loot boxes is illegal gambling. But they had a hard time winning this argument. Courts consider a game to be gambling if a user plays to win a prize. According to most courts, a "prize" means something that has value in the real world, not a soccer player card that only has a value in the game.[20] Plaintiffs stand a better chance of winning the gambling argument in games where players can exchange virtual goods for real money. Why? Because for judges this resembles physical casinos where players exchange their chips for money when they leave the building.[21]

Parents are losing because they struggle to fit loot boxes into what the law recognizes as gambling. But they also fail because judges do not view sales of items on virtual games as real. Judges hearing loot boxes cases frequently refer to a 2015 case where a judge declined to recognize an online casino game as gambling. The judge wrote: "[This is about] the need to draw clear and distinct lines between real and virtual worlds ... even in the age of the Internet there is a crucial distinction between that which is pretend and that which is real and true."[22]

So far, plaintiffs are losing cases. This does not mean they will not eventually win. We saw this happen with tobacco litigation.[23] But just as importantly, loot boxes are only the tip of the iceberg. The lawsuits introduce judges to the addictive nature of online games. Court filings tell many stories, like the story of C.W., describing how the addictive nature of these games compels kids to spend money on in-game purchases to acquire loot boxes.

Rebecca White, C.W.'s mother, filed a lawsuit on his behalf against Epic Games, the manufacturer of Fortnite. The complaint recounts how C.W. played Fortnite for more than six hours a day – frequently through the night – adversely affecting his sleep and overall health. He often purchased loot boxes when he was tired, after long hours of gaming or at night. The plaintiffs argued: "These games are highly addictive, designed deliberately so, and tend to compel children playing them to make purchases."[24] Lawsuits against game manufacturers highlighted that the games are made for kids, most players are kids, and game manufacturers *know* it. In a lawsuit against Overwatch, plaintiffs described the cartoonish appearance of the game. The characters are fantastical with human attributes. The world is animated imaginary and colorful.[25]

This all rings a bell. These arguments echo the words of one of the lawyers who litigated the tobacco companies in the third, and eventually successful, wave of litigation: "You addicted me, and you knew it was addicting and now you say it is my fault."[26] Plaintiffs suing Blizzard, the manufacturer of Overwatch, went even further and explicitly connected the actions of the gaming industry to those of the tobacco industry. They argued: "Not unlike Big Tobacco's 'Joe Camel' advertising campaign, Blizzard profits from creating addictive behaviors in kids to generate huge revenues for the Company."[27]

In 2019, the FTC joined other regulators around the world in considering concerns about loot boxes. Many stakeholders, including gaming industry representatives, participated in an FTC workshop. In 2020, the FTC concluded the workshop without taking specific action, but the Commission did announce it will continue to monitor loot boxes and take appropriate steps.[28]

The US gaming industry, facing backlash from near and far, attempted to preempt legal action in the United States. Like the tech industry through the privacy battles, game-makers took baby-steps toward self-regulation. During the FTC workshop in 2019 (and after China announced its law mandating disclosure of winning odds), the ESA announced that, by the end of 2020, Microsoft, Nintendo, and Sony would require disclosure of loot box odds. The gaming industry has also started slowly moving toward a rating system that incorporated loot boxes. In 2018, the ESRB required game-makers to place the label "In-Game-Purchases" on games featuring loot boxes, among other microtransactions. By 2020, responding to further pressure, the ESRB updated the In-Game Purchases label to "In-Game Purchases (Includes Random Items)." Still, the ESRB refused to include the words "loot boxes" on its labels.[29]

The fate of loot boxes is still unclear. But regardless of its resolution it serves to connect the past and the future. The war over loot boxes is familiar. It incorporates many moves from the battles of the past. It also sheds more specific light on what struggles to contain technology overuse are likely to look like.

Parents' Litigation: Going to the Core

It is unsurprising that parents' litigation focused on loot boxes. After all, the idea of kids gambling made loot boxes the tech industry's lowest hanging fruit. But in Quebec things happened differently. Parents and their attorneys suing Fortnite did not focus on loot boxes. They went to the heart of the matter: the addictiveness of Fortnite itself. The plaintiffs suing in *F.N.* v. *Epic Games* struck the two vulnerabilities of the personal responsibility argument: the involvement of minors and covert corporate intent to addict.

F.N. represented their child L.N. as one of the lead plaintiffs in the Quebec class action. The complaint described what happened to L.N. when he started playing Fortnite as a 9-year-old. L.N., who had not really played video games before, began playing almost daily. Since then, he has stopped hanging out much with other kids. When he did get together with friends, it looked different. They no longer spent time outdoors playing basketball or indoors in the winter playing board games. Instead, they only played Fortnite. When L.N. played Fortnite with friends, he used aggressive language. L.N. also got very angry when his parents tried to make him take a break and argued that Fortnite is the only activity available to him because: "in the winter it is cold and in the summer it rains." The complaint stated that Fortnite made L.N. dependent on the game. He needed to play several hours a day. His playing affected several spheres of his life and transformed his social interactions. The attorneys drafting the complaint phrased it to show it is addiction, by using terms that fit the WHO definition of Gaming Disorder and the DSM definition of Internet Gaming Disorder. L.N.'s parents stated that, had they known the risks, they would have prohibited L.N. from downloading the game or at least would have taken care from the start to prevent L.N. from becoming dependent on the game.[30]

L.N.'s story is typical, but the case itself is ground-breaking. F.N.'s lawyers are arguing that Fortnite is as addictive as cocaine. They claim that Epic, Fortnite's manufacturer, purposefully designed an addictive product, using experts to do that. They are saying that not only did Epic know the health risks to users of creating dependency, but it also failed to disclose the risks to its users. The plaintiffs sued under Quebec's consumer protection laws, which are in some ways unique.[31] But their argument rings an old bell. They composed it of the building blocks that eventually defeated the tobacco industry (and apply across legal systems): the addictive design, knowledge of the addictiveness of the design, and failure to warn users.

This lawsuit is crucial for its indirect implications. By arguing that Fortnite's designs are addictive, it focuses the floodlights on the way the technology industry uses addictive strategies not just in Fortnite or even just in online gaming. The lawsuit highlights Fortnite's use of the variable reward technique: its reliance on luck – not skill – and on random rewards. As discussed, tech companies apply the variable reward technique ubiquitously: through likes and notifications in social networks or through swiping on dating apps. F.N.'s lawsuit also under-scores how Fortnite takes advantage of teens' desire to be socially accepted and their fear of missing out (FOMO). The lawsuit describes how kids playing on Fortnite judge and ridicule each other for the virtual items and costumes they buy through in-game purchases. It details how Fortnite's marketing created a vicious cycle through which kids feel like they need to purchase more to be socially accepted. Social networks, especially Instagram, manipulate kids' need for social accept-ance even further. Finally, the game never ends. There are different challenges each day, which bring with them rewards; the game changes every ten weeks, which incentivizes the player to keep going. Like the infinite scroll or the automatic play of the next video on YouTube, there is no natural stopping point. The design manipulates kids' stimuli perception and reaction instincts.[32]

The media covered the Quebec Fortnite lawsuit extensively. Once the first news came out that the lawsuit was about to be filed, hundreds of parents flocked to join.[33] Epic may eventually settle to avoid reaching the discovery stage. Discovery is risky. The court may compel Epic to reveal internal documents about Fortnite's design and what it knew about how addictive the game is, especially among kids. Regardless, the train has already left the station. And unsurprisingly, parents' lawsuits against social media causing harm through addicting their kids quickly followed suit.[34]

In 2021, the attorneys general also took action. Forty-four state attorneys general signed a letter to Facebook quoting studies on the impact of Instagram on kids by enhancing FOMO and body image concerns. They warned that "[u]se of social media can be detrimental to the health and well-being of children, who are not equipped to navigate the challenges of having a social media account." The attorneys general called on Facebook to halt its plan to create an Instagram for young children.[35]

Attorneys general represented the interests of the public when they sued the tobacco industry during the third and critical litigation wave. The analogy between tobacco abuse and technology overuse was not lost here. "Big Tobacco understood that the younger you got to someone, the easier you could get them addicted to become a lifelong user," Doug Peterson, Nebraska's attorney general, said. "I see some comparisons to social media platforms."[36] Attorneys general representing the interests of children have targeted a vulnerable spot in the personal responsibility argument. In recent years, state attorneys general have become increasingly involved in regulating Big Tech through privacy lawsuits. Their letter to Facebook indicates they will likely not shy away from intervening on the overuse front.

Winds from Abroad: Ordering Redesign

I often advise students on their papers. After years of researching technology overuse, I was finally approached by a student who wanted to write a paper on the topic. I like talking to students about their paper ideas. My students are in their 20s and their experiences with technology are usually different from mine. I learn from them, and in turn I guide them to select a well-defined topic for their paper. In this conversation, however, I was less effective than usual. I had too much to say. Instead of helping him focus, I threw too many ideas his way. I explained that, so far, the research shows that kids are more impacted (compared to adults) by technology overuse. I jumped from topic to topic about what could be done. Eventually, our roles switched. The student stopped me and asked: "Professor Bernstein, but what do you want to happen?" That gave me a pause. What would I want to happen if I lived in the perfect law professor world? A world in which the policy solutions that we law professors prescribe become a legal reality. I immediately thought about my own kids. My kids do not play many online games. My 14-year-old twins started high school at that time and had not yet joined any social networks. My answer surprised me as well. It was stronger than I expected. I told the student: "I have children, and I wish that they could not use social networks until they turned eighteen."

As I said it my mind started wandering. Should this be the goal? Are we at a point at which we should ban access to social media? To online games? To certain online games? To certain social networks? The experience of some countries in Southeast Asia in restricting kids' access to online gaming came to mind. In these countries, concerns about technology addiction, especially gaming addiction, took center stage much earlier and more prominently than in the rest of the world. In South Korea, it started with several high-profile deaths. In 2010, a 32-year-old man played a game called "StarCraft" for five days without stopping to rest; he eventually dropped dead in the middle of the game. That same year, a 25-year-old woman pleaded guilty to negligent homicide after her infant died while she was spending up to ten hours a day playing an online game. Ironically, her favorite game was "Prius Online," in which she cared for a virtual girl as she gained magical powers and grew older.[37] But then attention turned to kids. In 2015, Reuters reported that, according to recent government data, one in ten South Korean children between the age of 10 and 19 is addicted to the Internet. Other reports indicated that the number could be much higher.[38]

Shutdown Systems

Countries such as Thailand, South Korea, Vietnam, Japan, and China experimented with a restrictive option to limit kids' access to online gaming. They implemented what has become known as "A Shutdown System" or "Cinderella Laws." Under this system, governments require game service providers to block access to their online games during specific times of the day. For example, in 2011, South Korea legally required online game providers to restrict gaming access by kids under 16 from midnight to 6am. While some of these countries – including Thailand – retracted the system, others – specifically Japan and China – adopted even more restrictive versions.[39] For example, in 2019, China restricted minors to playing video games for one and a half hours on weekdays and three hours on weekends and holidays. It also prohibited them from playing between 10pm and 8am. This meant minors were allowed to play thirteen and a half hours a week. The government required video-game service providers to verify identities to ensure compliance by minors.[40] Then, in 2021, as a state-owned media outlet decried the "spiritual opium" of gaming, China went further. It capped kids' playing time to three hours per week, encouraging them instead to spend more time outside.[41] That same year, China went beyond online gaming and implemented the Shutdown System on social media as well. As a result, kids under 14 using Douyin, the Chinese version of TikTok, are limited to forty minutes a day, and they cannot access it at all from 10pm to 6am.[42]

Other governments, not just totalitarian regimes like China, are still experimenting with the Shutdown option. Clearly, countries that chose to implement it did so because they perceived an ominous threat to kids from technology overuse, particularly online gaming. Countries that decided to retract the system did so, apparently, because of mixed results regarding its effectiveness. While some studies showed a decrease in the number of kids playing games after midnight and in overall gaming time, other studies did not show statistically significant results. Studies also highlighted adverse side effects. Some players got upset and felt they wanted to play more immediately after being forced to stop.[43] But then, shutdown systems, like government action about loot boxes, influenced game-makers' decisions. For example, in 2021, after China legislated its most restrictive shutdown measures, Epic Games announced that it would close its Chinese Fortnite version.[44]

Selective Shutdown

The Shutdown System is the most restrictive option, but not the only one. A variation is the Selective Shutdown Policy. South Korea has replaced its mandatory Shutdown System with a voluntary self-exclusion system. Under the Selective Shutdown Policy, a minor's guardian can request game vendors to block their child's gaming for certain hours.[45] This allows more flexibility to limit gaming time according to the needs of the specific child.

The Fatigue System

Another system that China implemented in 2007 to combat gaming addiction is called the Fatigue System. China required online game providers to monitor their users' playtime and to discourage underage players from playing for too long. After three hours of playing, a minor could get only half the experience points needed to advance in the game and after five hours a minor player could receive no experience points. In addition, after five hours of gameplay, a player would receive notifications every fifteen minutes that they had entered unhealthy game time and should stop immediately. While some sources found the system was effective, others claimed it was too difficult to implement and could be circumvented, for example, by kids using adults' identification.[46]

China is a major innovator in regulating online games and social networks. Although doubtless driven by the politics of its totalitarian regime, China shares its concern about addiction among youth with other countries in Southeast Asia that have adopted similar policies. Across the globe, countries are gearing up to take stronger measures to protect kids, particularly targeting online games and social media. These countries could benefit by studying the Southeast Asian experience.

In the United States: Options on the Table

By the time the COVID pandemic broke in early 2020, public concern about the harms of excessive screen time had reached America's legislative halls. Congressmen started promoting bills to curtail technology overuse, focusing mostly on children and/or social networks. Then came the pandemic and not much happened for over a year. But by 2021, the media reported regularly on the cost of pandemic screen life for kids, and legislative activity unsurprisingly resumed.

As usually happens, some bills died, while others may still proceed. But regardless, they point to routes already considered and indirectly highlight options that may still be on the table. Most proposals for legislative action combined several of the following elements together, while making choices as to the breadth of each restriction:

- targeting children or the public at large;
- focusing on all types of websites or only on social media;
- prohibiting specific addictive elements, including auto play, engagement badges (like snapstreaks), the infinite scroll, and alerts that encourage spending more time on an app when the user is not on it;
- taking a broader catch-all approach by prohibiting any feature that encourages additional engagement with the platform, thereby leaving the door open to prohibiting new manipulative features;
- requiring sites to design default time limits for users to spend on the platform – for example, thirty minutes on a social network – though still allowing the user an option to extend the time;
- requiring sites to provide notifications once a user spent a certain amount of time on the platform, usually every thirty minutes;
- creating a federal tort for social media harm by making social media companies liable for any harm (physical or mental) caused to kids; and
- creating a private right of action for individuals to sue, providing for enforcement by the attorney general, or providing that a violation falls under the FTC's jurisdiction.[47]

These are not the only options. To make an informed choice, we need to place side by side the full spectrum of options. Southeast Asian countries implemented the Mandatory or Selective Shut Down Systems and the Fatigue System. These systems may appear like totalitarian measures unsuitable in a Western democracy. But shutdown systems do not bar all access to games and social networks: they restrict access and limit time. We, in fact, endorse stronger measures by completely barring minors' access to cigarettes and alcohol. We hesitate here both because of the novelty and China's association with these systems. But mostly we are unsure because of our perception of harm. Public understanding of the harms of social media and games is still developing. Adoption of a shutdown-type system is likely to depend on how severe we think the harm is and the feasibility of verifying age to implement the system.

Other alternatives go further. But looking back to past battles and their tipping points, we have taken some of these measures before:

- *Likes and Comments:* Prohibiting comments and likes on social networks or on any social network accessible to kids under 18. Of course, likes and comments form the backbone of social networks. They also combine two of the psychological mechanisms that make these networks so addictive for kids: the intermittent reward model and the need to be socially accepted. No doubt these features play a central role in prolonging users' time on the networks and in making sure they keep returning. Without likes and comments, much of the allure may be gone and time on the network will likely diminish.

- *Pay Per Time:* Social media is free. Games are mostly free. But what if they were not? What if users had to pay? Taxes on cigarettes made them prohibitively expensive, and effectively reduced the number of smokers. Consider social media and games charging per time spent. Replacing the business model, which currently subsists on time and attention, with a Pay as You Go model. Changing the business model would in practice mostly target kids because their resources are most limited. A teen cannot go on unlimited rides in an amusement park with her friends because the rides are costly. Under the same business model, she will now be unable to afford spending all night on Instagram.

- *Prohibit Social Media Access by Minors:* The challenge of prohibiting manipulative features is that new ones will always come along. We will be playing an endless game of cat and mouse. We also know that once a kid gets on a social network her social life becomes largely virtual with, by now well-documented, effects on her mental well-being. In a way it is a point of no return. But what if they do not start? What if they wait until they are 18? We prohibit kids under 18 from purchasing cigarettes. We do it for a reason: it reduces the likelihood that they will become smokers as adults and improves their overall health. Social media networks require critical mass. Once a teen's friends are no longer there, even the temptation to go on it diminishes. If only adults over 18 could enter the social traps of Instagram or Facebook, the potential harmful impact would be much diluted.

Takeaway Points

- The fight against loot boxes illustrates how strategies of past battles apply to the realities of technology overuse:
  - game-makers raise the personal responsibility argument and extend it to parents;
  - abroad, some regulators restricted loot boxes, and the industry rushed to redesign games;
  - in the United States, reacting to legal pressure, the industry took voluntary steps to incorporate ratings, warnings, and information on loot boxes;
  - parents' class actions against game-makers target the vulnerabilities of the personal responsibility argument: marketing to minors and the tech industry's knowledge of the addictive qualities of its products.
- Countries in Southeast Asia accumulated over a decade of experience by legally implementing and assessing shutdown and fatigue systems to battle kids' addiction to online gaming.
- In the United States, legislators assess different options to protect kids on social media and other online platforms, including: requiring default settings for limiting time and notifications of time spent; prohibiting addictive features; and creating a tort liability for social networks.
- Other options to consider are: eliminating likes and comments on social media; adopting a pay-per-time model; and prohibiting social media access by minors.

12 ACUPUNCTURE FOR CHANGE

Reviving Antitrust: Old Tools for the New Economy

I graduated from law school in the mid-1990s with a concentration in intellectual property law. I was interested in the new economy; in technology; in legal change. After law school, I moved from the United States to Israel, where I started working in a leading law firm in Tel-Aviv. The law firm was as old school as could be, and so were many of its clients. I hoped to work on intellectual property cases, but – to my dismay – the law firm assigned me to work on antitrust cases. Antitrust was the antithesis of where I expected to start my career. I viewed it as the law of brick and mortar. Indeed, antitrust law grew regulating the old economy; railroad and oil companies dominate the classic antitrust court cases.[1]

Antitrust enforcement started in earnest in Israel in the mid-1990s. The State of Israel founded a government agency dedicated to the enforcement of antitrust laws, which began by targeting the pillars of the centralized Israeli economy. Quite a few of my firm's clients found themselves at the center of antitrust investigations. I recall attending 7am client meetings with heads of industries, walking into rooms so thick with cigarette smoke that I could barely see the faces of the older men sitting there. To my 28-year-old self, nothing was further away from technology law than the practice of antitrust.

A quarter of a century later, things have changed. Today, antitrust seems to be all about technology. Could a revival of antitrust enforcement cure the evils of Big Tech? For decades, we have seen antitrust enforcers laying low, while tech companies have risen high. The giants of Silicon Valley have operated largely undisturbed. Examples are plentiful. Facebook implemented CEO Mark Zuckerberg's strategy: "It is better to buy than compete." It purchased companies either to operate them under its wings or to shutter them.[2] The purchase of Instagram was a watershed moment. In 2012, when Facebook realized it could not beat Instagram's photo-sharing app, it went ahead and bought it. For years, most people thought that Facebook and Instagram were competitors. Many people had no idea that they were part of one large conglomerate. Then, in 2014, Facebook determined that WhatsApp posed a risk to its business. It feared that WhatsApp would leverage its very successful messaging app to enter social networking and threaten Facebook's control of that market. Facebook solved the problem by paying $22 billion to buy a five-year-old company with about fifty workers. By buying WhatsApp, Facebook buried WhatsApp's alternative ad-free business model.[3]

Facebook is by no means a unique player flexing its muscles in Silicon Valley. Google, Amazon, and Uber employed their own strategies to leverage their powerful positions. For example, Google pays Apple $12 billion a year to make it the default search engine on the Apple iPhone. As discussed in Chapter 8, we usually do not change our default settings. This means that Google has guaranteed that most iPhone users will use its search engine and see the ads it displays.[4]

Despite all of this and much more, Big Tech remained "the good guys" for years. The public believed it and the government rarely posed challenges. But around 2018–19, things changed. The government embarked on an antitrust crusade against Big Tech. The FTC, the Department of Justice, and dozens of state attorneys general sued Facebook, Google, Amazon, and Uber for antitrust violations.[5] Simultaneously, Congress held hearings and congressmen proposed multiple bills to curtail Big Tech through legislation.[6]

Why is antitrust the first round of artillery against Big Tech? Big Tech (as the name implies) refers to several globally known large players. Antitrust law often comes into action when large companies threaten competition. Its goal is to increase competition. The idea is that if more firms compete, companies will need to lure consumers by coming up with new ideas, and innovation will lead to better and cheaper products.[7] To achieve all this, antitrust law prohibits unreasonable behaviors by businesses that could inhibit competition. One restriction prohibits mergers between companies that will lessen competition or create a company likely to have a monopoly over the market.[8] For example, antitrust authorities could have tried to block the merger between Facebook and Instagram when it happened or to dismantle it.[9] Another restriction prohibits monopolies from operating in a way that unreasonably excludes competitors.[10] For example, the DOJ is suing Google for maintaining its monopoly in the US search engine market by abusing its power. Specifically by signing exclusionary contracts, like its contract with Apple, which prevents other search engines from competing over iPhone users.[11]

If successful, recent actions by antitrust authorities may break up companies like Meta, which now holds Facebook, WhatsApp, and Instagram. Judges may decide to restrict large companies like Google and Amazon and prevent them from taking anticompetitive actions. Successful antitrust actions could also indirectly help resolve the technology overuse problem. How? Right now, we have one dominant model: the business model that relies on our data and time and receives its revenue from ads. But antitrust action that enhances competition could lead to innovative business models that are not crucially dependent on user time.

One option is a subscription, advertising-free model. Instead of getting a product for free (while indirectly paying with time and data), a user would pay a monthly subscription fee. Facebook gobbled up WhatsApp, which offered a privacy-enhancing, advertising-free model. If Facebook had not purchased WhatsApp, this kind of social network could have already been our reality. We could also imagine a universe in which businesses compete to sell products with no manipulative features. Parents would likely be the first in line to purchase games or social network opportunities that their child could use to enjoy and socialize, but would not be devoured by.[12]

Now consider the "Pay as You Go" model, discussed in Chapter 11. A user would not need to pay any money upfront. Companies would charge a price depending on how much time the user spends online. Kids' resources are generally limited to their allowance or money they can make from odd jobs. They may limit prolonged online gaming or social networking if costs escalate.

At first blush, antitrust enforcement sounds very promising. And it is happening. The train has already left the station. So why can't a movement to curtail overuse hatch all its eggs in the antitrust basket? The problem lies in defining when markets are not functioning properly. When should the antitrust enforcer intervene?

For decades, the views of a group of scholars and judges called the "Chicago School" prevailed. They determined that the goal of antitrust law is to promote "consumer welfare." And they determined what is good for consumers through an economic lens. According to Richard Posner, one of the founders of the Chicago School: "the true meaning of justice is efficiency." As a result, antitrust law protected against economic injuries such as high price, inadequate supply or quality, reduced innovation, and consumer choice.[13] However, in practice, courts rarely found that there was an antitrust violation without high prices.[14]

This approach to antitrust may have made sense in the old economy: an economy dominated by oil and railroad tycoons, insurance, and telephone companies. But it is less suitable for the online economy and especially inappropriate for tackling the harms of technology overuse. First, Facebook, Google, Epic Games, and other technology companies offer their products for "free" to the public. Courts, trained to look for a high price as a tell-tale sign of consumer harm, are unlikely to decide that people are harmed when they get something for free.[15] We know that free is not free, and we pay dearly with data and time. But on its face, it seems, at least, that high prices are not an issue of the Internet economy.

Second, manipulative designs cause us to spend more time online and consume more – whether playing Roblox, scrolling through Instagram, or reading information on Reddit. But under our antitrust laws, consumption that is spiraling out of control (with unlimited supply) is not an injury. What counts as an injury is the opposite: inadequate supply and reduced consumption. In other words, not having enough. Still, saying that more is always better makes no sense. This is akin to allowing the manufacturer of OxyContin to count the additional pills consumed by the addicts it created as bolstering consumer welfare.[16] Even worse, courts consider companies that convince consumers to buy more of a product to be healthy, competitive businesses. This means that the bar is high. A court needs to determine that a manipulative design coerces consumers to avoid competitors' products to find an antitrust violation.[17]

Third, courts look for economic injuries, like high prices, to find that a firm committed an antitrust violation. But the injuries caused by technology overuse are different. They are injuries to mental health, general well-being, and social cohesion, which are considered social injuries.[18] Courts' reluctance to find antitrust violations when companies violated users' privacy is telling of their potential approach to overuse.[19]

It sounds like, then, that looking to antitrust to fix the woes of technology overuse is bad news. But new winds are now blowing.[20] In 2017, Lina Khan, an unknown 29-year-old Yale Law School student, published a student note titled: "Amazon's Antitrust Paradox" in the *Yale Law Journal.* Publishing a student note in a prestigious law journal can help a student attain a Supreme Court clerkship or launch an academic career as a law professor. But Khan's student note got her much further. In 2021, President Biden appointed her, at the age of 32, to enforce the federal government's antitrust laws.

What was so special about Khan's law review note? Khan's note challenged the prevailing Chicago School paradigm. It argued that Amazon, the retail conglomerate, which sells, delivers, publishes, and does just about everything, uses its enormous size to price products below cost. Smaller businesses cannot afford to do this and are unable to compete with Amazon. By looking closely at Amazon, Khan showed that measuring harm to competition through high price and low output does not work. Doing so allows giants like Amazon to slip below the antitrust radar.[21]

If anything published in a law review could be a blockbuster, Khan's student note was one. *The New York Times* described it as "reframing decades of monopoly law." Khan became a celebrity in the legal world and Congress, before even passing the bar exam and becoming a lawyer.[22] Khan's appointment to head the FTC, together with the lawsuits and Congressional action that preceded it, signaled a moment of transformation: an end to restraint in antitrust enforcement and a rethinking of antitrust law's obsession with price and economic injuries.[23]

While change is in the air for antitrust enforcement and Big Tech, scholars recently started looking at how Big Tech's manipulation of time online can trigger antitrust scrutiny. We already saw that applying antitrust law to Big Tech may require departing from its current application. But how to accomplish change?

Since my days as a law school student, I have been fascinated with legal transformation. Every year, when I teach a course about privacy law, I tell my students in the first class that it is also a course about legal change. Privacy law constantly evolves, mostly because it must address new technologies that threaten privacy in novel ways. It originated from the challenge of the first snapshot camera and today is grappling with GPS providing location information and facial imaging algorithms.[24] But technology and law are at odds because the former is forward-looking, constantly evolving, while the latter is backward-looking, relying on past legal precedents.

Over the years, different methods to create legal change have developed. One method is by being cautious and taking smaller steps. Those implementing it often argue that they are not really advocating for change, but simply clarifying what the law allowed for all along.[25] Some proposals seek to apply antitrust tools to the technology overuse problem by making tweaks to the traditional economic framework. One approach suggests that when a product is addictive (as are designs to manipulate our attention), courts should not consider increased consumption to be a sign of efficiency and healthy competition. So, basically, antitrust law should stay as it is with an exception for addictive products.[26] Another approach does not try to stir antitrust away from economic injuries. Instead, it points out that the mental health harms of manipulative designs are economic injuries – they cost money. Money is lost through missed workdays, reduced productivity, cost of treatment, and elevated unemployment.[27] A third proposal still relies on high price as an indicator of an antitrust problem, but argues that a "free" product does not mean that the price is zero. It is just paid using a different currency; we pay with data.[28] Similarly, we pay with time. Under this approach, tech companies cannot escape antitrust liability just because the indicator of a problem, a high monetary price, is missing.

Sometimes legal change is more dramatic; in this case, straying further away from the economic model. One proposal suggests that the way abusive design manipulates our free will amounts to coercion, and not persuasion. Antitrust law considers persuading consumers to be a mark of healthy competition, but it may view differently coercing them to turn away from a superior product. Under this approach, our attention is finite, and when consumers compulsively use one platform, for example, spend all their time on Instagram, Instagram's design is precluding them from trying out another, maybe better, option.[29]

While many want antitrust law to change, others believe that reining in Big Tech through antitrust law is misguided, doomed to fail, or both. Some believe that Big Tech's bigness is good for consumers. For example, they point out that Google uses its bigness to make its search services better, can license Android for free, helps lower the price of iPhones and iPads, and spurs innovation.[30] The technology industry, however, will use, and already is using, its vast resources to fight antitrust enforcement. Republicans and Democrats may work together to regulate Big Tech, but they have different motivations, and this fragile coalition could crack.[31]

As we have seen, change is possible, but it is hard to come by. Antitrust law is no exception. Antitrust action will take time. A lot of time. And it may still fail. Regulators hope to break up Meta, which now holds Facebook, Instagram, and WhatsApp. But history gives us some perspective. In 1956, antitrust authorities failed to break up the Bell System monopoly after a seven-year fight. They then went after IBM. That fight lasted thirteen years, and in 1982 it ended in failure. Then in 1998, the government took action against Microsoft and the court ruled it should be broken up. But three years later, Microsoft won an appeal. It ended up settling and staying intact.[32]

Antitrust, like every litigation process, can be long and may potentially fail. But with antitrust, even a win will take a long time to manifest change, because it can affect the overuse problem only indirectly. A successful antitrust action would increase competition in the technology industry and could result in business models that do not rely on abusive designs and user time as a resource. Still, growing competition takes time. It is especially time-consuming when a business is dependent on network effects.

What are network effects? Network effects exist when we are more likely to want a product or service if more people use it, especially when there is a critical mass of people using it.[33] I use Facebook because most of my friends and colleagues are on Facebook. It is an age thing. My college-aged son's network is Instagram. And although I maintain an Instagram account, and have some followers on Instagram, I have never posted there. Instagram does not appeal to me because I can interact with fewer people who are relevant to my life. I would not consider migrating there unless the bulk of my friends and contacts did.

Network effects are strong for social media; they are also quite significant for online gaming. Network effects are a considerable barrier to competition. Since the purpose of a social network is to interact with a network of contacts, it is very difficult for a new social network platform to replace a popular one. The new one needs a critical mass of users for people to migrate there. Users are less likely to switch networks because they have invested "sunk costs" in the familiar one.[34] My sunk costs in Facebook are fifteen years of expanding my network: preferring the profiles of some online friends over others (whether for their honest posts or for being on top of certain news events); a photo collection I can look back at; and groups I like, which took me time to find, like my Israeli feminist poetry group. While all this does not mean that antitrust cannot eventually produce new business models that will not rely on addictive designs, it means there are barriers which will make it harder. Harder means more years until the elimination of abusive designs.

Antitrust law emerges as an important pressure point that could make an impact in the future. It is important because it is in motion. Still, more direct modes of action exist, especially when products are dangerous. Think about cars: we would not just prohibit a merger to create competition for safer cars. We have direct regulations for air bags and seat belts. Recently, calls are intensifying for a federal agency that will regulate technology.[35] For the time being, though, the FTC is expanding its role in a way that could provide more immediate results to contain overuse.

Dark Patterns and Deceptive Practices

Sometimes, ideas take some time to catch on, but then they catch on fire. This happened even to the Internet. In my early 20s,

I visited my brother who lived in Paris. We wanted to take the train to go out of town, and I recall how surprised I was when he turned to a device, consisting of a small monitor and a keyboard next to his phone, and reserved our tickets. The year was 1991, and normally we would have had to go to the train station or make a phone call to get tickets. It turned out that my brother had used Minitel – a videotext system, popular in France since the mid-1980s. It gave the French population many of the advantages of the Internet a decade earlier than the rest of the world. They could go online to book travel, bank, shop for groceries, use messaging services, look for jobs, and play interactive games. Interestingly, in 1982, companies launched similar services that used the same technology in many other countries, including the United States, sixteen Western European countries, and Japan. But these services just didn't catch on.[36]

Harry Brignull is a British user-experience designer, who also had an important idea, which took some years to catch on. In 2010, he coined the term "Dark Patterns." Brignull defined Dark Patterns as: "tricks used in websites and apps that make you do things that you didn't mean to, like buying or signing up for something." He also started a website to spread awareness and to shame companies that used dark patterns.[37] Eleven years later, Brignull spoke at an FTC workshop dedicated to dark patterns. Brignull explained that he meant the term "dark patterns" to communicate the designs' unscrupulous nature and also the fact that they can be shadowy and hard to pin down. He added that when he started his website, he was quite naïve. He thought he could eradicate dark patterns by shaming the companies that used them and encouraging designers to use a code of ethics. He then acknowledged that it didn't really work and more action is needed to regulate dark patterns.[38]

Brignull is disappointed with his initial course of action, but his website, darkpatterns.org, still lives on. In the website's "Hall of Shame," he aggregates tweets about dark patterns. One of the tweets he shared reads: "The @nytimes should be ashamed of its dark patterns behavior for canceling. I didn't have to engage a human to start my subscription, I shouldn't to end it. When I click cancel I get a page that offers 'several ways,' but none that are immediate." He then displays the options featured, which are "Chat with a Customer Care advocate" or "Give us a call."[39]

Although shaming didn't work, Brignull's "Dark Patterns" concept caught fire. It spread everywhere. From the FTC to Congressional bills.[40] And some states, quick to move, enacted laws restricting the use of dark patterns.[41] Undoubtedly, many people are talking about dark patterns. But what do they mean? And how are the manipulative designs that hook us on to our screens related to dark patterns?

Most commonly, dark patterns are considered designs that manipulate a user's autonomy in making decisions and choices.[42] Initial actions are targeting dark patterns that cause us to spend money we do not intend to spend. The FTC is going after online companies using dark patterns for subscriptions. These businesses frequently use dark patterns to make it easy to subscribe, but hard to unsubscribe. It has the dynamic of the famous Eagles song "Hotel California": "You can check out any time you like, but you can never leave."[43]

To research this book, I subscribed to quite a few online publications. At a certain point, I realized that the cost of one subscription had jumped to nearly $40 per month. I did not recall consenting to pay this price and wanted to unsubscribe. I then discovered that I could not do this online. Instead, the publication required that I call them. Getting around to making that phone call took me six months. In the meantime, the publication gained another $240 in my subscription fees. Since then, the FTC has announced that companies will face legal action if they do not make cancellation easy.[44] This is just one of many dark patterns. Dark patterns involve different techniques that make consumers pay or give information without really intending to, including hidden costs. I am frequently surprised when I purchase plane tickets that, just when I am about to click pay, the ticket price significantly increases through additional costs that I did not see when selecting the ticket.[45]

Dark patterns, though, are not just about direct monetary costs. Designs that hook us into our devices and affect our autonomy and ability to choose how we spend our time are also dark patterns.[46] Most people have no idea that their favorite social network is brilliantly configured to extend the time they spend on it; they simply think they like it a lot. Even people who read or hear about addictive technology design fail to fully comprehend it because the traps are invisible. The traps are concealed because they are based on expert knowledge of human vulnerability that lies beyond the average consumer's understanding. Legal scholars Jamie Luguri and Lior Strahilevitz found that covert dark patterns are more dangerous than explicit ones and present a stronger case for regulation. Their research revealed that when a dark pattern is so aggressive that consumers notice it, consumers are more likely to oppose it. But the dark patterns that invisibly control our time are as stealthy as can be. They are less likely to cause a public relations problem for the businesses using them and are unlikely to go away without regulation.[47]

Now, how can regulating dark patterns help resolve technology overuse problems? Sam's addiction to Minecraft and how it came about is all too common and can illustrate how things can change. I met Sam's parents years ago when our kids attended the same preschool, and we remained friends as our kids grew up. When Sam was 11, his parents learned about an educational video game called Minecraft. They downloaded it for him and were happy that Sam enjoyed playing the game. By the time Sam turned 13, though, he often played twelve hours a day on non-school days. He also spent a lot of time watching Minecraft videos on YouTube. Sam rarely did his homework and was at a risk of flunking out of school. He did not interact much with his parents or younger sister. He got intensely angry when his parents tried to stop him from playing. They wished they had never let him start playing.

Minecraft gets many kids hooked through a combination of manipulative designs that qualify as dark patterns. One study of the addictiveness of online games even gave Minecraft the dubious title of being "The Most Addictive Game on the Market."[48] Sam's parents exhausted every home strategy available. They thought they were buying an educational game that Sam could enjoy and learn from. Minecraft's designers never revealed that a team of psychologists, adept at cognitive hooking, implemented dark patterns that impeded Sam's autonomy and undermined his ability to decide when to stop playing and for how much time he would play.

The natural place to look for regulating dark patterns is to the FTC. The FTC can act to sanction "deceptive and unfair trade practices."

It can do even more to protect children.[49] The FTC's move to regulate dark patterns is not surprising. For some years now, it has expanded what it considers to be deceitful.[50] Lies are an obvious target. When a company promises its consumers to do one thing and then does another, the FTC finds that the company has acted deceptively. It did so when Snapchat promised its users that their snaps would disappear, while, in fact, people captured them in many ways, including simply by taking a screenshot.[51] But, the FTC has gone beyond "broken promises"; it acts when a company deceives its customers by failing to reveal information. The FTC also prosecutes deceptive actions where consumers' reasonable expectations have been breached.[52] Looking at the use of dark patterns as a breach of consumers' expectations is a natural extension.[53] When they purchased Minecraft, Sam's parents did not think they were giving their son a game that would subvert his autonomous decision-making over time. They would have never bought it had they known. Dark patterns are, in their very essence, violations of consumers' reasonable expectations.

The FTC could regulate dark patterns as deceptive practices,[54] but this will accomplish change only through baby steps. Congress could take stronger measures by specifically empowering the FTC to regulate dark patterns. There is movement on both fronts. But as often happens, change is coming locally from the states. California is one of the states already regulating dark patterns. Most notably, California became a trailblazer through its privacy legislation. California's strict privacy law changed data collection practices across the United States. The regulation of dark patterns could follow a similar trend.[55]

Takeaway Points

- Pressuring through antitrust:
  - Wheels are in motion to enforce antitrust law to regulate Big Tech and encourage competition.
  - Competition in the tech industry could lead to business models that do not rely on user time and addictive designs.
  - While antitrust enforcement could help resolve the overuse problem in the long run, it is likely to take time, and cannot serve as more than an ancillary solution to the urgent overuse problem.

- Regulating addictive design as dark patterns and deceptive practices:
  - Addictive designs qualify as dark patterns, which are designs that manipulate a user's autonomy in making decisions and choices.
  - The FTC can regulate, and already is regulating, dark patterns as deceptive practices.
  - States are also emerging as players in regulating dark patterns.

EPILOGUE

I was finalizing this book, while juggling the usual frenzy of the end of the academic year. On a Saturday morning, I ordered bagels for my kids for breakfast through a phone delivery app, hoping to gain a few hours to write. After I placed the order, I received a confirmation text with an estimated delivery time. Twenty minutes later, as I settled down to work, I received another text letting me know my order was on the way. Then the doorbell rang, and the bagels arrived. I placed the bagels in the kitchen and sat down at my desk again, attempting to write. At that point I received a third text notifying me that my order had arrived. Every time a text arrived, I picked up my phone automatically and, without noticing, clicked on a few more apps. Despite my best efforts, I started work an hour later than intended that morning.

It was 2022, and I knew I could do better. But too often I kept forgetting to pay attention to my mindless phone clicking. I could have turned off the default notification settings of the delivery app. But I didn't. By then, I knew too well that our technologies are geared to overuse. After five years of speaking with parents and working on this book, I had no doubt we cannot win individually against an invisible and ever-evolving rival – that we have no choice but to do so collectively.

We now know we never chose this. We never autonomously decided to enter this symbiotic relationship with our devices. We were the frog in the technology industry's pot of water. The frog, which did not notice until the water boiled, and it could no longer leap out.

We kept believing that technology and progress would improve our lives. So, we waited and watched the science wars. But now we know the costs. For ourselves and mostly for our children, we can no longer afford to wait. Nor should we. Had we really been the choice-makers, we would never have chosen this.

We now also know who is calling the shots and why. The technology industry uses manipulative designs and sophisticated algorithms to prolong our time online. Tech companies do so to feed their business model and increase their advertising revenues. The tech industry's business model does not incentivize tech companies to find ways to reduce our time online. To the contrary, it gives them every motivation to constantly seek new, stealthy ways to manipulate us and consume more of our attention. Unsurprisingly, the titans of Silicon Valley, since the heyday of the privacy scandals, have always waived the self-regulation flag. While offering digital well-being tools, tech companies operated behind a cloak of non-transparency to produce ever-more sophisticated manipulative designs.

Going forward means finding a better balance between our technologies and ourselves. It does not mean returning to the twentieth century, by shedding our screens and online connections. Instead, it turns on placing our humanity above our technology. We can do so by redesigning technology to eliminate addictive designs and putting ourselves back in the driver's seat. It requires redirecting our energies from fighting failing individual battles to acting collectively. This action needs to take multiple different routes simultaneously. The paths go through town municipalities, states legislatures, courts, and all the way to the FTC and Congress. The past has shown that one failure is not necessarily a defeat, and that it takes consistent pressure on many fronts to make headway.

We have seen that both the past and the present give hope for the future. By looking into the past, we can predict the hidden curves down the road. We can prepare for the tech industry's future moves: the personal responsibility argument and the First Amendment defense. We can then hone in on their vulnerabilities. We have also seen that the movement to contain technology overuse has already taken off. It is active both in the United States and abroad. Parents and regulators have targeted the soft underbelly of the tech industry by suing and seeking to regulate game-makers and social networks' harms to kids. As more damning evidence leaks out of Silicon Valley's fortress, the movement can continue to grow. It can do so through changing education policies; as well as through antitrust and deceptive practices enforcement. Like the tobacco and food industries, the tech industry is unlikely to submit to change without a fight. But knowing all we know now, neither should we.

ACKNOWLEDGMENTS

Society's views of the role of technology in everyday life transformed significantly during the years in which I lectured parents and worked on this book. They shifted from growing awareness of technology overuse; to acceptance of technological immersion as a necessity during pandemic lockdown; and, finally, to a growing realization of the costs of overuse. Some of those I owe thanks to for the insights of this book cannot be named. Many are anonymous because they always were. These include the people waiting in line staring at their phones or tourists standing with their backs to the sunset intent on taking pictures. Some are anonymous because they chose to remain so. They came to me after lectures or confided in me as friends. To all of them I am grateful. Without their honesty and faith that something could and should be done, this book would not have been written. I am also grateful to the schools, which hosted my parents' lectures and provided the springboard for many of these conversations.

I developed many of the ideas in this book through exchanges with colleagues and students in conferences, colloquiums, and faculty workshops at Yale Law School, University of Chicago Law School, NYU School of Law, Sandra D. O'Connor College of Law – Arizona State University, University of California Irvine School of Law, Rutgers Law School, Health Law Professors Conference at the Northeastern University School of Law, University of Wisconsin Law School, New York Area Family Law Scholars Workshop at Cardozo School of Law,

Seton Hall University School of Law, Maurice A. Deane School of Law at Hofstra University, Haifa University Faculty of Law, The Haim Striks School of Law at the College of Management Academic Studies, and the Digital Well Being Festival.

Many generously read drafts of different parts of the manuscript, provided encouragement, guidance, vision, and support, and the book is here and much richer thanks to them. I would like to thank them in alphabetical order, and apologize in advance to anyone I have missed: Lori Andrews, Lisa Bernstein, Michal Bernstein, Derek Black, Gregory Day, Christina Dechen, Robert Dreesen, Sheldon Evans, Barbara Fedders, Apollonia Fortuna, Brett Frischmann, Douglas Gentile, Eric Goldman, Suzanne Kim, Orly Lobel, Jacqui Lipton, Irina Manta, Florencia Marotta-Wurgler, Sagit Mor, Andrew Moshirnia, Frank Pasquale, Marina Romashko, Barbara Stark, Zvi Triger, Rebecca Tushnet, and Sam Weinstein.

My former and current colleagues at Seton Hall Law School also provided feedback, support, and wisdom. I would particularly like to thank Charles Sullivan, Solangel Maldonado, Michael Ambrosio, Kristen Boon, Angela Carmella, Carl Coleman, Doron Dorfman, Thomas Healy, Laura Hoffman, Marina Lao, Andrea McDowell, David Opderbeck, and Tara Ragone.

I was extremely fortunate to have a uniquely talented group of research assistants. I am particularly grateful for the incredible work of Catherine (Katie) Salerno, Carmen Abrazado, Madeline (Maddie) Diab, and Eve Litvak, whose superb work and dedication went well beyond the call of duty and brought the book to the finish line. I would also like to thank the research assistants who worked on earlier parts of the book for their expert assistance. These include: Kamille Perry, David Batista, Andrew Broome, Meagan Free, Nathaniel Karni-Schmidt, Jonathan Trinidad Lira, Melanie Lupsa, and Kevin Monaghan. In addition, I am grateful to my assistant Matthew Friedman and to the Seton Hall University School of Law for providing research funding and a sabbatical to work on this project.

I would like to thank my agent Don Fehr for his guidance. I am also grateful to my editor Matt Gallaway for his enthusiasm for the project and for steering it forward expertly toward publication, together with the whole team at Cambridge University Press, including Jadyn Fauconier-Herry, Claire Sissen, and Sophie Rosinke.

This book is dedicated to my children Yonatan, Daniella, and Ytamar. As I proudly saw them growing up and making their independent and deliberate screen choices, I knew this book was written for them. Finally, I would like to thank my partner Jed Schwartz who accompanied the evolution of this book from a seed idea to completion, with love, kindness, and endless patience.

NOTES

Chapter 1

1 Joshua Boyd, *The History of Facebook: From Basic to Global Giant*, BRANDWATCH (Jan. 25, 2019), www.brandwatch.com/blog/history-of-facebook/; Susannah Fox & Lee Rainie, *The Web at 25 in the U.S.*, PEW RSCH. CTR. (Feb. 27, 2014), www.pewresearch.org/internet/2014/02/27/the-web-at-25-in-the-u-s/; *With Smartphone Adoption on the Rise, Opportunity for Marketers Is Calling*, NIELSEN (Sep. 15, 2019), www.nielsen.com/us/en/insights/article/2009/with-smartphone-adoption-on-the-rise-opportunity-for-marketers-is-calling/.

2 Jingjing Jiang, *How Teens and Parents Navigate Screen Time and Device Distractions*, PEW RSCH. CTR. (Aug. 22, 2018), www.pewresearch.org/internet/2018/08/22/how-teens-and-parents-navigate-screen-time-and-device-distractions/; *Connected and Content: Managing Healthy Technology Use*, Am. Psych. Ass'n. (Nov. 1, 2017), www.apa.org/topics/healthy-technology-use.

3 CAL NEWPORT, *DIGITAL MINIMALISM: ON LIVING BETTER WITH LESS TECHNOLOGY* 202 (Penguin Random House 2019).

4 Eileen Brown, *Americans Spend Far More Time on Their Smartphones than They Think*, ZDNET (Apr. 28, 2019), www.zdnet.com/article/americans-spend-far-more-time-on-their-smartphones-than-they-think/; Jingjing Jiang, *How Teens and Parents Navigate Screen Time and Device Distractions*, PEW RSCH. CTR. (Aug. 22, 2018), www.pewresearch.org/internet/2018/08/22/how-teens-and-parents-navigate-screen-time-and-device-distractions/.

5 Lauren E. Willis, *Deception by Design*, 34 HARV. J. L. & TECH. 34, 115, 132–34 (2020).

6 Daniel Susser et al., *Technology, Autonomy, and Manipulation*, INTERNET POL'Y REV. 1 (Jun. 2019); JOSEPH RAZ, *THE MORALITY OF FREEDOM* 369 (Oxford Clarendon Press 1986); GERALD DWORKIN, *THE NATURE OF AUTONOMY* (Cambridge University Press 1988); Daniel Susser et al., *Online Manipulation: Hidden Influences in a Digital World*, 4 GEO. L. TECH. REV. 1, 13 (2019); Julie

Cohen, *Examined Lives: Informational Privacy and the Subject as Object*, 52 STAN. L. REV. 1373 (2000).

7 BRETT M. FRISCHMANN & EVAN SELINGER, RE-ENGINEERING HUMANITY 209–10 (Cambridge University Press 2018); Daniel Susser *et al.*, *Technology, Autonomy, and Manipulation*, INTERNET POL'Y REV. 1, 31 (Jun. 2019).

8 Daniel Susser *et al.*, *Online Manipulation: Hidden Influences in a Digital World*, 4 GEORGETOWN L. TECH. REV. 16 (2019); BRETT M. FRISCHMANN & EVAN SELINGER, RE-ENGINEERING HUMANITY 209–10, 225–27 (Cambridge University Press 2018).

9 Daniel Susser *et al.*, *Technology, Autonomy, and Manipulation*, 8 INTERNET POL'Y REV. 1, 5, 13 (Jun. 2019).

10 DAN ARIELY, PREDICTABLY IRRATIONAL: THE HIDDEN FORCES THAT SHAPE OUR DECISIONS xvi (Harper Perennial 2008).

11 Jon D. Hanson & Douglas A. Kysar, *Taking Behavioralism Seriously: The Problem of Market Manipulation*, 74 N.Y.U. L. REV. 747 (1999); Ryan M. Calo, *Digital Market Manipulation*, 82 GEO. WASH. L. REV. 1010 (2013).

12 Cass R. Sunstein, *Fifty Shades of Manipulation*, 1 J MKTG. BEHAV. 5 (2015).

13 *Sensory Experiences Drive 9 Out of 10 Shoppers Back to Stores, Says Global Mood Media Study*, BLOOMBERG (Jan. 14, 2019), www.bloomberg.com/press-releases/2019-01-15/sensory-experiences-drive-9-out-of-10-shoppers-back-to-stores-says-global-mood-media-study; Ronald E. Milliman, *Using Background Music to Affect the Behavior of Supermarket Shoppers*, 46 J. MKTG 86 (1982).

14 Ryan M. Calo, *Digital Market Manipulation*, 82 GEO. WASH. L. REV. 995, 1032 (2014).

15 Cass R. Sunstein, *Fifty Shades of Manipulation*, 1 J. MKTG. BEHAV. 4–7 (2015); Brett Frischmann, Nudging Humans, 36 J. KNOWLEDGE CULTURE & POL. 129 (2022).

16 Daniel Susser *et al.*, *Technology, Autonomy, and Manipulation*, 8 INTERNET POL'Y REV. 1 (Jun. 2019).

17 Daniel Susser *et al.*, *Online Manipulation: Hidden Influences in a Digital World*, 4 GEO. L. TECH. REV. 14 (2019).

18 BRETT M. FRISCHMANN & EVAN SELINGER, RE-ENGINEERING HUMANITY 250 (Cambridge University Press 2018).

19 DELOITTE, 2018 GLOBAL MOBILE CONSUMER SURVEY: US EDITION (2018); *What Students Are Saying about How Much They Use Their Phones, and Whether We Should Be Worried*, N.Y. TIMES (Feb. 6, 2020), www.nytimes.com/2020/02/06/learning/what-students-are-saying-about-how-much-they-use-their-phones-and-whether-we-should-be-worried.html.

20 Gaia Bernstein, *When New Technologies Are Still New: Windows of Opportunity for Privacy Protection*, 51 VILL. L. REV. 921 (2006).

21 JONATHAN BARNES (ed.), THE COMPLETE WORKS OF ARISTOTLE 28, 32 (Princeton University Press 1992).

22 ROBERT NOZICK, ANARCHY, STATE, AND UTOPIA 48–51 (Blackwell Publishing 1974); Aartya Sen, *Freedom of Choice: Concept and Content*, 32 EUR. ECON. REV. 269 (1988); BRETT M. FRISCHMANN & EVAN SELINGER, RE-ENGINEERING HUMANITY 244–47 (Cambridge University Press 2018).

23 Thomas M. Scanlon, *The Significance of Choice*, The Tanner Lectures on Human Values 149 (1986).

24 EDWARD L. DECI & RICHARD M. RYAN, INTRINSIC MOTIVATION AND SELF-DETERMINATION IN HUMAN BEHAVIOR (Plenum Press 1985).

25 ALEX PATTAKOS, *PRISONERS OF OUR THOUGHTS: VIKTOR FRANKEL'S PRINCIPLES FOR DISCOVERING MEANING IN LIFE AND WORK* vii (Berrett-Koehler Publishers 2008).

26 Steven J. Phillipson, *Choice*, THE CTR. FOR COGNITIVE-BEHAV. PSYCHOTHERAPY, www.ocdonline.com/choice (last visited Jan. 16, 2022).

27 BJÖRN BARTLING et al., *The Intrinsic Value of Decision Rights*, 86 ECONOMETRICA 2005 (2014); DAVID OWENS et al., *The Control Premium: A Preference for Payoff Autonomy*, 6 AM. ECON. J. MICROECONOMICS 138 (2014); NICOLA J. BOWN et al., *The Lure of Choice*, 16 J. BEHAV. DECISION MAKING 297 (2003).

28 JALĀL AL-DĪN RŪMĪ, *THE ESSENTIAL RUMI* (Coleman Barks and John Moyne trans., HarperOne 2004).

29 RANDY SUSAN MEYERS, *ACCIDENTS OF MARRIAGE* (Washington Square Press 2015).

30 Martha DeGrasse, *4 Ways COVID-19 Is Changing Mobile Phone Usage*, FIERCEWIRELESS (Apr. 8, 2020), www.fiercewireless.com/wireless/three-ways-covid-19-changing-mobile-phone-usage; GLOBAL WEB INDEX, CORONAVIRUS RESEARCH APRIL 2020 SERIES 4: MEDIA CONSUMPTION AND SPORT (2020).

31 *Survey Shows Parents Alarmed as Kids' Screen Time Skyrockets during COVID-19 Crisis*, PARENTSTOGETHER (Apr. 23, 2020), https://parents-together.org/survey-shows-parents-alarmed-as-kids-screen-time-skyrockets-during-covid-19-crisis/.

32 Fred Imbert, *Big Tech Went from Growth Stocks to Wall Street's Treasury Bond Substitute during the Coronavirus*, CNBC (Jul. 10, 2020), www.cnbc.com/2020/07/10/big-tech-went-from-growth-stocks-to-wall-streets-treasury-bond-substitute-during-the-coronavirus.html; Matthew Haag, *Manhattan Faces a Reckoning If Working from Home Becomes the Norm*, N.Y. TIMES (May 12, 2020), www.nytimes.com/2020/05/12/nyregion/coronavirus-work-from-home.html; GLOBAL WEB INDEX, CORONAVIRUS RESEARCH APRIL 2020 SERIES 4: MEDIA CONSUMPTION AND SPORT (2020).

33 Monica Anderson & Emily A. Vogels, *Americans Turn to Technology during COVID-19 Outbreak, Say an Outage Would Be a Problem*, PEW RSCH. CTR. (Mar. 31, 2020), www.pewresearch.org/fact-tank/2020/03/31/americans-turn-to-technology-during-covid-19-outbreak-say-an-outage-would-be-a-problem/.

34 Julia Sklar, *"Zoom Fatigue" Is Taxing the Brain. Here's Why That Happens*, NAT'L. GEOGRAPHIC (Apr. 24, 2020), www.nationalgeographic.com/science/2020/04/coronavirus-zoom-fatigue-is-taxing-the-brain-here-is-why-that-happens/.

35 JULIA E. SEAMAN et al., *GRADE INCREASE: TRACKING DISTANCE EDUCATION IN THE UNITED STATES* (Babson Survey Research Group 2018).

36 R. H. Lossin & Andy Battle, *Resisting Distance Learning*, BOS. REV. (Apr. 30, 2020), http://bostonreview.net/forum/higher-education-age-coronavirus/r-h-lossin-andy-battle-resisting-distance-learning.

37 Ryan N. Gajarawala, *Better Late than Zoom: Opinion: The Harvard Crimson*, HARV. CRIMSON (Apr. 21, 2020), www.thecrimson.com/article/2020/4/21/editorial-better-late-than-zoom/.

38 *See* AZITA NAHAI, *TRAUMA TO DHARMA: TRANSFORM YOUR PAIN INTO PURPOSE* (AnR Books 2018).

Chapter 2

1 *Teen Who Killed over Video Game Gets 23 Years*, NBC NEWS (Jun. 16, 2009), www.nbcnews.com/id/wbna31387876; Marvin Fong, *Daniel Petric Killed Mother, Shot Father Because They Took Halo 3 Video Game, Prosecutors Say*, THE PLAIN

Dealer (Mar. 28, 2019), www.cleveland.com/metro/2008/12/boy_killed_mom_ and_shot_dad_ov.html; Mike Tobin, *Wellington Teen Daniel Petric Gets 23 Years to Life in Prison for Killing His Mother*, The Plain Dealer (Mar. 27, 2019), www .cleveland.com/metro/2009/06/lorain_county_teen_who_killed.html.

2 "Internet Gaming Disorder," in American Psychiatric Association, Diagnostic Statistical Manual of Mental Health Disorders (5th ed. 2013); Ranna Parekh, *Internet Gaming*, American Psychiatric Association (Jun. 2018), www.psychiatry.org/patients-families/internet-gaming#:~:text=The% 20DSM%2D5%20notes%20that,of%20social%20media%20or%20smartphones.

3 The 11th Revision of the International Classification of Diseases (ICD-11) was released in 2018. *Inclusion of "Gaming Disorder" in ICD-11*, World Health Organization (Sep. 14, 2018), www.who.int/news/item/14-09-2018-inclusion-of-gaming-disorder-in-icd-11.

4 *Inclusion of "Gaming Disorder" in ICD-11*, World Health Organization (Sep. 14, 2018), www.who.int/news/item/14-09-2018-inclusion-of-gaming-disorder-in-icd-11; *Addictive Behaviors: Gaming Disorder*, World Health Organization (Oct. 22, 2020), www.who.int/news-room/questions-and-answers/item/addictive-behaviours-gaming-disorder#:~:text=Gaming%20disorder%20is%20defined%20in, the%20extent%20that%20gaming%20takes; *ICD-11 for Mortality and Morbidity Statistics*, World Health Orgization, https://icd.who.int/browse11/l-m/en#/ http://id.who.int/icd/entity/1448597234. The DSM-5 proposed nine criteria for Internet Gaming Disorder. When five are met, a person qualifies for the diagnosis. These include preoccupation with Internet gaming, experienced withdrawal, developed tolerance, loss of control, continued use, mislead others, use as escape, reduced interests, and risked opportunities. "Internet Gaming Disorder," in American Psychiatric Association, Diagnostic Statistical Manual of Mental Health Disorders (5th ed. 2013).

5 Rashmi Parmar & Julian Lagoy, *Is Video Game Addiction a Disorder?*, Psychiatric Times (Oct. 4, 2021), www.psychiatrictimes.com/view/is-video-game-addiction-a-disorder; Sarah M. Coyne et al., *Pathological Video Game Symptoms from Adolescence to Emerging Adulthood: A 6-Year Longitudinal Study of Trajectories, Predictors, and Outcomes*, 56 Dev. Psych. 1385 (2020); Laura Stockdale & Sarah M. Coyne, *Video Game Addiction in Emerging Adulthood: Cross-Sectional Evidence of Pathology in Video Game Addicts as Compared to Matched Healthy Controls*, 225 J Affective Disorders 265 (2018); Cecilie Schou Andreassen et al., *The Relationship between Addictive Use of Social Media and Video Games and Symptoms of Psychiatric Disorders: A Large-Scale Cross-Sectional Study*, 30 Psych. Addictive Behav. 252 (2016). Research results are inconclusive on whether there is an association with increased aggression. Craig A. Anderson & Karen E. Dill, *Video Games and Aggressive Thoughts, Feelings, and Behavior in the Laboratory and in Life*, 78 J. Personality Soc. Psych. 772 (2018); Andrew K. Przybylski & Netta Weinstein, *Violent Video Game Engagement Is Not Associated with Adolescents' Aggressive Behaviour: Evidence from a Registered Report*, 6 Royal Soc'y Open Sci. 171474 (2019); Rashmi Parmar & Julian Lagoy, *Is Video Game Addiction a Disorder?*, Psychiatric Times (Oct. 4, 2021), www.psychiatrictimes.com/view/is-video-game-addiction-a-disorder.

6 Luca Milani et al., *Internet Gaming Addiction in Adolescence: Risk Factors and Maladjustment Correlates*, 16 Int'l J Mental Health and Addiction 888 (2018).

7 Daria J. Kuss & Mark D. Griffiths, *Internet and Gaming Addiction: A Systematic Literature Review of Neuroimaging Studies*, 2 BRAIN SCI. 327 (2012).

8 Rashmi Parmar & Julian Lagoy, *Is Video Game Addiction a Disorder?*, PSYCHIATRIC TIMES (Oct. 4, 2021), www.psychiatrictimes.com/view/is-video-game-addiction-a-disorder; Mira Fauth-Bühler & K. Mann, *Neurobiological Correlates of Internet Gaming Disorder: Similarities to Pathological Gambling*, 64 ADDICT BEHAV. 349 (2017).

9 Rashmi Parmar & Julian Lagoy, *Is Video Game Addiction a Disorder?*, PSYCHIATRIC TIMES (Oct. 4, 2021), www.psychiatrictimes.com/view/is-video-game-addiction-a-disorder; Mattias J. Koepp *et al.*, *Evidence for Striatal Dopamine Release during a Video Game*, 393 NATURE 266 (1998).

10 Andrew K. Przybylski *et al.*, *Internet Gaming Disorder: Investigating the Clinical Relevance of a New Phenomenon*, 174 AM. J. PSYCHIATRY 230 (2017); Christopher J. Ferguson & John Colwell, *Lack of Consensus among Scholars on the Issue of Video Game "Addiction,"* 9 PSYCH. POPULAR MEDIA 359 (2020); Alan Mozes, *1 in 20 College Students Has "Internet Gaming Disorder," Study Finds*, U.S. NEWS (Jul. 7, 2021), www.usnews.com/news/health-news/articles/2021-07-07/1-in-20-college-students-has-internet-gaming-disorder-study-finds.

11 60.8 percent of scholars agreed that pathological video game use could be a mental health problem, but 30.4 percent remained skeptical. Rashmi Parmar & Julian Lagoy, *Is Video Game Addiction a Disorder?*, PSYCHIATRIC TIMES (Oct. 4, 2021), www.psychiatrictimes.com/view/is-video-game-addiction-a-disorder.

12 Marc Palaus *et al.*, *Neural Basis of Video Gaming: A Systematic Review*, FRONTIERS IN HUMAN NEUROSCIENCE 248 (May 2017); Rashmi Parmar & Julian Lagoy, *Is Video Game Addiction a Disorder?*, PSYCHIATRIC TIMES (Oct. 4, 2021), www.psychiatrictimes.com/view/is-video-game-addiction-a-disorder.

13 Kimberly S. Young, *Psychology of Computer Use: XL. Addictive Use of the Internet: A Case That Breaks the Stereotype*, 79 PSYCHOLOGICAL REPORTS 899 (1996); Elias Aboujaoude & Lina Gega, *Editorial Perspective: Missing the Forest for the Trees – How the Focus on Digital Addiction and Gaming Diverted Attention Away from Wider Online Risks*, 26 CHILD AND ADOLESCENT MENTAL HEALTH 369 (2021); Elias Aboujaoude, *Problematic Internet Use: An Overview*, 9 WORLD PSYCHIATRY 85 (2010).

14 Tayana Panova & Xavier Carbonell, *Is Smartphone Addiction Really an Addiction?*, 7 J. BEHAV. ADDICTIONS 252 (2018).

15 Cecilie Schou Andreassen *et al.*, *The Relationship between Addictive Use of Social Media and Video Games and Symptoms of Psychiatric Disorders: A Large-Scale Cross-Sectional Study*, 30 PSYCH. ADDICTIVE BEHAV. 252 (2016) (pointing to research showing that gaming addiction and Internet addiction often co-occur); Vikram R. Bhargava & Manuel Velasquez, *Ethics of the Attention Economy: The Problem of Social Media Addiction*, 31 BUSINESS ETHICS Q. 321 (2021).

16 Georgia Wells *et al.*, *Is Facebook Bad for You? It Is for about 360 Million Users, Company Surveys Suggest*, WALL ST. J. (Nov. 5, 2021), www.wsj.com/articles/facebook-bad-for-you-360-million-users-say-yes-company-documents-facebook-files-11636124681?mod=article_inline.

17 Andrew K. Przybylski *et al.*, *Internet Gaming Disorder: Investigating the Clinical Relevance of a New Phenomenon*, 174 AM. J. PSYCHIATRY 230 (2017). The goal of this study was to examine overall prevalence of gaming addiction and the authors concluded that it is less common than other studies indicated. The authors composed

the study with four age groups. The data on the prevalence of each symptom for the two younger age groups yields information that does not qualify for the clinical definition of addiction, but sheds light on technology overuse.

18 Monica Anderson & Jingjing Jiang, *Teens, Social Media and Technology 2018*, PEW RSCH. CTR. (2018).

19 VICTORIA RIDEOUT & MICHAEL B. ROBB, *THE COMMON SENSE CENSUS: MEDIA USE BY TEENS AND TWEENS* (Common Sense Media 2019). These numbers include watching television, which is on the decline, and online video watching, which is on the incline.

20 Jean M. Twenge, *iGEN: WHY TODAY'S SUPER-CONNECTED KIDS ARE GROWING UP LESS REBELLIOUS, MORE TOLERANT, LESS HAPPY – AND COMPLETELY UNPREPARED FOR ADULTHOOD* ch. 3 (Artia Books 2017).

21 Michael Shankleman *et al.*, *Adolescent Social Media Use and Well-Being: A Systematic Review and Thematic Meta-Synthesis*, 6 ADOLESCENT RSCH. REV. 471, 479 (2021); HARRY KIMBALL & YAKIRA COHEN, *CHILDREN'S MENTAL HEALTH REPORT: SOCIAL MEDIA, GAMING AND MENTAL HEALTH* (Child Mind Institute 2019).

22 For a general overview, *see* Gadi Lissak, *Adverse Physiological and Psychological Effects of Screen Time on Children and Adolescents: Literature Review and Case Study*, 164 ENV'T RSCH. 149 (2018). For attention, *see* Ra Chaelin K. Cho *et al.*, *Association of Digital Media Use with Subsequent Symptoms of Attention-Deficit/Hyperactivity Disorder among Adolescents*, 320 JAMA PEDIATRICS 255 (2018) (a longitudinal study finding an association between media digital use and ADHD symptoms). For sleep, *see* Lauren Hale & Stanford Guan, *Screen Time and Sleep among School-Aged Children and Adolescents: A Systematic Literature Review*, 21 SLEEP MED. REV. 50 (2015). For impulsivity, *see* Michelle D. Guerrero *et al.*, *24-Hour Movement Behaviors and Impulsivity*, 144 PEDIATRICS 1673 (2019).

23 Daniel R. Anderson & Tiffany A. Pempek, *Television and Very Young Children*, 48 AM. BEHAV. SCIENTIST 505 (2005); Gabrielle A. Strouse *et al.*, *Co-Viewing Supports Toddlers' Word Learning from Contingent and Noncontingent Video*, 166 J. EXPERIMENTAL CHILD PSYCH. 310 (2018); Stephanie Pappas, *What Do We Really Know about Kids and Screens?*, 51 MONITOR ON PSYCH. 42 (2020).

24 Scott Gilbertson, *11 Great Games to Educate and Entertain Your Kids at Home*, WIRED (Mar. 25, 2020), www.wired.com/story/best-educational-games-for-kids/.

25 Sheri Madigan *et al.*, *Association between Screen Time and Children's Performance on a Developmental Screening Test*, 173 JAMA PEDIATRICS 244 (2019).

26 Sheri Madigan *et al.*, *Association between Screen Time and Children's Performance on a Developmental Screening Test*, 173 JAMA PEDIATRICS 244 (2019).

27 John Hutton, Jonathan Dudley, & Tzipi Horowitz-Kraus, *Associations between Screen-Based Media Use and Brain White Matter Integrity in Preschool-Aged Children*, 174 JAMA PEDIATRICS 1 (2020); Tzipi Horowitz-Kraus & John S. Hutton, *Brain Connectivity in Children Is Increased by the Time They Spend Reading Books and Decreased by the Length of Exposure to Screen-Based Media*, 107 ACTA PAEDIATRICA 685 (2018); Hongmei Wang *et al.*, *The Alteration of Gray Matter Volume and Cognitive Control in Adolescents with Internet Gaming Disorder*, 9 FRONTIERS IN BEHAV. NEUROSCIENCE 1 (2015); Martin P. Paulus *et al.*, *Screen Media Activity and Brain Structure in Youth: Evidence for Diverse Structural Correlation Networks from the ABCD Study*, 185 NEUROIMAGE 140 (2019).

28 Mark Zuckerberg, *Bringing the World Closer Together*, FACEBOOK (Mar. 15, 2021), www.facebook.com/notes/393134628500376/.

29 Jonathan Haidt & Jean Twenge, *Social Media Use and Mental Health: A Review* (unpublished manuscript) (on file at tinyurl.com/SocialMediaMentalHealthReview); Jean M. Twenge & Eric Farley, *Not All Screen Time Is Created Equal: Associations with Mental Health Vary by Activity and Gender*, 56 SOC. PSYCHIATRY PSYCHIATRIC EPIDEMIOLOGY 207 (2021).

30 Jonathan Haidt & Jean Twenge, *Social Media Use and Mental Health: A Review* (unpublished manuscript) (on file at tinyurl.com/SocialMediaMentalHealthReview). While nearly all researchers now agree that there is an association between time spent using social media and mental health problems, there is heated disagreement about the size and significance of these effects. *See* Andrew K. Przybylski & Netta Weinstein, *A Large-Scale Test of the Goldilocks Hypothesis: Quantifying the Relations between Digital-Screen Use and the Mental Well-Being of Adolescents*, 28 PSYCH. SCI. 204 (2017) (finding smaller effects). Jean M. Twenge & Keith Campbell, *Media Use Is Linked to Lower Psychological Well-Being: Evidence from Three Datasets*, 90 PSYCHIATRY Q. 311 (2019) (finding significant effects).

31 Jonathan Haidt & Jean Twenge, *Social Media Use and Mental Health: A Review* (unpublished manuscript) (on file at tinyurl.com/SocialMediaMentalHealthReview). *See also* Yvonne Kelly *et al.*, *Social Media Use and Adolescent Mental Health: Findings from the UK Millennium Cohort Study*, 6 ECLINICALMEDICINE 59 (2019); Jean M. Twenge & Eric Farley, *Not All Screen Time Is Created Equal: Associations with Mental Health Vary by Activity and Gender*, 56 SOC. PSYCHIATRY PSYCHIATRIC EPIDEMIOLOGY 207 (2021).

32 Jonathan Haidt & Jean Twenge, *Social Media Use and Mental Health: A Review* (unpublished manuscript) (on file at tinyurl.com/SocialMediaMentalHealthReview); Jean M. Twenge & Keith Campbell, *Media Use Is Linked to Lower Psychological Well-Being: Evidence from Three Datasets*, 90 PSYCHIATRY Q. 311 (2019).

33 Michael Shankleman *et al.*, *Adolescent Social Media Use and Well-Being: A Systematic Review and Thematic Meta-Synthesis*, 6 ADOLESCENT RSCH REV. 471, 492 (2021).

34 *See* Jonathan Haidt & Jean Twenge, *Is There an Increase in Adolescent Mood Disorders, Self-Harm, and Suicide since 2010 in the USA and UK? A Review* (unpublished manuscript) (on file with NYU); Ramin Mojtabai *et al.*, *National Trends in the Prevalence and Treatment of Depression in Adolescents and Young Adults*, 138 PEDIATRICS 1 (2016); Jean M. Twenge *et al.*, *Age, Period, and Cohort Trends in Mood Disorder Indicators and Suicide-Related Outcomes in a Nationally Representative Dataset, 2005–2017*, 128 J. ABNORMAL PSYCH. 185 (2019); Katherine M. Keyes *et al.*, *Recent Increases in Depressive Symptoms among US Adolescents: Trends from 1991 to 2018*, 54 SOC. PSYCHIATRY AND PSYCHIATRIC EPIDEMIOLOGY 987 (2019); Melissa C. Mercado *et al.*, *Trends in Emergency Department Visits for Nonfatal Self-Inflicted Injuries among Youth Aged 10 to 24 Years in the United States, 2001–2015*, 318 JAMA 1931 (2017).

35 Jonathan Haidt & Jean Twenge, *Social Media Use and Mental Health: A Review* (unpublished manuscript) (on file at tinyurl.com/SocialMediaMentalHealthReview) (reviewing the relevant experiments and finding that eight out of thirteen showed significant effects, usually an improvement of a mental health aspect or well-being after removing social media for a few weeks). But *see* Jeffrey A. Hall *et al.*, *Experimentally Manipulating Social Media Abstinence: Results of a*

Four-Week Diary Study, 24 MEDIA PSYCH. 259 (not finding a significant effect of social media on mental health).

36 Melissa Hunt *et al.*, *No More FOMO: Limiting Social Media Decreases Loneliness and Depression*, 37 J. SOC AND CLINICAL PSYCH. 751 (2018).

37 Georgia Wells *et al.*, *Facebook Knows Instagram Is Toxic for Teen Girls, Company Documents Show*, WALL ST. J. (Sep. 14, 2021), www.wsj.com/articles/facebook-knows-instagram-is-toxic-for-teen-girls-company-documents-show-11631620739.

38 NICHOLAS KARDARAS, GLOW KIDS: HOW SCREEN ADDICTION IS HIJACKING OUR KIDS – AND HOW TO BREAK THE TRANCE 14 (St. Martin's Press 2016).

39 Sarah E. Domoff *et al.*, *Development and Validation of the Problematic Media Use Measure: A Parent Report Measure of Screen Media "Addiction" in Children*, 8 PSYCH. POPULAR MEDIA CULTURE 2 (2019).

40 NICHOLAS KARDARAS, GLOW KIDS: HOW SCREEN ADDICTION IS HIJACKING OUR KIDS – AND HOW TO BREAK THE TRANCE 20 (St. Martin's Press 2016).

41 Andrew Perrin, *5 Facts about Americans and Video Games*, PEW RSCH. CTR. (Sep. 17, 2018), www.pewresearch.org/fact-tank/2018/09/17/5-facts-about-ameri cans-and-video-games/.

42 Rashmi Parmar & Julian Lagoy, *Is Video Game Addiction a Disorder?*, PSYCHIATRIC TIMES (Oct. 4, 2021), www.psychiatrictimes.com/view/is-video-game-addiction-a-disorder; Cecile Schou Andreassen *et al.*, *The Relationship between Addictive Use of Social Media and Video Games and Symptoms of Psychiatric Disorders: A Large-Scale Cross-Sectional Study*, 30 PSYCH. ADDICTIVE BEHAV. 252 (2016) (citing younger age as a factor increasing the risk for gaming disorder); Douglas A. Gentile *et al.*, *Internet Gaming Disorder in Children and Adolescents*, 104 PEDIATRICS S81 (2017) (finding that IGD prevalence rates range between ~1 and 9 percent, depending on age and country); Luca Milani *et al.*, *Internet Gaming Addiction in Adolescence: Risk Factors and Maladjustment Correlates*, 16 INT'L J. MENTAL HEALTH AND ADDICTION 888 (finding that IGD prevalence depended on age, gender, and country).

43 Amy Orben & Andrew K. Przybylski, *Screens, Teens, and Psychological Well-Being: Evidence from Three Time-Use-Diary Studies*, 30 PYSCH. SCI. 682 (2019) (finding that screen time did not have noticeable effects on teen psychological well-being); Jean M. Twenge *et al.*, *Underestimating Digital Media Harm*, 4 NATURE HUM. BEHAV. 346 (2020) (criticizing the methodology of the research used by Przybyiski and Orben).

44 *HEVGA Opposes World Health Organization's Proposed "Gaming Disorder,"* HIGHER EDUC. VIDEO GAME ALL. (Jan. 4, 2018), https://hevga.org/article_writeups/higher-education-video-game-alliance-opposes-world-health-organizations-gaming-dis order/.

45 Gaia Bernstein & Zvi Triger, *Over-Parenting*, 44 UC DAVIS L. REV. 1221 (2010); Holly H. Schiffrin *et al.*, *Helping or Hovering? The Effects of Helicopter Parenting on College Students' Well-Being*, 23 J. CHILD AND FAMILY STUD 548 (2013); Veronica Darlow *et al.*, *The Relationship between Helicopter Parenting and Adjustment to College*, 26 J. CHILD AND FAMILY STUD 2291 (2017); Kayla Reed *et al.*, *Helicopter Parenting and Emerging Adult Self-Efficacy: Implications for Mental and Physical Health*, 25 J. CHILD AND PARENTING STUD 3136 (2016).

46 Stephen Whiting *et al.*, *Physical Activity, Screen Time, and Sleep Duration of Children Aged 6–9 Years in 25 Countries: An Analysis within the WHO European Childhood Obesity Surveillance Initiative (COSI) 2015–2017*, 14 OBESITY FACTS 32

(2021); James J. Ashton & R. Mark Beattie, *Screen Time in Children and Adolescents: Is There Evidence to Guide Parents and Policy?*, 3 LANCET CHILD & ADOLESCENT HEALTH 292 (2019).

47 Georgia Wells *et al.*, *Facebook Knows Instagram Is Toxic for Teen Girls, Company Documents Show*, WALL ST. J. (Sep. 14, 2021), www.wsj.com/articles/facebook-knows-instagram-is-toxic-for-teen-girls-company-documents-show-11631620739; Jeff Horwitz, *The Facebook Whistleblower, Frances Huagen, Says She Wants to Fix the Company, Not Harm It*, WALL ST. J. (Oct. 3, 2021), www.wsj.com/articles/facebook-whistleblower-frances-haugen-says-she-wants-to-fix-the-company-not-harm-it-11633304122.

48 *Guidelines on Physical Activity, Sedentary Behavior and Sleep for Children under 5 Years of Age*, WORLD HEALTH ORGANIZATION (Apr. 2, 2019), www.who.int/publications/i/item/9789241550536; *WHO Guidelines on Physical Activity and Sedentary Behaviour*, WORLD HEALTH ORGANIZATION (Nov. 25, 2020), www.who.int/publications/i/item/9789240015128; Mary Alvord, *Digital Guidelines: Promoting Healthy Technology Use for Children*, AM. PSYCH. ASS'N. (Dec. 12, 2019), www.apa.org/topics/social-media-internet/technology-use-children.

49 Gaia Bernstein, *When New Technologies Are Still New: Windows of Opportunity for Privacy Protection*, 51 VILL. L. REV. 921 (2006).

50 ALAN LIGHTMAN, THE DIAGNOSIS (1st ed. Pantheon 2000).

51 SHERRY TURKLE, RECLAIMING CONVERSATION (Penguin Books 2016).

52 *UK: A Third of UK Families Use Phones during Meal Times*, AVIVA (Feb. 17, 2017), www.aviva.com/newsroom/news-releases/2017/02/uk-a-third-of-uk-families-use-phones-during-meal-times-17739/.

53 SHERRY TURKLE, ALONE TOGETHER: WHY WE EXPECT MORE FROM TECHNOLOGY AND LESS FROM EACH OTHER (Basic Books 2012).

54 BRENE BROWN, DARING GREATLY: HOW THE COURAGE TO BE VULNERABLE TRANSFORMS THE WAY WE LIVE, LOVE, PARENT AND LEAD 149–50 (reprint ed., Avery Publishing Group 2015).

55 Emily A. Vogels, *The State of Online Harassment*, PEW RSCH. CTR. (Jan. 13, 2021), www.pewresearch.org/internet/2021/01/13/the-state-of-online-harassment/.

56 Sounman Hong & Sun Hyoung Kim, *Political Polarization on Twitter: Implications for the Use of Social Media in Digital Governments*, 33 GOV'T INFO. Q. 777 (2016).

57 Dan Milmo, *Rohingya Sue Facebook for £150bn over Myanmar Genocide*, THE GUARDIAN (Dec. 6, 2021), www.theguardian.com/technology/2021/dec/06/rohingya-sue-facebook-myanmar-genocide-us-uk-legal-action-social-media-violence; Karen Hao, *The Facebook Whistleblower Says Its Algorithms Are Dangerous. Here's Why*, MIT TECH. REV. (Oct. 5, 2021); FRANK PASQUALE, NEW LAWS OF ROBOTICS: DEFENDING HUMAN EXPERTISE IN THE AGE OF AI 89–118 (Harvard University Press 2020).

58 Jeff Horwitz & Deepa Seetharaman, *Facebook Executives Shut down Efforts to Make the Site Less Divisive*, WALL ST. J. (May 26, 2020), www.wsj.com/articles/facebook-knows-it-encourages-division-top-executives-nixed-solutions-11590507499.

59 For an instrumental theory of autonomy, *see e.g.* Eric Racine, M. Ariel Cascio, & Aline Bogossian, *Instrumentalist Analyses of the Functions of Health Ethics Concepts and Principles: Methodological Guideposts*, 17 AM. J. BIOETHICS 16 (2017).

Chapter 3

1 Gaia Bernstein, *In the Shadow of Innovation*, 31 CARDOZO L. REV. 2257 (2010).

2 Buzz Aldrin, *You Promised Me Mars Colonies. Instead, I Got Facebook. We've Stopped Solving Big Problems*, 115 MIT TECH. REV. 26 (2012).

3 Gaia Bernstein, *The Socio-Legal Acceptance of New Technologies: A Close Look at Artificial Insemination*, 77 WASH. L. REV. 1035 (2002).

4 Gaia Bernstein, *The Socio-Legal Acceptance of New Technologies: A Close Look at Artificial Insemination*, 77 WASH. L. REV. 1035, 1037 (2002).

5 JOHANN HARI, STOLEN FOCUS: WHY YOU CAN'T PAY ATTENTION AND HOW TO THINK DEEPLY AGAIN (Crown 2022).

6 Bianca Bosker, *The Binge Breaker: Tristan Harris Believes Silicon Valley Is Addicting Us to Our Phones. He's Determined to Make Us Stop*, THE ATLANTIC (Nov. 2016), www.theatlantic.com/magazine/archive/2016/11/the-binge-breaker/501122/.

7 *Whistleblower Hearing before the Subcomm. on Consumer Prot., Prod. Safety, and Data Sec. of the Sen. Comm. on Com., Sci. and Transp.*, 117th Cong. (Oct. 5, 2021) (written statement of Frances Haugen, former employee of Facebook), www.commerce.senate.gov/services/files/FC8A558E-824E-4914-BEDB-3A7B1190BD49; Jeff Horwitz et al., *A Wall Street Journal Investigation: The Facebook Files*, WALL ST. J. (Sep.–Oct. 2021), www.wsj.com/articles/the-facebook-files-11631713039? mod=series_facebookfiles; Victor Ordonez, *Key Takeaways from Facebook Whistleblower Frances Haugen's Senate Testimony*, ABC NEWS (Oct. 5, 2021), https://abcnews.go.com/Politics/key-takeaways-facebook-whistleblower-frances-hau gens-senate-testimony/story?id=80419357.

8 Michael D. Zeiler, *Fixed-Interval Behavior: Effects of Percentage Reinforcement*, 17 J. EXPERIMENTAL ANALYSIS BEHAV. 177 (March 1972); NATASHA DOW SCHUL, ADDICTION BY DESIGN: GAMBLING IN LAS VEGAS (Princeton University Press 2014, new in paper ed.).

9 See ADAM ALTER, IRRESISTIBLE: THE RISE OF ADDICTIVE TECHNOLOGY AND THE BUSINESS OF KEEPING US HOOKED 76–77 (Penguin 2017); Tristan Harris, *How Technology Is Hijacking Your Mind – from a Magician and Google Design Ethicist*, MEDIUM (May 18, 2016).

10 Mike Allen, *Sean Perker Unloads on Facebook: "God Only Knows What It's Doing to Our Children's Brains,"* AXIOS: TECHNOLOGY (Nov. 9, 2017), www.axios.com/sean-parker-unloads-on-facebook-2508036343.html.

11 ADAM ALTER, IRRESISTIBLE: THE RISE OF ADDICTIVE TECHNOLOGY AND THE BUSINESS OF KEEPING US HOOKED 141 (Penguin 2017); Tristan Harris, *How Technology Is Hijacking Your Mind – from a Magician and Google Design Ethicist*, MEDIUM (May 18, 2016); Avery Hartmans, *These Are the Sneaky Ways Apps Like Instagram, Facebook, Tinder, Lure You in and Get You Addicted*, BUSINESS INSIDER: TECH (Feb. 17, 2018), www.businessinsider.com/how-app-developers-keep-us-addicted-to-our-smartphones-2018-1; Mayank Gupta & Aditya Sharma, *Fear of Missing Out: A Brief Overview of Origin, Theoretical Underpinnings and Relationship with Mental Health*, 9 WORLD J. CLIN. CASES 4881 (Jul. 6, 2021).

12 Lizette Chapman, *Inside the Mind of a Snapchat Streaker*, BLOOMBERG (Jan. 30, 2017), www.bloomberg.com/news/features/2017-01-30/inside-the-mind-of-a-snap chat-streaker.

13 See Brian Wansink, James E. Painter, & Jill North, *Bottomless Bowls: Why Visual Cues of Portion Size May Influence Intake*, 13 OBESITY RES. 93 (Jan. 2005).

14 Tristan Harris, *How Technology Is Hijacking Your Mind – from a Magician and Google Design Ethicist*, MEDIUM (May 18, 2016).

15 *See* CAL NEWPORT, *DIGITAL MINIMALISM: ON LIVING BETTER WITH LESS TECHNOLOGY* xiv (Penguin Random House 2019).

16 CAL NEWPORT, *DIGITAL MINIMALISM: ON LIVING BETTER WITH LESS TECHNOLOGY* 24 (Penguin Random House 2019).

17 CAL NEWPORT, *DIGITAL MINIMALISM: ON LIVING BETTER WITH LESS TECHNOLOGY* 69 (Penguin Random House 2019) (emphasis added).

18 NIR EYAL, *HOOKED: HOW TO BUILD HABIT-FORMING PRODUCTS* (Penguin 2014).

19 NIR EYAL, *INDISTRACTABLE: HOW TO CONTROL YOUR ATTENTION AND CHOOSE YOUR LIFE* 25 (Bloomsbury 2019).

20 NIR EYAL, *INDISTRACTABLE: HOW TO CONTROL YOUR ATTENTION AND CHOOSE YOUR LIFE* 37, 129–30 (Bloomsbury 2019).

21 NIR EYAL, *INDISTRACTABLE: HOW TO CONTROL YOUR ATTENTION AND CHOOSE YOUR LIFE* 37, 49, 129–30 (Bloomsbury 2019).

22 *See* Oren Soffer, *The Eraser and the Anti-Eraser: The Battle over Colour Television in Israel*, 30 MEDIA, CULTURE & SOCIETY 759 (2008).

23 Victoria Rideout & Michael B. Robb, *The Common Sense Census: Media Use by Tweens and Teens*, COMMON SENSE MEDIA 3 (2019).

24 NIR EYAL, *INDISTRACTABLE: HOW TO CONTROL YOUR ATTENTION AND CHOOSE YOUR LIFE* 49 (Bloomsbury 2019).

25 *See* Michael Moss, *HOOKED: FOOD, FREE WILL, AND HOW THE FOOD GIANTS EXPLOIT OUR ADDICTIONS* 169–70, 182 (Penguin Random House 2021).

26 Daniel Svensson, *Digital Wellbeing, According to Google* (MSc thesis, Lund University, 2019), https://lup.lub.lu.se/luur/download?func=downloadFile&recordOId=8976353&fileOId=8981518.

27 GOOGLE DIGITAL WELLBEING, https://wellbeing.google/ (last visited Jan. 17, 2022).

28 *See* Alberto Monge Roffarello & Luigi De Russis, *The Race towards Digital Wellbeing: Issues and Opportunities*, CHI 2019: PROCEEDINGS OF THE 2019 CHI CONFERENCE ON HUMAN FACTORS IN COMPUTING SYSTEMS 2.

29 *See* Alberto Monge Roffarello & Luigi De Russis, *The Race towards Digital Wellbeing: Issues and Opportunities*, CHI 2019: PROCEEDINGS OF THE 2019 CHI CONFERENCE ON HUMAN FACTORS IN COMPUTING SYSTEMS 2, 11.

30 Daniel Bader, *Digital Wellbeing Has Been Forgotten, But We Need It Now More than Ever*, ANDROID CENTRAL (Sep. 20, 2020); GOOGLE DIGITAL WELLBEING: OUR COMMITMENT, https://wellbeing.google/ (citing a 2019 YouGov.com survey reporting that one in three US adults has taken active steps to improve digital wellbeing in the prior year).

31 Daniel Bader, *Digital Wellbeing Has Been Forgotten, But We Need It Now More than Ever*, ANDROID CENTRAL (Sep. 20, 2020).

Chapter 4

1 Smoking & Tobacco Use among Adults in the United States, CTR. FOR DISEASE CONTROL AND PREVENTION, www.cdc.gov/tobacco/data_statistics/fact_sheets/adult_data/cig_smoking/index.htm; RICHARD KLUGER, *ASHES TO ASHES: AMERICA'S HUNDRED-YEAR CIGARETTE WAR, THE PUBLIC HEALTH AND THE UNABASHED TRIUMPH OF PHILLIP MORRIS* 132 (First Vintage Books 2010).

2 In 2021, about 1 of every 100 middle school students (1.3 percent) and nearly 4 of every 100 high school students (3.8 percent) reported current use of two or more tobacco products in the past thirty days. Although 11.3 percent reported smoking electronic cigarettes and 1.9 percent reported smoking cigarettes. *Youth and Tobacco Use*, CTR. FOR DISEASE CONTROL AND PREVENTION, www.cdc.gov/ tobacco/data_statistics/fact_sheets/youth_data/tobacco_use/index.htm#:~:text=In% 202021%2C%20about%204%20of,use%20of%20a%20tobacco%20product.& text=In%202021%2C%20about%2011%20of,ever%20tried%20a%20tobacco %20product.

3 *See Nearly 800,000 Deaths Prevented Due to Decline in Smoking*, NAT'L INST. IN HEALTH (Mar. 14, 2012), www.nih.gov/news-events/news-releases/nearly-800000-deaths-prevented-due-declines-smoking.

4 *See* Robert L. Rabin, *A Sociological History of Tobacco Tort Litigation*, 44 STAN. L. REV. 853, 870–71 (1992); Michael S. Givel, *Tobacco Lobby Political Influence on US State Legislatures in the 1990s*, 10 TOBACCO CONTROL 124 (2001).

5 Albert G. Ingalls, *If You Smoke*, 154 SCI. AM. 310 (1936).

6 RICHARD KLUGER, ASHES TO ASHES: AMERICA'S HUNDRED-YEAR CIGARETTE WAR, THE PUBLIC HEALTH AND THE UNABASHED TRIUMPH OF PHILLIP MORRIS 106, 132, 152 (First Vintage Books 2010).

7 Roy Norr, *Cancer by the Carton*, READER'S DIGEST (Dec. 1952).

8 RICHARD KLUGER, ASHES TO ASHES: AMERICA'S HUNDRED-YEAR CIGARETTE WAR, THE PUBLIC HEALTH AND THE UNABASHED TRIUMPH OF PHILLIP MORRIS 153, 188 (First Vintage Books 2010).

9 RICHARD KLUGER, ASHES TO ASHES: AMERICA'S HUNDRED-YEAR CIGARETTE WAR, THE PUBLIC HEALTH AND THE UNABASHED TRIUMPH OF PHILLIP MORRIS 157–58, 191, 201 (First Vintage Books 2010).

10 RICHARD KLUGER, ASHES TO ASHES: AMERICA'S HUNDRED-YEAR CIGARETTE WAR, THE PUBLIC HEALTH AND THE UNABASHED TRIUMPH OF PHILLIP MORRIS 208–09, 211 (First Vintage Books 2010).

11 ALLAN M. BRANDT, THE CIGARETTE CENTURY: THE RISE, FALL, AND DEADLY PERSISTENCE OF THE PRODUCT THAT DEFINED AMERICA 210–39 (reprint ed., Basic Books 2009).

12 ALLAN M. BRANDT, THE CIGARETTE CENTURY: THE RISE, FALL, AND DEADLY PERSISTENCE OF THE PRODUCT THAT DEFINED AMERICA 210–39 (reprint ed., Basic Books 2009).

13 Federal Cigarette Labeling and Advertising Act 79 Stat. 282 Pub. L. No. 89-92 1 (1965).

14 ALLAN M. BRANDT, THE CIGARETTE CENTURY: THE RISE, FALL, AND DEADLY PERSISTENCE OF THE PRODUCT THAT DEFINED AMERICA 254–58 (reprint ed., Basic Books 2009).

15 Unlawful Advertisements on Medium of Electronic Communication, 15 USCA § 1335 (1971).

16 ALLAN M. BRANDT, THE CIGARETTE CENTURY: THE RISE, FALL, AND DEADLY PERSISTENCE OF THE PRODUCT THAT DEFINED AMERICA 268–71 (reprint ed., Basic Books 2009).

17 RICHARD KLUGER, ASHES TO ASHES: AMERICA'S HUNDRED-YEAR CIGARETTE WAR, THE PUBLIC HEALTH AND THE UNABASHED TRIUMPH OF PHILLIP MORRIS 309–27 (First Vintage Books 2010).

18 RICHARD KLUGER, *ASHES TO ASHES: AMERICA'S HUNDRED-YEAR CIGARETTE WAR, THE PUBLIC HEALTH AND THE UNABASHED TRIUMPH OF PHILLIP MORRIS* 325 (First Vintage Books 2010).

19 Robert Rabin, "The Third Wave of Tobacco Tort Litigation", in REGULATING TOBACCO 176, 184 (Sep. 2001) (Robert L. Rabin & Stephen D. Sugarman eds.); ALEXANDRA LAHAV, *IN PRAISE OF LITIGATION* (1st ed. Oxford University Press 2017); Michael J. Saks, *Do We Really Know Anything about the Behavior of the Tort Litigation System – and Why Not?*, 140 *U. PA. L. REV.* 1150 (Apr. 1992).

20 DONALD G. GIFFORD, *SUING THE TOBACCO AND LEAD PIGMENT INDUSTRIES: GOVERNMENT LITIGATION AS PUBLIC HEALTH PRESCRIPTION* 121–32; 171–85 (University of Michigan Press 2010); Richard L. Cupp, *A Morality Play's Third Act: Revisiting Addiction, Fraud and Consumer Choice in "Third Wave" Tobacco Litigation*, 46 KAN. L. REV. 465, 488 (1988).

21 *Latrigue v. R. J. Reynolds Tobacco Co.*, 317 F.2d 17, 22 (5th Cir. 1963); Patrick Luff, *Regulating Tobacco Through Litigation*, 47 ARIZ. STATE L.J. 125, 142 (2015).

22 *Latrigue v. R. J. Reynolds Tobacco Co.*, 317 F.2d 17, 36 (5th Cir. 1963); DONALD G. GIFFORD. *SUING THE TOBACCO AND LEAD PIGMENT INDUSTRIES: GOVERNMENT LITIGATION AS PUBLIC HEALTH PRESCRIPTION* 35–38 (University of Michigan Press 2010); MARTHA A. DERTHICK, *UP IN SMOKE: FROM LEGISLATION TO LITIGATION IN TOBACCO POLITICS* 29–31 (3rd ed., CQ Press 2011); James A. Henderson & Aaron D. Twerski, *Reaching Equilibrium in Tobacco Litigation*, 62 SC. L. REV. 67, 74 (2010).

23 *Horton v. American Tobacco Co.*, 667 Sp. 2d 1289, 1289–91 (Miss. 1995).

24 DONALD G.. GIFFORD, *SUING THE TOBACCO AND LEAD PIGMENT INDUSTRIES: GOVERNMENT LITIGATION AS PUBLIC HEALTH PRESCRIPTION* 39–40 (University of Michigan Press 2010); MARTHA A. DERTHICK, *UP IN SMOKE: FROM LEGISLATION TO LITIGATION IN TOBACCO POLITICS* 31–34 (3rd ed., CQ Press 2011); *Cipollone v. Liggett Group, Inc.*, 693 F. Supp. 208 (DNJ 1988) (in which the jury assigned 20 percent of the cause to the tobacco company, but the defendant did not pay damages because NJ law provided for no damages without at least 50 percent liability).

25 Robert Rabin, "The Third Wave of Tobacco Tort Litigation," in REGULATING TOBACCO 176, 181–182 (Robert L. Rabin & Stephen D. Sugarman eds., Oxford University Press 2001).

26 DONALD G. Gifford, *SUING THE TOBACCO AND LEAD PIGMENT INDUSTRIES: GOVERNMENT LITIGATION AS PUBLIC HEALTH PRESCRIPTION* 108 (University of Michigan Press 2010).

27 Robert Rabin, "The Third Wave of Tobacco Tort Litigation," in REGULATING TOBACCO 176, 186 (Robert L. Rabin & Stephen D. Sugarman eds., Oxford University Press 2001).

28 *Castano v. American Tobacco Co.*, 160 FRD 544 (ED La. 1995); Richard L. Cipp, *A Morality Plays Third Act: Revisiting Addiction, Fraud and Consumer Choice in "Third Wave" Tobacco Litigation*, 46 KAN. L. REV. 465, 473 (1998); Richard Kluger, *ASHES TO ASHES: AMERICA'S HUNDRED-YEAR CIGARETTE WAR, THE PUBLIC HEALTH AND THE UNABASHED TRIUMPH OF PHILLIP MORRIS* 760 (First Vintage Books 2010).

29 *Carter v. Brown & Williamson Tobacco Corp.*, 680 So.2d 546 (Fla. First DCA 1996).

30 Donald G. Gifford, Suing the Tobacco and Lead Pigment Industries: Government Litigation as Public Health Prescription 121–32 (University of Michigan Press 2010).

31 Smoke Free Air Act, NYC Admin. Code § 17-501 (2002).

32 Smoking Ban: Foreign Air Carriers, 14 CFR § 252.5 (2016).

33 Secondhand Smoke (SHS) Facts, Ctr. for Disease Control and Prevention, www.cdc.gov/tobacco/data_statistics/fact_sheets/secondhand_smoke/general_facts/index.htm.

34 Allan M. Brandt, The Cigarette Century: The Rise, Fall, and Deadly Persistence of the Product That Defined America 280–89 (Basic Books 2009).

35 Richard Kluger, Ashes to Ashes: America's Hundred-Year Cigarette War, the Public Health and the Unabashed Triumph of Phillip Morris 678 (First Vintage Books 2010).

36 Richard Kluger, Ashes to Ashes: America's Hundred-Year Cigarette War, the Public Health and the Unabashed Triumph of Phillip Morris 737 (First Vintage Books 2010).

37 Donald G. Gifford, Suing the Tobacco and Lead Pigment Industries: Government Litigation As Public Health Prescription 207 (University of Michigan Press 2010).

38 Allan M. Brandt, The Cigarette Century: The Rise, Fall, and Deadly Persistence of the Product That Defined America 289–90 (Basic Books 2009).

39 Donald G. Gifford, Suing the Tobacco and Lead Pigment Industries: Government Litigation As Public Health Prescription 106–07 (University of Michigan Press 2010); James A. Henderson & Aaron D. Twerski, Reaching Equilibrium in Tobacco Litigation, 62 S.C. L. Rev. 67, 75 (2010).

40 Frank J. Chaliupka et al., "The Politics of Tobacco Regulation in the United States," in Regulating Tobacco 11, 20 (Robert L. Rabin & Stephen E. Sugarman eds., Oxford University Press 2001).

41 Richard Kluger, Ashes to Ashes: America's Hundred-Year Cigarette War, the Public Health and the unabashed Triumph of Phillip Morris 679–80 (First Vintage Books 2010).

42 Allan M. Brandt, The Cigarette Century: The Rise, Fall, and Deadly Persistence of the Product that Defined America 298 (Basic Books 2009).

43 Allan M. Brandt, The Cigarette Century: The Rise, Fall, and Deadly Persistence of the Product that Defined America 308 (Basic Books 2009); Frank J. Chaliupka et al., "Taxing Tobacco: The Impact of Tobacco Taxes on Cigarette Smoking and Other Tobacco Use," in Regulating Tobacco 39 (Robert L. Rabin & Stephen E. Sugarman eds., Oxford University Press 2001).

44 Dorie E. Apollonio & Stanton A. Glantz, Minimum Ages of Legal Access for Tobacco in the United States from 1863 to 2015, 106 Am. J. Pub. Health 1200 (2016).

45 S2833. Assemb. Reg. Sess. 2019-20 (N.Y. 2019).

46 Surgeon General's Report, Preventing Tobacco Use among Adults and Youth 710 (Nat'l Ctr. for Chronic Disease Prevention and Health Promotion 2012); Dorie E. Apollonio & Stanton A. Glantz, Minimum Ages of Legal Access for Tobacco in the United States from 1863 to 2015, 106 Am. J. Pub. Health 1200 (2016).

47 *Youth Tobacco Surveillance – United States, 2001–2002*, Ctr. for Disease Control and Prevention, www.cdc.gov/Mmwr/preview/mmwrhtml/ss5503a1 .htm (finding that 80 percent of tobacco users started using before they turned 18).

48 Nancy A. Rugotti, "Reducing the Supply of Tobacco to Youth," in *Regulating Tobacco* 143, 143–57 (Robert L. Rabin & Stephen E. Sugarman eds., Oxford University Press 2001).

49 *Cigarette Tax Increases vs. Cigarette Company Price Increases*, Campaign for Tobacco-Free Kids, www.tobaccofreekids.org/assets/factsheets/0210.pdf; Frank J. Chaliupka, Melanie Wakefield, & Christina Czart, "The Politics of Tobacco Regulation in the United States," in *Regulating Tobacco* 11 (Robert L. Rabin & Stephen E. Sugarman eds., Oxford University Press 2001); *Cigarette Tax Increases by State per Year 2000–2019*, Campaign for Tobacco-Free Kids, www .tobaccofreekids.org/assets/factsheets/0275.pdf.

50 *Income Statistics for New York Zip Codes*, Income by Zipcode, www .incomebyzipcode.com/newyork.

51 Frank J. Chaliupka *et al.*, "Taxing Tobacco: The Impact of Tobacco Taxes on Cigarette Smoking and Other Tobacco Use," in *Regulating Tobacco* 39 (Robert L. Rabin & Stephen E. Sugarman eds., Oxford University Press 2001); Tobacco, World Health Organization (Jul. 26, 2021), www.who.int/news-room/fact-sheets/detail/tobacco.

Chapter 5

1 *The Health Effects of Overweight and Obesity*, Centers for Disease Control and Prevention, www.cdc.gov/healthyweight/effects/index.html.

2 Trust for America's Health, The State of Obesity 5 (2021), https://doi.org/ 10.1377/hlthaff.28.5.w822, www.tfah.org/wp-content/uploads/2021/09/2021 ObesityReport_Fnl.pdf (claiming that obesity increased annual medical expenses in the United States by $149 billion); John Cawley *et al.*, *Direct Medical Costs of Obesity in the United States and Most Populous States*, 27 J. Managed Care & Specialty Pharmacy 354, 361 (2021) (asserting that the direct medical costs of obesity in adults reached $260.6 billion in 2016).

3 *Economic Costs of Obesity*, National League of Cities, www .healthycommunitieshealthyfuture.org/learn-the-facts/economic-costs-of-obesity/#: ~:text=The%20estimated%20annual%20health%20care,spending%20in%20the %20United%20States.

4 David S. Freedman, *Obesity – United States, 1988–2008*, Centers for Disease Control and Prevention (Jan. 14, 2011).

5 Katherine M. Flegal *et al.*, *Prevalence and Trends in Obesity among US Adults, 1999–2008*, 303 *JAMA* 235 (2010).

6 Cynthia Ogden & Margaret Carroll, *Prevalence of Obesity among Children and Adolescents: United States, Trends 1963–1965 through 2007–2008*, Centers for Disease Control and Prevention, www.cdc.gov/nchs/data/hestat/obesity_child_ 07_08/obesity_child_07_08.htm#.

7 Sheryl Gay Stolberg, *Childhood Obesity Battle Is Taken up by First Lady*, N.Y. Times (Feb. 9, 2010), www.nytimes.com/2010/02/10/health/nutrition/10obesity .html.

8 MICHAEL MOSS, *HOOKED: FOOD, FREE WILL, AND HOW THE FOOD GIANTS EXPLOIT OUR ADDICTIONS* xxv–xxvi (Random House 2021) (describing how food companies design their food to make us eat more by, for example, making it sweeter).

9 Anthony Winson, *The Demand for Healthy Eating: Supporting a Transformative Food "Movement,"* 74 RURAL SOCIOLOGY 584 (2010); MICHAEL POLLAN, *IN DEFENSE OF FOOD: AN EATER'S MANIFESTO* (Penguin Press 2008); *Americans' Views about and Consumption of Organic Foods*, PEW RSCH. CTR. (Dec. 1, 2016), www.pewresearch.org/science/2016/12/01/americans-views-about-and-consumption-of-organic-foods/.

10 Robert A. Sedler, *An Essay on Freedom of Speech: The United States Versus the Rest of the World*, 377 MICH STATE L. REV. 384 (2006).

11 Colleen Smith, *A Spoonful of (Added) Sugar Helps the Constitution Go down: Curing the Compelled Commercial Speech Doctrine with FDA's Added Sugar Rule*, 71 FOOD DRUG L.J. 442, 450–451 (2016). Cigarette companies had mixed results with these First Amendment challenges. *See e.g. Disc. Tobacco City & Lottery Inc. v. United States*, 64 F.3d 509 (6th Cir. 2012); *R. J. Reynolds Tobacco Co. v. United States Food & Drug Admin.*, 696 F.3d 1205 (D.C. Cir. 2012).

12 *Am. Bev. Ass'n v. City & City of San Francisco*, 916 F.3d 749 (9th Cir. 2019).

13 Felix T. Wu, *The Commercial Difference*, 58 WM. & MARY L. REV. 2005 (2017); Martin H. Redish, *Compelled Commercial Speech and the First Amendment*, 94 NOTRE DAME L. REV. 1749 (2019); Eugene Volokh, *The Law of Compelled Speech*, 97 TEX. L. REV. 355–95 (2018).

14 MICHAEL MOSS, *HOOKED: FOOD, FREE WILL, AND HOW THE FOOD GIANTS EXPLOIT OUR ADDICTIONS* (Random House 2021); Anahad O'Connor, *Coca-Cola Funds Scientists Who Shift Blame for Obesity Away from Bad Diets*, N.Y. TIMES (Aug. 9, 2015), https://well.blogs.nytimes.com/2015/08/09/coca-cola-funds-scientists-who-shift-blame-for-obesity-away-from-bad-diets/; Anahad O'Connor, *How the Sugar Industry Shifted Blame to Fat*, N.Y. TIMES (Sep. 12, 2016), www.nytimes.com/2016/09/13/well/eat/how-the-sugar-industry-shifted-blame-to-fat.html.

15 *Zauderer v. Off. of Disciplinary Couns. of Sup. Ct. of Ohio*, 471 U.S. 626, 651 (1985).

16 David S. Ludwig, *Relation between Consumption of Sugar-Sweetened Drinks and Childhood Obesity: A Prospective, Observational Analysis*, 357 THE LANCET 505 (2001); Vasanti S. Malik *et al.*, *Sugar-Sweetened Beverages, Obesity, Type 2 Diabetes Mellitus, and Cardiovascular Disease Risk*, 121 CIRCULATION 1356 (2010).

17 Sarah A. Roache *et al.*, *Big Food and Soda Versus Public Health: Industry Litigation against Local Government Regulations to Promote Healthy Diets*, 45 FORDHAM URB. L.J. 1051, 1063–1064 (2018); Maira Bes-Rastrollo *et al.*, *Financial Conflicts of Interest and Reporting Bias Regarding the Association between Sugar-Sweetened Beverages and Weight Gain: A Systematic Review of Systematic Reviews*, 10 PLOS MED. 1, 2 (2013).

18 MARION NESTLE, *SODA POLITICS: TAKING ON BIG SODA (AND WINNING)* 107 (Oxford University Press 2015).

19 MARION NESTLE, *SODA POLITICS: TAKING ON BIG SODA (AND WINNING)* 108 (Oxford University Press 2015).

20 *Am. Bev. Ass'n v. City & Cnty. S. F.*, 916 F.3d 749, 761 (9th Cir. 2019) (Judge Ikuta, concurring). The majority opinion based its decision that the law violates the First

Amendment on the possibility that the rectangular border that covers 20 percent of the ad could drown the beverage companies' message and effectively rule out having an ad in the first place. *Am. Bev. Ass'n v. City & Cnty. S. F.*, 916 F.3d 749, 756–57 (9th Cir. 2019).

21 *N.Y. State Res't Ass'n v. N.Y. City Bd. of Health*, 556 F.3d 114, 114, 120–21, 131, 134, 136 (1st Cir. 2009).

22 *Grocery Mfr.'s Ass'n v. Sorrell*, 102 F. Supp. 3d 583, 620, 622–25, 629 (D. Vt. 2015).

23 *Krommenbock v. Post Foods LLC*, No. 16-cv-04958-WHO, 2018 LEXIS 42938. at *1–4 (N.D. Cal. Mar. 15, 2018).

24 *Grocery Mfr.'s Ass'n v. Sorrell*, 102 F. Supp. 3d 583, 620, 622–25, 629 (D. Vt. 2015); *Krommenbock v. Post Foods LLC*, No. 16-cv-04958-WHO, 2018 LEXIS 42938. at *7–12 (N.D. Cal. Mar. 15, 2018).

25 *Grocery Mfr.'s Ass'n v. Sorrell*, 102 F. Supp. 3d 583, 635–41 (D. Vt. 2015).

26 Eric A. Finkelstein & Laurie Zuckerman, *The Fattening of America* 143 (Wiley 2007); *Pelman v. McDonald's Corp.*, 237 F. Supp. 2d 512, 515, 519 (2003).

27 *Pelman v. McDonald's Corp.*, 237 F. Supp. 2d 512, 517–19, 530–31 (2003).

28 Adam Benforado *et al.*, *Broken Scales: Obesity and Justice in America*, 53 Emory L.J. 1645 (2004).

29 *Pelman v. McDonald's Corp.*, 237 F. Supp. 2d 512, 533 (2003).

30 *Pelman v. McDonald's Corp.*, 237 F. Supp. 2d 512, 533 (2003).

31 H. R. 554, 109th Cong. § 2(a)(4) (2005).

32 Grace Thompson, *How Commonsense Consumption Acts Are Preventing "Big Food" Litigation*, 41 Seattle Univ. L. Rev. 695 (2018); Deborah Rhode, *Obesity and Public Policy: A Roadmap for Reform*, 22 Va. J. Soc. Pol'y & L. 491, 520–21 (2015).

33 Colin Campbell, *Bloomberg Says Government "Probably" Shouldn't Force People to Exercise*, The Observer (Mar. 8, 2013), https://observer.com/2013/03/bloom berg-says-government-probably-shouldnt-force-people-to-exercise/.

34 Sarah A. Roache *et al.*, *Big Food and Soda Versus Public Health: Industry Litigation against Local Government Regulations to Promote Healthy Diets*, 45 Fordham Urb. L.J. 1051, 1067–68 (2018); *In re. N.Y. Statewide Coal. of Hisp. Chambers of Com. v. N.Y. City Dep't of Health & Mental Hygiene*, 16 N.E.3d 538, 542 (N.Y. 2014); Deborah Rhode, *Obesity and Public Policy: A Roadmap for Reform*, 22 Va. J. Soc. Pol'y & L. 491, 509–10 (2015).

35 *Bloomberg's War on Sugar*, N.Y. Amsterdam News (Apr. 16, 2013), https://amsterdamnews.com/news/2013/04/16/bloombergs-war-on-sugar/.

36 Brad Hamilton, *Bloomberg's Ban Prohibits 2-Liter Soda with Your Pizza and Some Nightclub Mixers*, N.Y. Post (Feb. 24, 2013), https://nypost.com/2013/02/24/bloom bergs-ban-prohibits-2-liter-soda-with-your-pizza-and-some-nightclub-mixers/.

37 Ron Dicker, *"Nanny Bloomberg" Ad in New York Times Targets N.Y. Mayor's Anti-Soda Crusade (PHOTO)*, Huffington Post (Dec. 16, 2017), www.huffpost .com/entry/nanny-bloomberg-ad-in-new_n_1568037.

38 Marion Nestle, *Soda Politics: Taking on Big Soda (and Winning)* 85 (Oxford University Press 2015); Richard H. Thaler & Cass R. Sunstein, *Libertarian Paternalism*, 93 Am. Econ. Rev. 175, 175, 179 (2003); Lawrence O. Gostin, *Bloomberg's Health Legacy: Urban Innovator or Meddling Nanny?*, 43 Hastings Ctr. Rpt. 19 (2013).

39 David Adam Friedman, *Public Health Regulation and the Limits of Paternalism*, 46 CONN. L. REV. 1687, 1687 (2014).

40 David L. Shapiro, *Courts, Legislatures and Paternalism*, 74 VA. L. REV. 519 (1988); Eric Lode, *Slippery Slope Arguments and Legal Reasoning*, 87 CAL. L. REV. 1469 (1999); Eugene Volokh, *The Mechanisms of the Slippery Slope*, 116 HARV. L. REV. 1028 (2003).

41 Gerald Dworkin, *Paternalism*, 56 THE MONIST 64, 65 (1972); M. Todd Henderson, *The Nanny Corporation*, 76 U. CHI. L. REV. 1517, 1527 (2009); CASS SUNSTEIN & RICHARD A. THALER, NUDGE: IMPROVING DECISIONS ABOUT HEALTH, WEALTH AND HAPPINESS (Yale University Press 2008).

42 SARAH CONLY, AGAINST AUTONOMY: JUSTIFYING COERCIVE PATERNALISM 5 (Cambridge University Press 2013).

43 Yilin Yoshida & Eduardo J. Simoes, *Sugar-Sweetened Beverage, Obesity, and Type 2 Diabetes in Children and Adolescents: Policies, Taxation, and Programs*, 18 CURRENT DIABETES REP. 31 (2018); Maria Luger *et al.*, *Sugar-Sweetened Beverages and Weight Gain in Children and Adults: A Systematic Review from 2013 to 2015 and a Comparison with Previous Studies*, 10 OBESITY FACTS 674–93 (2017).

44 Yichen Zhong *et al.*, *The Short-Term Impacts of the Philadelphia Beverage Tax on Beverage Consumption*, 44 AM. J. PREVENTIVE MED 26, 26–34 (2018); Anurag Sharma *et al.*, *The Effects of Taxing Sugar-Sweetened Beverages Across Different Income Groups*, 23 HEALTH ECON. 1159 (2014); Barbara Bennett Woodhouse & Charles F. Woodhouse, *Children's Rights and the Politics of Food: Big Food Versus Little People*, 56 FAM. CT. REV. 287, 299 (2018); Sarah A. Roache *et al.*, *Big Food and Soda Versus Public Health: Industry Litigation against Local Government Regulations to Promote Healthy Diets*, 45 FORDHAM URB. L.J. 1051, 1060–61 (2018).

45 Matthew M. Lee *et al.*, *Sugar-Sweetened Beverage Consumption 3 Years after the Berkeley, California, Sugar-Sweetened Beverage Tax*, 109 AM. J. PUB. HEALTH 637 (2019).

46 Eric A. Finkelstein, *Impact of Targeted Beverage Taxes on Higher-and Lower-Income Households*, 170 ARCHIVES OF INTERNAL MED. 2028, 2033 (2010); Eric Finkelstein *et al.*, *Pros and Cons of Proposed Interventions to Promote Healthy Eating*, 27 AM. J. PREVENTIVE MED. 163, 169 (2003); Roland Strum *et al.*, *Soda Taxes, Soft Drink Consumption and Children's Body Mass Index*, 29 HEALTH AFFAIRS 1052 (2010); Ryan Edwards, *Commentary: Soda Taxes, Obesity, and the Shifty Behavior of Consumers*, 52 PREVENTIVE MED. 417 (2011); Maira Bes-Rastrollo *et al.*, *Impact of Sugars and Sugar Taxation on Body Weight Control: A Comprehensive Literature Review*, 24 OBESITY 1410 (2016).

47 *How Do State and Local Soda Taxes Work?*, TAX POLICY CENTER, www.taxpolicycenter.org/briefing-book/how-do-state-and-local-soda-taxes-work.

48 John Geluardi, *The Richmond Soda War*, EAST BAY EXPRESS (Oct. 24, 2012), https://eastbayexpress.com/the-richmond-soda-war-1/.

49 Caleb Nelson, *Preemption*, 86 VA. L. REV. 225 (2000).

50 Paul A. Diller, *Reorienting Home Rule: Part 2 – Remedying the Urban Disadvantage through Federalism and Localism*, 77 LA. L. REV. 1045 (2017); Sarah A. Roache *et al.*, *Big Food and Soda Versus Public Health: Industry Litigation against Local Government Regulations to Promote Healthy Diets*, 45 FORDHAM URB. L.J. 1051,

1062–1063 (2018); Laura Hoffman, *The Fight over Fizz: Soda Taxes as a Means of Curbing Childhood Obesity?*, 5 PITT. J. ENV'T & PUB. HEALTH L. 123 (2011).

51 Ariz. Rev. Stat. §§ 42-6004, 42-6015 (2016); Mich. Compiled L. §§ 135.123.711–135.123.713 (2017).

52 Cal. Rev. & Tax. Code § 7284-10 (2018).

53 Jacob Gershman, *How Sweet It Is: Lawsuit Accuses Honey Nut Cheerios of Deceptive Health Claims*, WALL ST. J. (Sep. 15, 2016), https://blogs.wsj.com/law/2016/09/15/how-sweet-it-is-class-action-alleges-honey-nut-cheerios-misleads-consumers/; *Truxel v. Gen. Mills Sales, Inc.*, No. C 16-04957 JSW, 2019 LEXIS 144871 (N.D. Cal. Aug. 13, 2019).

54 Ben & Jerry's, www.benjerry.com/.

55 Letter from Micahel F. Jacobson, Exec. Dir., Ctr. for Sci. in the Pub. Interest to Paul Polman, CEO, Unilever (Aug. 12, 2010), https://cspinet.org/sites/default/files/attachment/benandjerrysunileverletter.pdf.

56 April Fulton, *Ben & Jerry's Takes "All Natural" Claims off Ice Cream Labels*, NAT'L PUB. RADIO (Sep. 27, 2010), www.npr.org/sections/health-shots/2010/09/27/130158014/ben-jerry-s-takes-all-natural-claims-off-ice-cream-labels.

57 Melissa Mortazavi, *Tort as Democracy: Lessons from the Food Wars*, 57 ARIZ. L. REV. 929, 968–72 (2015).

58 Jennifer Lee, *Reading the Tea Leaves, Snapple Refreshes Itself*, N.Y. TIMES (Feb. 19, 2009), http://cityroom.blogs.nytimes.com/2009/02/19/reading-the-tea-leaves-snapple-refreshes-itself/?_php=true&_type=blogs&_r=0.

59 Jacques Wilson, *Kraft Changing Some Mac & Cheese Products*, CNN (Nov. 4, 2013), www.cnn.com/2013/11/01/health/kraft-macaroni-cheese-dyes/index.html; Martha C. White, *Kraft Reveals Revamped Mac and Cheese, 50 Million Boxes Later*, N.Y. TIMES (Mar. 20, 2016), www.nytimes.com/2016/03/21/business/media/kraft-reveals-revamped-mac-and-cheese-50-million-boxes-later.html; *Frequently Asked Questions*, KRAFT, www.kraftmacandcheese.com/faq; Paul Harries, *Kraft Meets with Bloggers Protesting Chemical Additives in Mac'n'Cheese*, THE GUARDIAN (Apr. 2, 2013), www.theguardian.com/business/2013/apr/02/kraft-bloggers-chemical-additives-macncheese.

60 Roni Caryn Rabin, *The Chemicals in Your Mac and Cheese*, N.Y. TIMES (Jul. 12, 2017), www.nytimes.com/2017/07/12/well/eat/the-chemicals-in-your-mac-and-cheese.html.

61 Corrado Rizzi, *Unhappy Cows: Ben & Jerry's Ice Cream Ingredients Are Not "Humanely" Sourced, Lawsuit Alleges*, CLASSACTION.ORG (Jul. 12, 2018), www.classaction.org/blog/unhappy-cows-ben-and-jerrys-ice-cream-ingredients-are-not-humanely-sourced-lawsuit-alleges.

62 Joe Satran, *Trader Joe's Lawsuit over "Evaporated Cane Juice" Part of Firm's Crusade against Mislabeled Foods*, HUFFINGTON POST (Mar. 31, 2013), www.huffpost.com/entry/trader-joes-lawsuit-evaporated-cane-juice_n_2980706. See e.g. *Kane v. Chobani, Inc.*, 973 F. Supp. 2d 1120 (N.D. Cal. 2014); *Gitson v. Trader Joe's Co.*, No. 13-cv-01333-WHO, 2013 LEXIS 144917 (N.D. Cal. Oct. 4, 2013); *Pratt v. Whole Food Market California, Inc.*, No. 5:12-cv-05652-EJD, 2015 LEXIS 134968 (N.D. Cal. Sep. 30, 2015).

63 FOOD AND DRUG ADMINISTRATION, *Ingredients Declared as Evaporated Cane Juice: Guidance for Industry* (2016); Melissa Mortazavi, *Tort as Democracy: Lessons from the Food Wars*, 57 ARIZ. L. REV. 929, 929–61 (2015).

64 World Health Organization, Evaluating Implementation of the WHO Set of Recommendations on the Marketing of Foods and Non-Alcoholic Beverages to Children (2018).

65 Marion Nestle, Soda Politics: Taking on Big Soda (and Winning) 157 (Oxford University Press 2015).

66 Children's Food and Beverage Advertising Initiative (CFBAI), BBB Nat'l Programs, www.bbbprograms.org/programs/cfbai.

67 Marion Nestle, Soda Politics: Taking on Big Soda (and Winning) 109 (Oxford University Press 2015).

68 Lorillard Tobacco Co. v. Reilly, 533 U.S. 525 (2001).

69 Ellen A. Black, Menu Labeling: The Unintended Consequences to the Consumer, 69 Food Drug L.J. 531, 532–33 (2014); Dale Junkel et al., Solution or Smokescreen? Evaluating Industry Self-Regulation of Televised Food Marketing to Children, 19 Comm. L. & Pol'y 264, 275–79 (2014).

70 Angela J. Campbell, Rethinking Children's Advertising Policies for the Digital Age, 29 Loy. Consumer L. Rev. 1, 11, 33–35 (2016); Dale Junkel et al., Solution or Smokescreen? Evaluating Industry Self-Regulation of Televised Food Marketing to Children, 19 Comm. L. & Pol'y 264, 285 (2014).

71 David Adam Friedman, Public Health Regulation and the Limits of Paternalism, 46 Conn. L. Rev. 1687, 1720 (2014).

72 Tools for Schools: Focusing on Smart Snacks, USDA (Aug. 22, 2019), www.fns.usda .gov/cn/tools-schools-focusing-smart-snacks.

73 Dominique G. Ruggieri & Sarah B. Bass, A Comprehensive Review of School-Based Body Mass Index Screening Programs and Their Implications for School Health: Do the Controversies Accurately Reflect the Research?, 85 J. Sch. Health 61 (2015).

74 Wanting Lin et al., The Association between State Physical Education Laws and Student Physical Activity, 58 Am. J. Preventive Med. 436 (2020).

75 Andrew Condiles, How Voluntary Is Voluntary: Designing Wellness Programs to Fit the Participant, 18 Appalachian. J. L. 1 (2018); Zachary Maciejewski, Saving Money on Health Insurance Just Got a Lot Easier … Or Did It? The Preserving Employee Wellness Programs Act and Its Impact on the Future of Employee Health, 95 Ind. J. L. Supp. 28 (2019).

76 Childhood obesity rates were high in 2019 (19.3 percent) and significantly increased during the pandemic (22.4 percent). Martha Njolomole, CDC: School Closures Accelerated Weight Gain and Obesity among Kids, American Experiment (Sep. 21, 2021), www.americanexperiment.org/cdc-school-closures-accelerated-weight-gain-and-obesity-among-kids.

Chapter 6

1 See Yochai Benkler, The Wealth of Nations: How Social Production Transforms Markets and Freedom (Yale University Press 2006).

2 Tim Wu, The Attention Merchants: The Epic Scramble to Get Inside Our Heads (First Vintage Books 2017).

3 Many scholars wrote work that contributed to the emergence of that movement. For a small sampling, which includes some of the earlier work, see e.g. Daniel Solove, Conceptualizing Privacy, 90 Cal. L. Rev. 1087 (2002); Julie Cohen, Examined Lives: Informational Privacy and the Subject as Object, 52 Stan. L. Rev. 1373

(2000); Anita Allen, *Coercing Privacy*, 40 WILLIAM. & MARY L. REV. 723 (1999); Paul Schwartz, *Privacy and Democracy in Cyberspace*, 52 VAND. L. REV. 1609 (1999).

4 Casey Newton, *In a Leaked Memo, Facebook Executive Describes the Consequences of Its Growth-at-all Costs Mentality*, THE VERGE (Mar. 29, 2022), www.theverge .com/2018/3/29/17178086/facebook-growth-memo-leak-boz-andrew-bosworth.

5 *Meta Reports Fourth Quarter and Full Year 2021 Results*, PR NEWSWIRE (Feb. 2, 2022), https://investor.fb.com/investor-news/press-release-details/2022/ Meta-Reports-Fourth-Quarter-and-Full-Year-2021-Results/default.aspx.

6 Salvador Rodriguez, *Instagram Surpasses 2 Billion Monthly Users While Powering through a Year of Turmoil*, CNBC (Dec. 14, 2021), www.cnbc.com/2021/12/14/ instagram-surpasses-2-billion-monthly-users.html.

7 David Prosser, *How Cooby Plans to Make WhatsApp Work Better for Businesses*, FORBES (Mar. 7, 2022), www.forbes.com/sites/davidprosser/2022/03/07/how-cooby-plans-to-make-whatsapp-work-better-for-businesses/?sh=4d5066662ad3.

8 ROGER MCNAMEE, ZUCKED: WAKING UP TO THE FACEBOOK CATASTROPHE 89 (Penguin Publishing Group 2019).

9 *See e.g.* Lawrence Lessig, *Open Code and Open Societies: Values of Internet Governance*, 74 CHI.-KENT L. REV. 1405 (1999).

10 Brief for Amicus Curiae Law Professors & Scholars in Support of Appellee, *Authors Guild v. Google, Inc.*, No. 13-4829-CV, 2014 WL 3556331 at 1 (2d Cir. July 10, 2014); Brief of Digital Humanities and Law Scholars as Amici Curiae in Support of Defendant-Appellees, *Authors Guild v. Google, Inc.*, No. 13-4829-CV, 2014 WL 3556331 at 1 (2d Cir. July 10, 2014). *See also* RANA FOROOHAR, DON'T BE EVIL: THE CASE AGAINST BIG TECH (Currency 2019).

11 Spyros Kokolakis, *Privacy Attitudes and Privacy Behavior: A Review of Current Research on the Privacy Paradox Phenomenon*, 64 COMPUTERS & SEC. 122 (2017).

12 Betsy Schiffman, *Facebook CEO Apologizes, Lets Users Turn off Beacon*, WIRED (Dec. 5, 2007), www.wired.com/2007/12/facebook-ceo-apologizes-lets-users-turn-off-beacon/.

13 *Lane v. Facebook, Inc.*, No. C 08-3845 RS, 2009 WL 3458198 at *1 (N.D. Cal. Oct. 23, 2009).

14 Mark Zuckerberg, *Thoughts on Beacon*, FACEBOOK (Mar. 14, 2021), www .facebook.com/notes/facebook/thoughts-on-beacon/7584397130/.

15 *Our Mission*, META, https://about.facebook.com/company-info/.

16 *Our Mission*, META, https://about.facebook.com/company-info/.

17 *Purpose and Vision*, THE COCA-COLA COMPANY, www.coca-colacompany.com/ company/purpose-and-vision.

18 Mark Zuckerberg, *Bringing the World Together*, FACEBOOK (Jun. 22, 2017), www .facebook.com/notes/mark-zuckerberg/bringing-the-world-closer-together/ 10154944663901634/.

19 Susan P. Crawford, *Shortness of Vision: Regulatory Ambition in the Digital Age*, 74 FORDHAM L. REV. 695, 741–43 (2005); Jonathan L. Zittrain, *The Generative Internet*, 119 HARV. L. REV. 1974 (2006).

20 Harry Davies, *Ted Cruz Using Firm That Harvested Data on Millions of Unwitting Facebook Users*, THE GUARDIAN (Dec. 11, 2015), www.theguardian.com/us-news/ 2015/dec/11/senator-ted-cruz-president-campaign-facebook-user-data.

21 Matthew Rosenberg, Nicholas Confessore, & Carole Cadwalladr, *How Trump Consultants Exploited the Facebook Data of Millions*, N.Y. TIMES

(Mar. 17, 2018), www.nytimes.com/2018/03/17/us/politics/cambridge-analytica-trump-campaign.html.

22 Nick Statt, *Mark Zuckerberg Apologizes for Facebook's Data Privacy Scandal in Full-Page Newspaper Ads*, THE VERGE (Mar. 25, 2018), www.theverge.com/2018/3/25/17161398/facebook-mark-zuckerberg-apology-cambridge-analytica-full-page-newspapers-ads.

23 ROGER MCNAMEE, *ZUCKED: WAKING UP TO THE FACEBOOK CATASTROPHE* 120–49 (Penguin Publishing Group 2019).

24 Jefferson Graham, *Facebook Apologizes for Text Spam for 2FA Users: Here's How to Secure Your Account Wisely*, USA TODAY (Feb. 18, 2018), www.usatoday.com/story/tech/talkingtech/2018/02/16/how-secure-your-facebook-account-and-prevent-facebook-spamming-you-texts/345483002/.

25 Gabriel J. X. Dance et al., *Facebook Gave Device Makers Deep Access to Data on Users and Friends*, N.Y. TIMES (Jun. 3, 2018), www.nytimes.com/interactive/2018/06/03/technology/facebook-device-partners-users-friends-data.html.

26 Cecilia Kang, *FTC Approves Facebook Fine of about $5 Billion*, N.Y. TIMES (Jul. 12, 2019), www.nytimes.com/2019/07/12/technology/facebook-ftc-fine.html.

27 Tony Romm, *"It's about Time": Facebook Faces First Lawsuit from U.S. Regulators after Cambridge Analytica Scandal*, WASH. POST (Dec. 18, 2018), www.washingtonpost.com/technology/2018/12/19/dc-attorney-general-sues-facebook-over-alleged-privacy-violations-cambridge-analytica-scandal/; Cecilia Kang, *FTC Approves Facebook Fine of about $5 Billion* (Jul. 12, 2019), www.nytimes.com/2019/07/12/technology/facebook-ftc-fine.html; *Attorney General v. Facebook*, 2020 WL 742136 at *1 (Sup. Ct. of Mass. 2020); *In re. Facebook Biometric Information Privacy Litigation*, 185 F. Supp. 3d 1155 (N.D. Cal. 2016); Danielle Keats Citron, *The Privacy Policymaking of State Attorney Generals*, 92 NOTRE DAME L. REV. 747 (2016).

28 Jeff John Roberts, *Facebook Has Been Hit by Dozens of Data Lawsuits. And This Could Just Be the Beginning*, FORTUNE (Apr. 30, 2018), https://fortune.com/2018/04/30/facebook-data-lawsuits/.

29 *Williams v. Facebook, Inc.*, 384 F. Supp. 3d 1043 (N.D. Cal. 2018).

30 *Lundy v. Facebook, Inc.*, No. 18-cv-06793-JD, 2021 WL 4503071 at *1 (N.D. Cal. Sep. 30, 2021).

31 Jonathan Stempel, *Meta's Facebook to Pay $90 Million to Settle Privacy Lawsuit over User Tracking*, REUTERS (Feb. 15, 2022), www.reuters.com/technology/metas-facebook-pay-90-million-settle-privacy-lawsuit-over-user-tracking-2022-02-15.

32 Herb Weisbaum, *Trust in Facebook Has Dropped by 66 Percent since the Cambridge Analytica Scandal*, NBC NEWS (Apr. 11, 2018), www.nbcnews.com/business/consumer/trust-facebook-has-dropped-51-percent-cambridge-analytica-scandal-n867011.

33 In an NBC News/Wall Street Journal poll, 60 percent of those surveyed said they don't trust the company at all to protect personal information. Mark Murray, *Poll: Americans Give Social Media a Clear Thumbs-Down*, NBC NEWS (Apr. 5, 2019), www.nbcnews.com/politics/meet-the-press/poll-americans-give-social-media-clear-thumbs-down-n991086.

34 Chloe Watson, *The Key Moments from Mark Zuckerberg's Testimony to Congress*, THE GUARDIAN (Apr. 11, 2018), www.theguardian.com/technology/2018/apr/11/mark-zuckerbergs-testimony-to-congress-the-key-moments.

35 *See* LARRY LESSIG, *CODE: AND OTHER LAW OF CYBERSPACE* (Basic Books 1999).

36 On the dilemma of applying old law to new technologies or crafting specialized laws, *see* Gaia Bernstein, *Toward a General Theory of Law and Technology, Introduction*, 8 MINN. J. L. SCI. & TECH. 441 (2007); Andrea M. Matwyshyn, *Commerce, Development, Identity*, 8 MINN. J. L. SCI & TECH. 515 (2007); Gregory M. Mandel, *History Lessons for a General Theory of Law and Technology*, 8 MINN. J. L., SCI. & TECH. 551 (2007).

37 Kevin Maney, *The Law Can't Keep Up with Technology... and That's a Very Good Thing*, NEWSWEEK (Oct. 31, 2015), www.newsweek.com/government-gets-slower-tech-gets-faster-389073; Mark Fenwick *et al.*, *Regulation Tomorrow: What Happens When Technology Is Faster than the Law?*, 6 AM. UNIV. BUS. L. REV. 561 (2017).

38 Lyria Bennett Moses, *Recurring Dilemmas: The Law's Race to Keep up with Technological Change*, 7 U. ILL. J. L. TECH., & POL'Y 239 (2007).

39 Howard A. Shelanski, *Information, Innovation, and Competition Policy for the Internet*, 161 UNIV. PA. L. REV. 1663 (2013).

40 *See* Neil Weinstock Netanel, *Cyberspace Self-Governance: A Skeptical View from Liberal Democratic Theory*, 88 CAL. L. REV. 395 (2000) (analyzing the argument).

41 *See* Jay P. Kesan & Carol M. Hayes, *Liability for Data Injuries*, 2019 UNIV. ILL. L. REV. 295 (2019). On obstacles to privacy protection, *see* Felix T. Wu, *How Privacy Distorted Standing Law*, 66 DEPAUL L. REV. (2017).

42 On privacy and free speech, *see generally*: Neil M. Richards, *Reconciling Data Privacy and the First Amendment*, 52 UCLA L. REV. 1149 (2005); Danielle Keats Citron & Mary Anne Franks, *The Internet as a Speech Machine and Other Myths Confounding Section 230 Reform*, UNIVERSITY OF CHICAGO LEGAL FORUM, 45 (2020).

43 *Art. 3 GDPR Territorial Scope*, GENERAL DATA PROTECTION REGULATION, https://gdpr.eu/article-3-requirements-of-handling-personal-data-of-subjects-in-the-union/ (defining GDPR's territorial scope); Daphne Keller, *The Right Tools: Europe's Intermediary Liability Laws and the EU 2016 General Data Protection Regulation*, 33 BERKELEY TECH. L.J. 297, 347–48 (2018).

44 *See e.g.* Michael L. Rustad & Thomas H. Koenig, *Towards a Global Data Privacy Standard*, 71 FLA. L. REV. 18 (2019); Julie Brill, *Microsoft's Commitment to GDPR, Privacy and Putting Customers in Control of Their Own Data*, MICROSOFT (May 21, 2018), https://blogs.microsoft.com/on-the-issues/2018/05/21/microsofts-commitment-to-gdpr-privacy-and-putting-customers-in-control-of-their-own-data/.

45 CAL. CIV. CODE § 1798.100 (2018); Thorin Klosowski, *The State of Consumer Data Privacy Laws in the US (And Why It Matters)*, N.Y. TIMES (Sep. 6, 2021), www.nytimes.com/wirecutter/blog/state-of-privacy-laws-in-us/.

46 Ira S. Rubinstein, *Privacy Localism*, 94 WASH. L. REV. 101 (2018); Kristine Roach *et al.*, *Municipal Drone Policy*, SSRN (Apr. 30, 2018), https://papers.ssrn.com/sol3/papers.cfm?abstract_id=3168866.

47 S.F., Ca., S.F. Charter §16.130.

48 Jeffrey Mays, *New York City to Consider Banning Sale of Cellphone Location Data* (Jul. 23, 2019), www.nytimes.com/2019/07/23/nyregion/cellphone-tracking-location-data.html.

49 Lauren Feiner, *CEOs from Amazon, IBM, Salesforce and More Ask Congress to Pass a Consumer Data Privacy Law*, CNBC (Sep. 10, 2019), www.cnbc.com/2019/09/10/business-roundtable-urges-congress-to-pass-consumer-data-privacy-law.html.

50 Neil Richards, *Why Privacy Matters* (Oxford University Press 2021); Ari Ezra Waldman, *Industry Unbound: The Inside Story of Privacy Data and Corporate Power* (Cambridge University Press 2021); Frank Pasquale, *The Black Society: The Secret Algorithms that Control Money and Information* (Harvard University Press 2016); Neil Richards & Woodrow Hartzog, *A Duty of Loyalty for Privacy Law*, 99 *Wash. Univ. L. Rev.* 961 (2021).

Chapter 7

1 Richard Delgado & Jean Stefancic, *Must We Defend Nazis? Why the First Amendment Should Not Protect Hate Speech and White Supremacy* (New York University Press 2018); Jane R. Bambauer, *Snake Oil Speech*, 93 *Wash. L. Rev.* 73 (2018); Catharine A. MacKinnon, *Weaponizing the First Amendment: An Equality Reading*, 106 *Va. L. Rev.* 1223 (2020).

2 Ashutosh Bhagwat, *When Speech Is Not Speech*, 78 *Ohio State L.J.* 839, 845 (2017). It started with a Supreme Court decision that defined a cable television selection to include or not include broadcasting of local channels as speech. *Turner Broad Sys. v. F.C.C.*, 512 U.S. 622, 626 (1994).

3 *Brown v. Ent. Merchants*, 546 U.S. 786 (2011).

4 *Watters v. TSR, Inc.*, 904 F.2d 378 (6th Cir. 1990) (plaintiff argued that Dungeons and Dragons manufacturer was liable for son's suicide); Kyle Langvardt, *Regulating Habit-Forming Technology*, 88 *Fordham L. Rev.* 129, 167 (2019).

5 Kyle Langvardt, *Regulating Habit-Forming Technology*, 88 *Fordham L. Rev.* 129, 179 (2019); Ashutosh Bhagwat, *When Speech Is Not Speech*, 78 *Ohio State L.J.* 839, 845 (2017).

6 *See* Jane Bambauer, *Is Data Speech?*, 66 *Stan. L. Rev.* 57 (2014); Kyle Langvardt, *Regulating Habit-Forming Technology*, 88 *Fordham L. Rev.* 129, 184–85 (2019).

7 Alexis R. Auricella *et al.*, *Young Children's Screen Time: The Complex Role of Parent and Child Factors*, 36 *J. Applied Developmental Psych.* 11(2015); Jörg Matthes *et al.*, *Fighting over Smartphones? Parents' Excessive Smartphone Use, Lack of Control over Children's Use, and Conflict*, 116 *Computers in Human Behavior* 106618 (2021).

8 Matthew A. Lapierre & Meleah N. Lewis, *Should It Stay or Should It Go Now? Smartphones and Relational Health*, 7 *Psych. Popular Media Culture* 348 (2018); Mandy Oaklander, *How Your Smartphone Is Ruining Your Relationship*, TIME (Apr. 28, 2016), https://time.com/4311202/smartphone-relationship-cell-phone/.

9 Jeremy Bauer-Wolf, *Will Parents of College Students Who Died from Hazing Change Federal Law?*, Higher Educ. Dive (Oct. 28, 2019), www.highereddive.com/news/parents-lobby-for-anti-hazing-bill/565684/.

10 *Wait Until 8th*, www.waituntil8th.org/.

11 *Creating Community to Navigate Screen Time*, Screen Time Action Network, https://screentimenetwork.org; *Join the Dedicated Community of Advocates in the Screen Time Action Network*, Screen Time Action Network, https://fairplayforkids.org/screen-time-action-network/.

12 Richard H. Thaler & Cass R. Sunstein, *Nudge: Improving Decisions about Health, Wealth and Happiness* 6 (Penguin Group 2008).

13 David Adam Friedman, *Public Health Regulation and the Limits of Paternalism*, 46 *Conn. L. Rev.* 1687, 1698–99, 1705 (2014).

14 Richard H. Thaler & Cass R. Sunstein, *Nudge: Improving Decisions about Health, Wealth and Happiness* 5 (Penguin Group 2008); Julian Le Grand, *Government Paternalism: Nanny State or Helpful Friend* 105 (Princeton University Press 2015).

15 Julian Le Grand, *Government Paternalism: Nanny State or Helpful Friend* 105 (Princeton University Press 2015).

16 Julian Le Grand, *Government Paternalism: Nanny State or Helpful Friend* 111 (Princeton University Press 2015).

17 Julian Le Grand, *Government Paternalism: Nanny State or Helpful Friend* 105 (Princeton University Press 2015).

18 Zak Doffman, *Facebook's Bizarre Response to Privacy Scandals? New Pop-up Cafés*, Forbes (Aug. 27, 2019), www.forbes.com/sites/zakdoffman/2019/08/17/new-facebook-cafs-will-offer-privacy-check-ups-over-free-cappuccinos/#7d5df9613e95.

19 Jenna Wortham, *Obama Brought Silicon Valley to Washington*, N.Y. Times (Oct. 25, 2016), www.nytimes.com/2016/10/30/magazine/barack-obama-brought-silicon-valley-to-washington-is-that-a-good-thing.html; Sheelah Kolhatkar, *Lina Khan's Battle to Rein in Big Tech*, The New Yorker (Nov. 29, 2021), www.newyorker.com/magazine/2021/12/06/lina-khans-battle-to-rein-in-big-tech.

Chapter 8

1 Woodrow Hartzog, *Privacy's Blueprint: The Battle to Control the Design of New Technologies* 143 (Harvard University Press 2018). *See also* Lauren E. Willis, *Deception by Design*, 34 Harv. J. L. & Tech. 116, 121–51 (2020).

2 Woodrow Hartzog, *Privacy's Blueprint: The Battle to Control the Design of New Technologies* 35 (Harvard University Press 2018).

3 Woodrow Hartzog, *Privacy's Blueprint: The Battle to Control the Design of New Technologies* 134, 143–44 (Harvard University Press 2018).

4 Sigmund Freud, *The Ego and the Id* 25 (James Strachey ed., Joan Riviere trans., Hogarth Press 1927 [1923]).

5 Olga Khazan, *When Trans Fats Were Healthy*, The Atlantic (Nov. 8, 2013), www.theatlantic.com/health/archive/2013/11/when-trans-fats-were-healthy/281274/.

6 David Schleifer, *The Perfect Solution: How Trans Fats Became the Healthy Replacement for Saturated Fats*, 53 Tech & Culture 94 (2012).

7 Patricia V. Johnston, Ogden C. Johnson, & Fred. E. Kummerow, *Occurrence of Trans Fatty Acids in Human Tissue*, 126 Sci. 698 (1957); Brady Dennis, *Fred Kummerow, U. of I. Professor Who Fought against Trans Fats, Dies at 102*, Chi. Trib. (Jun. 2, 2017), www.chicagotribune.com/news/obituaries/ct-fred-kummerow-obituary-wapo-met-20170602-story.html; Katie Hafner, *Fred A. Kummerow, an Early Opponent of Trans Fats, Dies at 102*, N.Y. Times (Jun. 1, 2017), www.nytimes.com/2017/06/01/science/fred-kummerow-dead-biochemist-ban-trans-fatty-acids.html.

8 Brady Dennis, *Fred Kummerow, U. of I. Professor Who Fought against Trans Fats, Dies at 102*, Chi. Trib. (Jun. 2, 2017), www.chicagotribune.com/news/obituaries/ct-fred-kummerow-obituary-wapo-met-20170602-story.html; *Compl., Kummerow v. U.S. FDA, et al.*, No. 2:13CV02180, 2013 WL 4037924 (C.D. Ill. 2016).

9 *Trans Fat Is Double Trouble for Heart Health*, Mayo Clinic (Feb. 23, 2022), www.mayoclinic.org/diseases-conditions/high-blood-cholesterol/in-depth/trans-fat/art-20046114; David Resnik, *Trans Fat Bans and Human Freedom*, 10 Am. J. Bioethics 27 (2010).

10 Dariush Mozaffarian *et al.*, *Trans Fatty Acids and Cardiovascular Disease*, 354 New Eng. J. Med. 1601 (2006).

11 Marian Burros, *KFC Is Sued over the Use of Trans Fats in Its Cooking*, N.Y. Times A16 (Jun. 14, 2006); *Burger King Sued over Trans Fat in Oil*, L.A. Times (May 17, 2007), www.latimes.com/archives/la-xpm-2007-may-17-fi-fat17-story.html; Molly Selvin, *Lawyer Who Took on Oreos and McDonald's Fights on in Food War*, L.A. Times (Sep. 25, 2005), www.latimes.com/archives/la-xpm-2005-sep-25-fi-trans fat25-story.html.

12 *Food Labeling: Trans Fatty Acids in Nutrition Labeling, Nutrient Content Claims, and Health Claims*, 68 Fed. Reg. 41, 434 (Jan. 1, 2006) (codified at 21 CFR § 101.9 (c)(2)(i)).

13 *Shining the Spotlight on Trans Fats*, Harv. T.H. Chan Sch. Pub. Health: Nutrition Source, www.hsph.harvard.edu/nutritionsource/what-should-you-eat/fats-and-cholesterol/types-of-fat/transfats/.

14 *CDC Study Finds Levels of Trans-Fatty Acids in Blood of U.S. White Adults Has Decreased*, CDC Newsroom (Feb. 8, 2012), www.cdc.gov/media/releases/2012/p0208_trans-fatty_acids.html; Vivien L. Hendry *et al.*, *Impact of Regulatory Interventions to Reduce Intake of Artificial Trans-Fatty Acids: A Systematic Review*, 105 Am. J. Pub. Health e32 (2015) (additional studies affirmed the impact of trans-fat labeling requirements, but acknowledged the added effect of certain local authorities' regulations limiting trans-fat use by restaurants).

15 Joanne F. Guthrie *et al.*, "What People Know and Do Not Know about Nutrition," in Food & Rural Econ. Div., Econ. Rsch. Serv., USDA, Agric. Info. Bull. No. 750, America's Eating Habits: Changes and Consequences 243 (1999), www.ers.usda.gov/webdocs/publications/42215/5842_aib750m_1_.pdf?v=0.

16 Int'l Food Info. Council Found., 2008 Food & Health Survey: Consumer Attitudes Toward Food, Nutrition & Health 29–31 (2008), https://foodinsight.org/wp-content/uploads/2009/10/IFICFdn2008FoodandHealthSurvey.pdf.

17 Fadar O. Otite *et al.*, *Trends in Trans Fatty Acids Reformulations of US Supermarket and Brand-Name Foods from 2007 through 2011*, 10 Preventing Chronic Disease (2013), www.cdc.gov/pcd/issues/2013/12_0198.htm; Dariush Mozaffarian *et al.*, *Food Reformulations to Reduce Trans Fatty Acids*, 362 New Eng. J. Med. 2037 (2010); Sabrina Tavernise, *F.D.A. Ruling Would All But Eliminate Tran Fats*, N.Y. Times (Nov. 7, 2013), www.nytimes.com/2013/11/08/health/fda-trans-fats.html. Some studies showed that reduction of trans-fat was not consistent across products and through time; *see e.g.* Emily Y. Wang *et al.*, *The Impact of Mandatory Trans Fat Labeling on Product Mix and Consumer Choice: A Longitudinal Analysis of the US Market for Margarine and Spreads*, 64 Food Pol'y 63 (2016).

18 *FDA Takes Step to Remove Artificial Trans Fats in Processed Foods: Action Expected to Prevent Thousands of Fatal Heart Attacks*, ScienceDaily (Jun. 16, 2015), www.sciencedaily.com/releases/2015/06/150616160256.htm.

19 Brady Dennis, *Fred Kummerow, U. of I. Professor Who Fought against Trans Fat, Dies at 102*, Chi. Trib. (Jun. 2, 2017), www.chicagotribune.com/news/obituaries/ct-fred-kummerow-obituary-wapo-met-20170602-story.html.

20 *See* Ari Ezra Waldman, *Industry Unbound: The Inside Story of Privacy Data and Corporate Power* (Cambridge University Press 2021).

21 Woodrow Hartzog, *Privacy's Blueprint: The Battle to Control the Design of New Technologies* 23 (Harvard University Press 2018); Gaia Bernstein, *When New Technologies Are Still New: Windows of Opportunity for Privacy Protection*, 51 Vill. L. Rev. 921 (2006).

22 Julie E. Cohen, *Cyberspace as/and Space*, 107 Colum. L. Rev. 210, 225–27 (2007); Steve Woolgar, "Configuring the User: The Case of Usability Trials," in *A Sociology of Monsters: Essays on Power, Technology, and Domination* 59, 67–69 (John Law ed., Routledge 1991).

23 Ari Ezra Waldman, *Privacy's Law of Design*, 9 U.C. Irvine L. Rev. 1239, 1252–57 (2019).

24 Wiebe E. Bijker, *Of Bicycles, Bakelites, and Bulbs: Toward a Theory of Sociotechnical Change* 19–100 (MIT Press 1995).

25 Cass R. Sunstein, *How Change Happens* 125 (MIT Press 2019). People do often add apps, though, to replace default apps that come preloaded on a device. For example, iPhone users often install Google Chrome and Google Maps, although they could use Safari or Apple Maps.

26 Lauren Willis, *When Nudges Fail: Slippery Defaults*, 80 U. Chi. L. Rev. 1144 (2013); Lauren Willis, *Why Not Privacy by Default?* 29 Berk. Tech L.J. 61 (2014).

27 Tom Knowles, *I'm So Sorry, Says Inventor of Endless Online Scrolling*, The Times (Apr. 27, 2019), www.thetimes.co.uk/article/i-m-so-sorry-says-inventor-of-endless-online-scrolling-9lrv59mdk.

28 Omri Levi, *Cellular Phone with the Rabbi's Stamp: The Story of the Phone for the Ultra-Orthodox*, Ynet (Jan. 6, 2009), www.ynet.co.il/articles/0,7340,L-3650344,00.html (in Hebrew); Nechama Almog, *Samsung Has Launched Smartphones for the Ultra-Orthodox Sector*, People & Computers (Jun. 1, 2016), www.pc.co.il/featured/216020/ (in Hebrew); Yair Etinger, *Rabbi Elyashiv: Ultra-Orthodox Schools Will Not Admit Students Whose Parents Do Not Have a Kosher Phone*, Haaretz (Sep. 6, 2011), www.haaretz.co.il/1.1383251 (in Hebrew); Nathan Jeffay, *Kosher Smart Phone Arrives as Ultra-Orthodox Tech Taboo Shifts*, Forward (Sep. 18, 2013), https://forward.com/news/184099/kosher-smart-phone-arrives-as-ultra-orthodox-tech/?p=all.

29 *The Light Phone: Frequently Asked Questions*, www.thelightphone.com/faq.

30 Cass R. Sunstein, *How Change Happens* 155, 211–14 (MIT Press 2019).

31 Congress for the New Urbanism, *Charter of the New Urbanism*, www.cnu.org/who-we-are/charter-new-urbanism.

32 Rose Palazzolo, *Smokers Rally in New York to Protest Ban*, ABC News (Jan. 6, 2006), https://abcnews.go.com/Health/story?id=117545&page=1; Michael Brick, *Waiting to Inhale*, N.Y. Times (Jan. 4, 2004), www.nytimes.com/2004/01/04/nyregion/waiting-to-inhale.html; *Italians Fume over Cigarette Curb*, BBC News (Jan. 10, 2005), http://news.bbc.co.uk/2/hi/europe/4159587.stm.

33 Bin Jiang et al., *How to Waste a Break: Using Portable Electronic Devices Substantially Counteracts Attention Enhancement Effects of Green Spaces*, 51 Env't & Behav. 1133 (2018).

34 Cailey Rizzo, *These Hotels Are Making Guests VIPs If They Agree to Put Away Their Phones*, Travel + Leisure (Oct. 5, 2018), www.travelandleisure.com/hotels-resorts/wyndham-grand-phone-free-zones.

35 Carolina A. Miranda, *Why Can't We Take Pictures in Art Museums?*, ARTnews (May 13, 2013), www.artnews.com/art-news/news/photography-in-art-museums-2222/; Jay L. Zagorsky, *Why Taking Photographs Is Banned in Many Museums and Historic Places*, Observer (Oct. 12, 2016), https://observer.com/2016/10/why-taking-photographs-is-banned-in-many-museums-and-historic-places/.

36 Alex Ledsom, *The Mobile Phone Ban in French Schools, One Year On. Would It Work Elsewhwere?*, FORBES (Aug. 30, 2019), www.forbes.com/sites/alexledsom/2019/08/30/the-mobile-phone-ban-in-french-schools-one-year-on-would-it-work-else where/?sh=318329ae5e70; Abigail Johnson Hess, *Research Continually Shows How Distracting Cell Phones Are – So Some Schools Want to Ban Them*, CNBC (Apr. 2, 2019), www.cnbc.com/2019/01/18/research-shows-that-cell-phones-distract-stu dents–so-france-banned-them-in-school–.html.

Chapter 9

1 Nellie Bowles, *A Dark Consensus about Screens and Kids Begins to Emerge in Silicon Valley*, N.Y. TIMES (Oct. 26, 2018), www.nytimes.com/2018/10/26/style/ phones-children-silicon-valley.html; Nellie Bowles, *Silicon Valley Nannies Are Phone Police for Kids*, N.Y. TIMES (Oct. 26, 2018), www.nytimes.com/2018/10/ 26/style/silicon-valley-nannies.html; Emily Retter, *Billionaire Tech Mogul Bill Gates Reveals He Banned His Children from Mobile Phones until They Turned 14*, MIRROR (Jun. 27, 2018), www.mirror.co.uk/tech/billionaire-tech-mogul-bill-gates-10265298; Matt Richtel, *A Silicon Valley School That Doesn't Compute*, N.Y. TIMES (Oct. 22, 2011), www.nytimes.com/2011/10/23/technology/at-waldorf-school-in-silicon-valley-technology-can-wait.html.

2 Bianca Bosker, *The Binge Breaker: Tristan Harris Believes Silicon Valley Is Addicting Us to Our Phones. He's Determined to Make It Stop*, THE ATLANTIC (Nov. 2016), www.theatlantic.com/magazine/archive/2016/11/the-binge-breaker/ 501122/.

3 Bianca Bosker, *The Binge Breaker: Tristan Harris Believes Silicon Valley Is Addicting Us to Our Phones. He's Determined to Make It Stop*, THE ATLANTIC (Nov. 2016), www.theatlantic.com/magazine/archive/2016/11/the-binge-breaker/ 501122/.

4 Jeanne Fromer, *Expressive Incentives in Intellectual Property*, 98 VIRGINIA L. REV. 1745 (2012); Richard H. McAdams, *The Legal Construction of Norms: A Focal Point Theory of Expressive Law*, 86 VA. L. REV. 1649 (2000); Cass R. Sunstein, *On the Expressive Function of the Law*, 144 UNIV. OF PA. L. REV. 2021 (1996).

5 RICHARD H. THALER & CASS R. SUNSTEIN, NUDGE: IMPROVING DECISIONS ABOUT HEALTH, WEALTH, AND HAPPINESS (Yale University Press 2008).

6 Scholars researching the effectiveness of disclosures found many cases in which disclosures were made ineffectively, but also concluded that disclosures can be effective if done the right way. *See e.g.* Alessandro Aqcuisiti *et al.*, *Privacy and Human Behavior Age of Information*, 347 SCI. 509 (2015); OMRI BEN-SHAHAR & CARL E. SCHNEIDER, MORE THAN YOU WANTED TO KNOW: THE FAILURE OF MANDATED DISCLOSURE (Princeton University Press 2014); Lauren E. Wills, *Performance-Based Consumer Law*, 82 CHICAGO L. REV. 1309 (2015).

7 Florencia Marotta-Wurgler, *Does Contract Disclosure Matter?*, 168 J. INSTITUTIONAL AND THEORETICAL ECON. 94 (2012).

8 ARCHON FUNG *et al.*, FULL DISCLOSURE: THE PERILS AND PROMISE OF TRANSPARENCY 84–121 (Cambridge University Press 2007).

9 Ryan Bubb, *YMI? Why the Optimal Architecture of Disclosure Remains TBD*, 113 MICH. L. REV. 1021, 1029–30 (2015).

10 Christine Jolls, *Debiasing through Law and the First Amendment*, 67 STAN. L. REV. 1411, 1418–22 (2015); Alexia Brunet Marks, *Taming America's Sugar Rush: A Traffic-Light Label Approach*, 62 ARIZ. L. REV. 683 (2020).

11 ARCHON FUNG et al., *FULL DISCLOSURE: THE PERILS AND PROMISE OF TRANSPARENCY* 56–57 (Cambridge University Press 2007).

12 Sherry Emery et al., *The Effects of Smoking-Related Television Advertising on Smoking and Intentions to Quit among Adults in the United States: 1999–2007*, 102 AM. J. PUB. HEALTH 751 (2012); Rebecca Murphy-Hoefer et al., *Impact of the Tips from Former Smokers Campaign on Population-Level Smoking Cessation, 2012–2015*, 15 PREVENTING CHRONIC DISEASE 1 (2018); OFFICE ON SMOKING AND HEALTH, PREVENTING TOBACCO USE AMONG YOUTH AND YOUNG ADULTS: A REPORT OF THE SURGEON GENERAL (Centers for Disease Control and Prevention (US) 2012).

13 DONALD G. GIFFORD, *SUING THE TOBACCO AND LEAD PIGMENT INDUSTRIES: GOVERNMENT LITIGATION AS PUBLIC HEALTH PRESCRIPTION* 121–32; 171–85 (University of Michigan Press 2010); Rebecca Murphy-Hoefer et al., *Impact of the Tips from Former Smokers Campaign on Population-Level Smoking Cessation, 2012–2015*, 15 PREVENTING CHRONIC DISEASE 1 (2018).

14 David Gianatasio, *Ex-Smokers Fight for Dignity in CDC's Brutal New Anti-Smoking Ads*, ADWEEK (Mar. 19, 2012), www.adweek.com/creativity/ex-smokers-fight-dignity-cdcs-brutal-new-anti-smoking-ads-139063/.

15 *More than 100,000 Americans Quit Smoking Due to National Media Campaign*, CTR. FOR DISEASE CONTROL AND PREVENTION (Sep. 9, 2013), www.cdc.gov/media/releases/2013/p0909-tips-campaign-results.html; *Impact of First Federally Anti-Smoking Ad Campaign Remains Strong after Three Years*, CTR. FOR DISEASE CONTROL AND PREVENTION (Mar. 24, 2016), www.cdc.gov/media/releases/2016/p0324-anti-smoking.html.

16 Public Health Cigarette Smoking Act of 1969, 15 USC §§ 1331–38 (1970).

17 Yeoman Lowbrown, *12 Memorable American TV Commercials of the 1970s*, FLASHBAK (Sep. 29, 2014), https://flashbak.com/12-memorable-american-tv-commercials-of-the-1970s-21340/.

18 *Children: Food*, ADVERT. STANDARDS AUTH. (Jun. 29, 2017), www.asa.org.uk/advice-online/children-food.html#place.

19 *First Ads Barred under New Junk Food Rules*, BBC (Jul. 8, 2018), www.bbc.com/news/uk-44706755.

20 Matthew K. Parlow, *Healthy Zoning*, 44 FORDHAM URBAN L.J. 33, 43–44 (2017).

21 Douglas Gentile et al., *Media Ratings for Movies, Music, Video Games, and Television: A Review of the Research and Recommendations for Improvements*, 16 ADOLESCENT MEDICINE CLINICS 427, 440 (2005); Douglas Gentile et al., *Parents' Evaluation of Media Ratings a Decade after the Television Ratings Were Introduced*, 128 PEDIATRICS DIGEST 36 (2011).

22 Michigan Medicine – University of Michigan, *Nearly 9 in 10 Parents Say Teens Spend Too Much Time Gaming*, SCIENCEDAILY (Jan. 20, 2020), www.sciencedaily.com/releases/2020/01/200120113420.htm.

23 *Here's How Many People Play Fortnite*, GAMES RADAR (Jan. 17, 2022), www.gamesradar.com/how-many-people-play-fortnite/.

24 J. Clement, *Hours Spent Per Week Playing Fortnite According to Players in the United States as of February 2020*, STATISTA (May 27, 2021), www.statista.com/statistics/882113/time-spent-playing-fortnite/.

25 Jane Mavoa *et al.*, *Beyond Addiction: Positive and Negative Parent Perceptions of Minecraft Play*, CHILD PLAY'17: PROCEEDINGS OF THE ANNUAL SYMPOSIUM ON COMPUTER-HUMAN INTERACTION IN PLAY, Oct. 2017, 171.

26 Douglas Gentile, *Thinking More Broadly about Policy Responses to Problematic Video Game Use: A Response to Kiraly et al. (2018)*, 7 J. BEHAVIORAL ADDICTION 563 (2018).

27 Clayton Gillette, *Lock-In Effects in Law and Norms*, 78 B.U. L. REV. 817 (1998).

28 *Number of Monthly Active Instagram Users 2013–2021*, STATISTA (Feb. 8, 2022), www.statista.com/statistics/253577/number-of-monthly-active-instagram-users/.

29 *7 Facts about Americans on Instagram*, PEW RSCH. CTR. (Oct. 7, 2021), www .pewresearch.org/fact-tank/2021/10/07/7-facts-about-americans-and-instagram/; *Percentage of Teenagers in the United States Who Use Snapchat as of April 2018, by Age Group*, STATISTA (Jan. 28, 2022), www.statista.com/statistics/419400/us-teen-snapchat-users-age-reach/; Manish Singh, *TikTok Tops 2 Billion Downloads*, TECH CRUNCH (Apr. 29, 2020), https://techcrunch.com/2020/04/29/tiktok-tops-2-billion-downloads/#:~:text=The%20app%20has%20been%20downloaded,435.3%20mil lion%20of%20%24456%20million.

30 Arjun Panchadar, *Top Gamer "Ninja" Made $1 Million to Promote EA's "Apex Legends" Launch: Source*, REUTERS (Mar. 14, 2019), www.reuters.com/article/us-electronic-arts-apexlegends/top-gamer-ninja-made-1-million-to-promote-eas-apex-legends-launch-source-idUSKBN1QU2AC.

31 *FTC Staff Reminds Influencers and Brands to Clearly Disclose Relationship*, FTC (Apr. 19, 2017), www.ftc.gov/news-events/press-releases/2017/04/ftc-staff-reminds-influencers-brands-clearly-disclose; FTC, STATEMENT OF COMMISSIONER ROHIT CHOPRA REGARDING THE ENDORSEMENT GUIDES REVIEW COMMISSION FILE NO. P204500 (2020); F.TC, DISCLOSURES 101 FOR SOCIAL MEDIA INFLUENCERS (2019).

Chapter 10

1 Matt Richtel, *Children's Screen Time Has Soared in the Pandemic, Alarming Parents and Researchers*, N.Y. TIMES (Jan. 16, 2021), www.nytimes.com/2021/01/16/ health/covid-kids-tech-use.html.

2 Shelag Dolan, *Electronic Device Usage Nearly Doubled among US Kids during the Pandemic*, BUSINESS INSIDER (Nov. 5, 2020), www.emarketer.com/content/elec tronic-device-usage-nearly-doubled-among-us-kids-during-pandemic (reporting on a poll by Ipsos and The Global Myopia Awareness Coalition (GMAC)).

3 Jess Berthold, *Adolescents' Recreational Screen Time Doubled during Pandemic, Affecting Mental Health*, UNIV. OF CAL. S.F. (Nov. 1, 2021), www.ucsf.edu/news/ 2021/11/421701/adolescents-recreational-screen-time-doubled-during-pandemic-affecting-mental; Jason M. Nagata *et al.*, *Screen Time Use among US Adolescents during the COVID-19 Pandemic*, 176 JAMA PEDIATRICS 94 (2022), https:// jamanetwork.com/journals/jamapediatrics/fullarticle/2785686.

4 Elise Favis, *With Coronavirus Closing Schools, Here's How Video Games Are Helping Teachers*, WASH. POST (Apr. 15, 2020), www.washingtonpost.com/video-games/2020/04/15/teachers-video-games-coronavirus-education-remote-learning/; Paige Tutt, *From Headache to Helpful – Teachers on Using TikTok in the Classroom*, EDUTOPIA (Mar. 19, 2021), www.edutopia.org/article/headache-help ful-teachers-using-tiktok-classroom.

5 *Education*, ROBLOX, https://education.roblox.com/en-us/ (last visited Jan. 3, 2022).

6 *Training for Minecraft Educators*, MINECRAFT, https://education.minecraft.net/en-us/resources/get-trained (last visited Jan. 3, 2022).

7 Amelia Nierenberg & Adam Pasick, *Streaming Kindergarten on TikTok*, N.Y. TIMES (Sep. 18, 2020), www.nytimes.com/2020/09/18/us/remote-learning-tiktok.html.

8 Paige Tutt, *From Headache to Helpful – Teachers on Using TikTok in the Classroom*, EDUTOPIA (Mar. 19, 2021), www.edutopia.org/article/headache-helpful-teachers-using-tiktok-classroom.

9 ABCD Study, https://abcdstudy.org/ (last visited Jan. 3, 2022).

10 John Hutton, Jonathan Dudley, & Tzipi Horowitz-Kraus, *Associations between Screen-Based Media Use and Brain White Matter Integrity in Preschool-Aged Children*, 174 JAMA PEDIATRICS 1 (2020).

11 Tzipi Horowitz-Kraus & John S. Hutton, *Brain Connectivity in Children Is Increased by the Time They Spend Reading Books and Decreased by the Length of Exposure to Screen-Based Media*, 107 ACTA PAEDIATRICA 685 (2018) (study examined scans of 8–12-year-olds and found that kids who spent more time on screens showed decreased functional connectivity between the visual word form areas and areas related to processing language and cognitive control areas of the brains than kids who spent more time reading); Hingmei Wang *et al.*, *The Alteration of Gray Matter Volume and Cognitive Control in Adolescents with Internet Gaming Disorder*, 9 FRONTIERS IN BEHAV. NEUROSCIENCE, 1 (2015) (18-year-old college students with Internet gaming addiction showed less gray matter in certain brain areas compared to controls); Martin P. Paulus *et al.*, *Screen Media Activity and Brain Structure in Youth: Evidence for Diverse Structural Correlation Networks from the ABCD Study*, 185 NEUROIMAGE 140 (2019) (researchers found mixed results: (i) some heavy screen users showed cortical thinning at younger ages than expected; but this thinning is part of natural brain maturation, and the study did not explain the implications of the difference; (ii) some heavy users scored below the curve on aptitude tests, while others performed well).

12 Anderson Cooper, *Groundbreaking Study Examines Effects of Screen Time on Kids*, CBS NEWS (Dec. 9, 2018), www.cbsnews.com/news/groundbreaking-study-examines-effects-of-screen-time-on-kids-60-minutes/.

13 §2.22 Psychological Abuse, Comment (b) Restatement of the Law, Children and the Law – Draft; Diana Morelen & Anne Shaffer, *Understanding Clinical, Legal, and Ethical Issues in Child Emotional Maltreatment*, 21 MALTREATMENT & TRAUMA No. 2, 188, 196 (2012) ("difficult to substantiate cases of emotional maltreatment" – therefore, CPS is unlikely to investigate).

14 *See* Dan M. Kahan, *Social Influence, Social Meaning, and Deterrence*, 83 VA. L. REV. 349 (1997).

15 *The Global Climate Crisis: A Child Rights Crisis*, CHILD RIGHTS NOW! (Nov. 2019).

16 *Juliana v. United States*, OUR CHILD'S TRUST (last visited Jan. 8, 2022), www.ourchildrenstrust.org/juliana-v-us; *Juliana v. United States*, 947 F.3d 1159 (9th Cir. 2020).

17 Jeff McMahon, *Appellate Judge Sees Criminal Neglect in U.S. Response to Climate Change*, FORBES (Jun. 5, 2019), www.forbes.com/sites/jeffmcmahon/2019/06/05/childrens-climate-lawsuit-appellate-judge-sees-criminal-neglect/?sh=67020ce61126.

18 *Reimagining the Role of Technology in Education: 2017 National Education Technology Plan Update*, OFFICE OF EDUCATIONAL TECHNOLOGY (Jan. 2017); OECD, *Students, Computers and Learning: Making the Connection* (2015); Privacy Technical Assistance Center, *Protecting Student Privacy While Using*

Online Educational Services: Requirements and Best Practices, US DEPT. OF EDUC. (2014); Barbara Fedders, *The Constant and Expanding Classroom: Surveillance K–12 Public Schools*, 97 N.C. L. REV. 1673 (2019). *See also* AUDREY WATERS, TEACHING MACHINES: THE HISTORY OF PERONALIZED LEARNING (MIT Press 2021).

19 Lauren M. Singer & Patricia A. Alexander, *Reading on Paper and Digitally: What the Past Decades of Empirical Research Reveal*, 87 REV. EDUC. RSCH. (Dec. 2017).

20 Amanda C. G. Hall *et al.*, *On or Off Task: The Negative Influence of Laptops on Neighboring Students' Learning Depends on How They Are Used*, 153 COMPUT. & EDUC. 1 (2020); Ahlam Alghamdi *et al.*, *Online and Face-to-Face Classroom Multitasking and Academic Performance: Moderated Mediation with Self-Efficacy for Self-Regulated Learning and Gender*, 102 COMPUT. HUM. BEHAV. 214 (2020).

21 The study did show that technology in the classroom has certain positive results, such as improving computer proficiency and when used for certain interventions. Maya Escueta *et al.*, *Education Technology: An Evidence-Based Review* (Nat'l Bureau of Econ. Rsch., Working Paper No. 23744, 2017); *see also* C. K. Lo & K. F. Hew, *A Critical Review of Flipped Classroom Challenges in K–12 Education: Possible Solutions and Recommendations for Future Research*, 12 RSCH. & PRAC. IN TECH. ENHANCED LEARNING 1 (2017) (providing a literature review of flipped classroom studies).

22 OECD, *Students, Computers and Learning: Making the Connection* (2015). While the mega studies discuss the impact on digital divide generally, they do not provide data on the effect of integrating technology into the classroom on specific racial and ethnic groups.

23 OECD, *Students, Computers and Learning: Making the Connection* (2015). *See e.g.* Kevin Burden *et al.*, *Investigating the Use of Innovative Mobile Pedagogies for School-Aged Students: A Systematic Literature Review*, 136 COMPUT. & EDUC. 83 (2019) (focusing on teachers' need to adjust to implementing new technologies).

24 Office of Educational Technology, *Reimagining the Role of Technology in Education: 2017 National Education Technology Plan Update*, US Dep't. of Educ.

25 *See* Regulating Screen Time in Early and K–12 Education, H.R. 106, 192nd General Court § 2(c)(2) (2021). *See also* Report of the Special Rapporteur on the Right to Education; *Right to Education: Impact of the Covid-19 Crisis on the Right to Education; Concerns, Challenges and Opportunities*, presented to the Human Rights Council (Jun. 15, 2020) (warning against digitizing education and relying on private companies). *See also* MORGAN G. AMES, THE CHARISMA MACHINE: THE LIFE, DEATH AND LEGACY OF ONE LAPTOP PER CHILD (MIT Press 2019).

26 Public Health Law Center, *50 State Screen Time Regulations Dataset*, MITCHELL HAMILTON SCH. OF L. (2017), www.publichealthlawcenter.org/sites/default/files/50-State-Screen-Time-Regs-Dataset-May2017.pdf. For example, municipalities like Anchorage in California restrict all screen time for smaller kids: https://library.municode.com/ak/anchorage/codes/code_of_ordinances?nodeId=TIT16HE_CH16.55ANCHCALICO. *See* additional examples in Ark. R. 016.22.6-401; Okla. Admin. Code 340:110-3-289; Tex. 26 TAC § 746.2207; and Utah U.A.C. R430–50-18.

27 An Act regulating screen time in early and K–12 education, 2021 Massachusetts House Bill No. 106 (introduced Feb. 19, 2021).

28 Alissa J. Rubin & Elian Peltier, *France Bans Smartphones in Schools through 9th Grade. Will It Help Students?*, N.Y. TIMES (Sep. 20, 2018), www.nytimes.com/2018/09/20/world/europe/france-smartphones-schools.html.

29 Nicole Thieneman Maddox, *Chalk Talks: Silencing Students' Cell Phones beyond the Schoolhouse Gate: Do Public Schools' Cell Phone Confiscation and Retention Policies Violate Parents' Due Process Rights?*, 41 J. L. & EDUC. 261 (2012); Liz Langley, *Should Cell Phones Be Banned from American Classrooms?*, THE HILL (Nov. 26, 2019), https://thehill.com/changing-america/enrichment/education/ 471957-should-cellphones-be-banned-from-classrooms.

30 Desmond Brown, *Cellphone Ban in Ontario Classrooms Starts Today*, CBC NEWS (Nov. 3, 2019), www.cbc.ca/news/canada/toronto/cellphone-ban-ontario-classrooms-1.5346207; Edgar Sandoval *et al.*, *Department of Education Lifts Ban on Cell Phones in New York City Schools*, N.Y. DAILY NEWS (Mar. 2, 2015), www.nydailynews.com/new-york/dept-education-ends-cell-phone-ban-nyc-schools-article-1.2134970; Abigail Johnson Hess, *Research Continually Shows How Distracting Cell Phones Are – So Some Schools Want to Ban Them*, CNBC (Apr. 2, 2019), www.cnbc.com/2019/01/18/research-shows-that-cell-phones-distract-students–so-france-banned-them-in-school–.html.

31 Kathryn Greenaway, *Results of St-Thomas High School Cellphone Ban Are Positive*, MONTREAL GAZETTE (Feb. 26, 2020), https://montrealgazette.com/news/ local-news/west-island-gazette/results-of-st-thomas-high-school-cellphone-ban-are-positive.

32 Kathryn Greenaway, *Results of St-Thomas High School Cellphone Ban Are Positive*, MONTREAL GAZETTE (Feb. 26, 2020), https://montrealgazette.com/news/local-news/ west-island-gazette/results-of-st-thomas-high-school-cellphone-ban-are-positive.

Chapter 11

1 See C. Ip, *Why FIFA Ultimate Team Is Often Hated and Very Successful*, ENGADGET (Nov. 17, 2020), www.engadget.com/fifa-21-ultimate-team-loot-boxes-love-hate-153036039.html.

2 See Andrew E. Freedman, *What Are Loot Boxes? Gaming's Big Controversy Explained*, TOM'S GUIDE (Aug. 9, 2019), www.tomsguide.com/us/what-are-loot-boxes-microtransactions,news-26161.html [https://perma.cc/E3C9–25MH]. *See also* David Zendle *et al.*, *The Changing Face of Desktop Video Game Monetisation: An Exploration of Trends in Loot Boxes, Pay to Win, and Cosmetic Microtransactions in the Most-Played Steam Games of 2010–2019*, PSYARXIV PREPRINTS (Nov. 1, 2019), https://journals.plos.org/plosone/article?id=10.1371/journal.pone.0232780; David Zendle *et al.*, *Adolescents and Loot Boxes: Links with Problem Gambling and Motivations for Purchase*, 6 ROYAL SOC'Y OPEN SCI. 190049 (2019), http://dx.doi .org/10.1098/rsos.190049. Microtransactions and in-game purchases actually originated years earlier, in the 1990s, with Sega Dremacast's Download Content (DLC). DUSTIN HANSEN, GAME ON: VIDEO GAME HISTORY FROM PING PONG TO MARIO, MINECRAFT AND MORE 91 (Feiwel & Friends 2016).

3 See Daniel L. King & Paul H. Delfabbro, *Predatory Monetization Schemes in Video Games (e.g. "Loot Boxes") and Internet Gaming Disorder*, 113 ADDICTION 1967 (Nov. 2018).

4 Alex Wiltshire, *Behind the Addictive Psychology and Seductive Art of Loot Boxes*, PC GAMER (Sep. 28, 2017), www.pcgamer.com/behind-the-addictive-psychology-and-seductive-art-of-loot-boxes/.

5 *See* Daniel L. King & Paul H. Delfabbro, *Predatory Monetization Schemes in Video Games (e.g. "Loot Boxes") and Internet Gaming Disorder*, 113 ADDICTION 1967 (Nov. 2018); Interview by Terry Gross with Dr. Frances Jensen, *Why Teens Are Impulsive, Addiction-Prone and Should Protect Their Brains*, FRESH AIR (NPR radio broadcast originally broadcast Jan. 28, 2015).

6 *See* Kyle Langvardt, *Regulating Habit-Forming Technology*, 88 FORDHAM L. REV. 129, 140–41 (2019).

7 *See* Agneta Johansson *et al.*, *Risk Factors for Problematic Gambling: A Critical Literature Review*, 25 J. GAMBLING STUD. 67 (Mar. 2009).

8 Sean Kane, Founding Member of the Video Game Bar Association, Remarks at the FTC Workshop, *Inside the Game: Unlocking the Consumer Issues Surrounding Loot Boxes* 26 (Aug. 7, 2019) (transcript available at www.ftc.gov/system/files/docu ments/public_events/1511966/loot_boxes_workshop_transcript.pdf).

9 Makenna Kelly, *Game Studios Would Be Banned from Selling Loot Boxes to Minors under New Bill*, THE VERGE (May 8, 2019), www.theverge.com/2019/5/8/18536806/game-studios-banned-loot-boxes-minors-bill-hawley-josh-blizzard-ea.

10 Pat Vance, President of the Entertainment Software Rating Board, Remarks at the FTC Workshop, *Inside the Game: Unlocking the Consumer Issues Surrounding Loot Boxes* 176–77 (Aug. 7, 2019) (transcript available at www.ftc.gov/system/files/docu ments/public_events/1511966/loot_boxes_workshop_transcript.pdf).

11 *See* Philippe Vlaemminck & Robbe Verbecke, *The Gambling Law Review: Belgium*, THE LAW REVIEWS (Jun. 7, 2021), https://thelawreviews.co.uk/title/the-gambling-law-review/belgium; *see also* FEDERALE OVERHEIDSDIENST JUSTITIE KANSSPELCOMMISSIE, ONDERZOEKSRAPPORT LOOT BOXEN 17 (Apr. 2018) (Belg.), *translated in* FEDERAL PUBLIC SERVICE JUSTICE GAMING COMMISSION, RESEARCH REPORT ON LOOT BOXES 16 (Apr. 2018), www.skadden.com/-/media/files/publica tions/2019/08/video-gaming-egaming-law-update/fn12_onderzoeksrapportlootboxe nengelspublicatie.pdf?la=en.

12 *See* KANSSPELAUTORITEIT, ONDERZOEK NAAR LOOT BOXES; EEN BUIT OF EEN LAST? 15 (Apr. 19, 2018) (Neth.), *translated in* NETHERLANDS GAMING AUTHORITY, STUDY INTO LOOT BOXES: A TREASURE OR A BURDEN? (Apr. 10, 2018), https://kansspelautoriteit.nl/publish/library/17/study_into_loot_boxes_-_a_treasure_or_a_burden_-_eng.pdf; Matt Davidson, *The Netherlands Determines Some Loot Boxes Are Gambling*, IGN (Apr. 20, 2018), www.ign.com/articles/2018/04/20/the-nether lands-determines-some-loot-boxes-are-gambling. As for Japan, it has adopted a narrow law that prohibits "kompu gacha," games requiring players to open multiple loot boxes to achieve the "grand prize" by collecting a broad array of random items. Other gacha, or loot box, mechanisms are still permitted. *See* Andrew Vahid Moshirnia, *Precious and Worthless: A Comparative Perspective on Loot Boxes and Gambling*, 20 MINN. J. L., SCI. & TECH. 77, 103 (2019).

13 *See* Philippe Vlaemminck & Robbe Verbecke, *The Gambling Law Review: Belgium*, THE LAW REVIEWS (Jun. 7, 2021), https://thelawreviews.co.uk/title/the-gambling-law-review/belgium.

14 *See* John Woodhouse, *House of Commons Library: Loot Boxes in Video Games* 8 (Aug. 2, 2021), https://researchbriefings.files.parliament.uk/documents/CBP-8498/CBP-8498.pdf; *Proceso participativo sobre los mecanismos aleatorios de recompense (cajas botín)*, DIRECCIÓN GENERAL DE ORDENACIÓN DEL JUEGO (Feb. 19, 2021) (Spain), *translated in Machine at Participatory Process on Random Reward Mechanisms (Loot Boxes)*, DIRECTORATE GENERAL FOR THE REGULATION OF

GAMBLING (Feb. 19, 2021), www.ordenacionjuego.es/en/Noticia-Cajas-Botin (outlining the process by which members of the public can provide feedback on possible regulatory actions against loot boxes).

15 Joshua Robertson, *Australian MP Is Trying to Stop Publishers from Selling Loot Boxes to Minors*, THE GAMER (Jul. 14, 2021); HOUSE OF REPRESENTATIVES STANDING COMMITTEE ON SOCIAL POLICY AND LEGAL AFFAIRS, PARLIAMENT OF COMMONWEALTH OF AUSTRALIA, PROTECTING THE AGE OF INNOCENCE, REPORT OF THE INQUIRY INTO AGE VERIFICATION FOR ONLINE WAGERING AND ONLINE PORNOGRAPHY 89 (2020), https://parlinfo.aph.gov.au/parlInfo/download/committees/reportrep/024436/toc_pdf/Protectingtheageofinnocence.pdf;fileType=application/pdf.

16 Leon Y. Xiao, *People's Republic of China Legal Update: The Notice on the Prevention of Online Gaming Addiction in Juveniles*, 24 GAMING L. REV. 51, 52 (2020), www.liebertpub.com/doi/epdf/10.1089/glr2.2019.0002; Javier C. Hernandez & Albee Zhang, *90 Minutes a Day, Until 10 p.m.: China Sets Rules for Young Gamers*, N.Y. TIMES (Nov. 6, 2019), www.nytimes.com/2019/11/06/business/china-video-game-ban-young.html.

17 S. Dent, *China Forces Game Producers to Reveal Loot Box Odds*, ENGADGET (Dec. 12, 2016), www.engadget.com/2016/12/12/china-forces-game-producers-to-reveal-loot-box-odds. But studies showed that game-makers manipulated the probability disclosure requirement. *See e.g.* Keon Y. Xiao *et al.*, *Gaming the System: Suboptimal Compliance with Loot Box Probability Disclosure Regulations in China*, BEHAVIORAL PUBLIC POLICY I (Jul. 23, 2021).

18 S. 1629, 116th Cong. (2019) (a bill introduced by Senator Hawley "to regulate certain pay-to-win microtransactions and sales of loot boxes in interactive digital entertainment products, and for other purposes").

19 H.F. 1767, 91st Leg., Reg. Sess. (Minn. 2019). *See also* H.B. 2943, 102nd Gen. Assemb., Reg. Sess. (Ill. 2021).

20 States usually require gambling to include: (1) offering consideration, basically giving something of value; (2) playing a game of chance; and (3) potentially winning a prize. Sheldon Evans, *Pandora's Loot Box*, 90 GEO. WASH. L. REV. 376 (2022), https://papers.ssrn.com/sol3/papers.cfm?abstract_id=3733910 (discussing how courts evaluate value and arguing for a more expansive view of value of virtual goods so they will fall into the gambling category). *But see* Jerry Shen, *The Predatory Nature of Loot Boxes and the Need for Government Regulation*, 53 J. MARSHALL L. REV. 1085, 1113 (2020) (reporting that in Washington state, the courts have come to the opposite conclusion and determined that virtual currency has value).

21 *See* Sheldon Evans, *Pandora's Loot Box*, 90 GEO. WASH. L. REV. 376 (2022), https://papers.ssrn.com/sol3/papers.cfm?abstract_id=3733910; *see* Andrew Vahid Moshirnia, *Precious and Worthless: A Comparative Perspective on Loot Boxes and Gambling*, 20 MINN. J. OF L., SCI. & TECH. 77, 99 (2019).

22 *Mason v. Machine Zone, Inc.*, 140 F. Supp. 3d 457, 469 (D. Md. 2015); Interview with Timothy Blood, Attorney, Blood Hurst & O'Reardon, LLP (Apr. 29, 2021).

23 Plaintiffs are raising other arguments including violations of unfair competition, consumer protection, and false advertisement laws; minors' rights to rescind contracts; and unjust enrichment. *See Coffee* v. *Google, LLC*, No. 20-CV-03901-BLF, 2021 WL 493387 (N.D. Cal. Feb. 10, 2021); *C.W.* v. *Epic Games, Inc.*, No. 19-CV-03629-YGR, 2020 WL 6064422 (N.D. Cal. Oct. 14, 2020); *R. A.* v. *Epic Games, Inc.*, No. CV 19-1488-GW-EX, 2019 WL 6792801 (C.D. Cal. Jul. 30, 2019).

24 First Amended Complaint, at 2, *C.W., a minor, by and through his Guardian, Rebecca White* v. *Epic Games, Inc.*, No. 4:19cv3629-YGR, 2020 WL 1650496 (N.D. Cal. filed Feb. 13, 2020); *see also* Complaint, *K.W., a minor through K.W.'s guardian, Jillian Williams* v. *Epic Games, Inc.*, No. 3:21-cv-00976, 2021 WL 1954747 (N.D. Cal. filed Feb. 8, 2021) (arguing that Epic Games "misleads and manipulates minors" into contracts with real-world money as payment).

25 *See* Complaint, at 4-5, *K.W., a minor through K.W.'s guardian, Jillian Williams* v. *Epic Games, Inc.*, No. 3:21-cv-00976, 2021 WL 1954747 (N.D. Cal. filed Feb. 8, 2021); Complaint, at 2, *B.D., a minor by Stewart K. Dadmun* v. *Activision Blizzard, Inc.*, No. 37-2020-00020000-CU-BT-CTL (Cal. Super. Ct. filed Mar. 16, 2020).

26 RICHARD KLUGER, *ASHES TO ASHES: AMERICA'S HUNDRED-YEAR CIGARETTE WAR, THE PUBLIC HEALTH AND THE UNABASHED TRIUMPH OF PHILLIP MORRIS* 760 (First Vintage Books 2010).

27 Complaint, at 2, *B.D., a minor by Stewart K. Dadmun* v. *Activision Blizzard, Inc.*, No. 37-2020-00020000-CU-BT-CTL (Cal. Super. Ct. filed Mar. 16, 2020).

28 *See* FEDERAL TRADE COMMISSION (FTC), STAFF PERSPECTIVE ON FTC VIDEO GAME LOOT BOX WORKSHOP 7 (Aug. 1, 2020), www.ftc.gov/system/files/documents/reports/staff-perspective-paper-loot-box-workshop/loot_box_workshop_staff_perspective.pdf.

29 *See* FEDERAL TRADE COMMISSION (FTC), STAFF PERSPECTIVE ON FTC VIDEO GAME LOOT BOX WORKSHOP 6 (Aug. 1, 2020), www.ftc.gov/system/files/documents/reports/staff-perspective-paper-loot-box-workshop/loot_box_workshop_staff_perspective.pdf; Carl C. Jones, *The Fox in the Henhouse: The Failure of the Video Game Industry's Self-Regulation with Regard to Loot Boxes*, 24 CHAP. L. REV. 245, 245–81 (2020).

30 *See* Demande Remodifiée pour Autorisation d'Exercer Une Action Collective et pour se Voir Attribuer le Statut de Représentants, F.N. c. Epic Games Canada, No. 500-06-001024-195 (Can. Que. Cour Supérieure Jan. 11, 2021).

31 *See* Demande Remodifiée pour Autorisation d'Exercer Une Action Collective et pour se Voir Attribuer le Statut de Représentants, F.N. c. Epic Games Canada, No. 500-06-001024-195 (Can. Que. Cour Supérieure Jan. 11, 2021). Quebec has unique consumer laws, which provide strict liability if plaintiffs can show that there is addiction by design. Interview with Alessandra Esposito Chartrand, attorney representing plaintiffs in *FN* v. *Epic Games*, Mar. 29, 2021.

32 *See* Demande Remodifiée pour Autorisation d'Exercer Une Action Collective et pour se Voir Attribuer le Statut de Représentants at ¶ 19, 32, 51, 56, F.N. c. Epic Games Canada, No. 500-06-001024-195 (Can. Que. Cour Supérieure Jan. 11, 2021).

33 *See Lawsuit to Allege Fortnite as Addictive as Drugs*, REUTERS (Oct. 8, 2019), www.reuters.com/article/us-esports-fortnite-lawsuit/lawsuit-to-allege-fortnite-as-addictive-as-drugs-idUSKBN1WN20O; Edward C. Baig, *Epic Games Sued for Not Warning Parents "Fortnite" Is Allegedly as Addictive as Cocaine*, USA TODAY (Oct. 7, 2019), www.usatoday.com/story/tech/talkingtech/2019/10/07/fortnite-producer-epic-games-lawsuit-says-addictive-as-cocaine/3900236002/; Brendan Kelly, *Hundreds of Quebec Parents Flock to Fortnite Lawsuit*, MONTREAL GAZETTE (Oct. 11, 2019), https://montrealgazette.com/news/local-news/hundreds-of-quebec-parents-flock-to-fortnite-lawsuit.

34 Lida Alvim & Penelope Lopex, *Mom Sues Social Media Giants for Allegedly Driving Her 11-Year-Old Daughter to Suicide*, ABC NEWS (Feb. 4, 2022), https://abcnews.go.com/Health/mom-sues-social-media-giants-allegedly-driving-11/story?id=82652830.

35 Letter from National Association of Attorneys General to Mark Zuckerburg, CEO of Facebook (May 10, 2021), https://1li23g1as25g1r8so110zniw-wpengine.netdna-ssl.com/wp-content/uploads/2021/05/NAAG-Letter-to-Facebook-Final-1.pdf.

36 Adam Satariano & Ryan Mac, *Facebook Delays Instagram App for Users 13 and Younger*, N.Y. TIMES (Sep. 27, 2021), www.nytimes.com/2021/09/27/technology/facebook-instagram-for-kids.html.

37 *See* John D. Sutter, *Wired for Success or Destruction?*, CNN: GAMING REALITY (2012), www.cnn.com/interactive/2012/08/tech/gaming.series/korea.html.

38 *See* Melia Robinson, *Korea's Internet Addiction Crisis Is Getting Worse as Teens Spend up to 88 Hours a Week Gaming*, BUSINESS INSIDER: TECH (Mar. 26, 2015), www.businessinsider.com.au/south-korea-online-gaming-addiction-rehab-centers-2015-3.

39 Thailand was the first to try the system out (not as a formal law) in 2003, but withdrew it in 2005. *See* Orsolya Király *et al.*, *Policy Responses to Problematic Video Game Use: A Systematic Review of Current Measures and Future Possibilities*, 7 J. BEHAV. ADDICTIONS 503, 506–08 (2018), https://doi.org/10.1556/2006.6.2017.050.

40 *See* Leon Y. Xiao, *People's Republic of China Legal Update: The Notice on Further Strictly Regulating and Effectively Preventing Online Video Gaming Addiction in Minors (Published August 30, 2021, Effective September 1, 2021)*, OSF PREPRINTS (Aug. 30, 2021), https://doi.org/10.31219/osf.io/4fua8.

41 *See* Zheping Huang, *Unable to Win Beijing's Approval, Fortnite Gives up on China*, BLOOMBERG BUSINESSWEEK (Nov. 14, 2021), www.bloomberg.com/news/articles/2021-11-14/-fortnite-china-shutdown-game-makers-give-up-as-beijing-tightens-restrictions?srnd=premium&fr=operanews#xj4y7vzkg. Similarly, Japan's Kagawa Prefecture enacted a law in 2020 that severely limits the amount of time that kids under 18 years of age can spend playing games to sixty minutes a day during the week and ninety minutes a day during the weekend. The law even extends to smartphones, prohibiting their use past 10pm. *See* Anthony Puleo, *Japanese Prefecture Passes Law Severely Restricting How Much Kids Can Play Video Games*, GameRant (Apr. 5, 2020), https://gamerant.com/japan-anti-gaming-law/.

42 *See China: Children Given Daily Time Limit on Douyin – Its Version of TikTok*, BBC (Sep. 20, 2021), www.bbc.com/news/technology-58625934; Diksha Madhok, *The Chinese Version of TikTok Is Limiting Kids to 40 Minutes a Day*, CNN BUSINESS (Sep. 20, 2021), www.cnn.com/2021/09/20/tech/china-tiktok-douyin-usage-limit-intl-hnk/index.html; Alex Kantrowitz, *Five Ways China Is Trying to Unaddict Kids from Social Media*, BIG TECHNOLOGY (Nov. 24, 2021), https://bigtechnology.substack.com/p/five-ways-china-is-trying-to-unaddict.

43 *See* Orsolya Király *et al.*, *Policy Responses to Problematic Video Game Use: A Systematic Review of Current Measures and Future Possibilities*, 7 J. BEHAV. ADDICTIONS 503, 503–506 (2018), https://doi.org/10.1556/2006.6.2017.050.

44 *See Chinese Version of Fortnite to Close in November*, BBC NEWS (Nov. 1, 2021), www.bbc.com/news/technology-59121165.

45 *See* Leon Y. Xiao, *People's Republic of China Legal Update: The Notice on Further Strictly Regulating and Effectively Preventing Online Video Gaming Addiction in Minors (Published August 30, 2021, Effective September 1, 2021)*, OSF PREPRINTS (Aug. 30, 2021), https://doi.org/10.31219/osf.io/4fua8; Orsolya Király *et al.*, *Policy Responses to Problematic Video Game Use: A Systematic Review of Current Measures and Future Possibilities*, 7 J. BEHAV. ADDICTIONS 503, 508 (2018), https://doi.org/10.1556/2006.6.2017.050.

46 *See* Orsolya Király *et al.*, *Policy Responses to Problematic Video Game Use: A Systematic Review of Current Measures and Future Possibilities*, 7 *J. Behav. Addictions* 503, 508 (2018), https://doi.org/10.1556/2006.6.2017.050.

47 *See* Kids Internet Design and Safety Act ["KIDS Act"], S. 3411, 116th Cong. (introduced Mar. 5, 2020); Social Media Addiction Reduction Technology Act ["SMART Act"], S. 2314, 116th Cong. (introduced Jul. 30, 2019); Federal Big Tech Tort Act, H.R. 5449, 117th Cong. (introduced Sep. 30, 2021); The Social Media Platform Duty to Children Act, AB No. 2408 Cal. Stat. (introduced Mar. 15 2022).

Chapter 12

1 *Northern Sec. Co. v. United States*, 193 U.S. 197 (1904); *Standard Oil Co. v. United States*, 221 U.S. 1 (1911).

2 Am. Compl. at 24, 30, FTC v. *Facebook, Inc.*, No. 1:20-cv-03590-JEB (D.D.C. filed Aug. 19, 2021) (Onavo, a rapidly growing polling app that attained 2.5 million daily users within nine weeks of launching, is an example of a company that Facebook purchased and terminated).

3 Kelly A. Smith, *What's Going on with the Facebook Antitrust Lawsuit?*, Forbes (May 17, 2021), www.forbes.com/advisor/investing/update-facebook-antitrust-law suit/; Zephyr Teachout, Break 'Em Up: Recovering Our Freedom from Big Ag, Big Tech, and Big Money 41 (St. Martin's Press 2020); Am. Compl. at 20, 36, FTC v. *Facebook, Inc.*, No. 1:20-cv-03590-JEB (D.D.C. filed Aug. 19, 2021).

4 Kelly A. Smith, *What's Going on with the Facebook Antitrust Lawsuit?*, Forbes (May 17, 2021), www.forbes.com/advisor/investing/update-facebook-antitrust-law suit/; *Compl. United States v. Google, LLC*, No. 1:20-cv-03010-APM (D.D.C. filed Oct. 20, 2020).

5 *See e.g.* Compl. at 73, *New York v. Facebook, Inc.*, No. 1:20-cv-03589-JEB (D.D.C. filed Dec. 9, 2020), ECF No. 4 at 6; *Compl. United States v. Google, LLC*, No. 1:20-cv-03010-APM (D.D.C. filed Oct. 20, 2020); *Pl.'s Compl. District of Columbia v. Amazon.com, Inc.* (D.D.C. filed May 2021) *Pl.'s Compl. United States v. Uber Tech., Inc.*, No. 3:21-cv-08735 (N.D. Cal. filed Nov. 10, 2021), ECF No. 21-8735.

6 *See e.g.* American Innovation and Choice Online Act, S. 2992, 117th Cong. (2021); Ending Platform Monopolies Act, H.R. 3825, 117th Cong. (2021); Platform Competition and Opportunity Act, S. 3192, 117th Cong. (2021); Platform Competition and Opportunity Act, H.R. 3826, 117th Cong. (2021).

7 Gregory Day, *Antitrust, Attention and the Mental Health Crisis*, Minn. L. Rev. (forthcoming) (manuscript at 42) (on file with SSRN).

8 Clayton Act, 15 USC § 18 (2012) (barring transactions that may substantially lessen competition or lead to a monopoly); US Dep't of Justice & Fed. Trade Comm'n, Horizontal Merger Guidelines at 2 (Aug. 19, 2010), www.justice.gov/atr/hori zontal-merger-guidelines-08192010 (explaining how mergers can affect competition and innovation).

9 *See* 15 USC § 18a(i)(1); Am. Compl. at 76, FTC v. *Facebook, Inc.*, No. 1:20-cv-03590-JEB (D.D.C. filed Aug. 19, 2021). Marina Lao, *Reimagining Merger Analysis to Include Intent*, 71 Emory L.J. 1035 (2022) (discussing mergers in digital markets).

10 15 USC § 2 (1890) (while § 2 of the Sherman Act usually involves refusals to deal or exclusive dealing, it also applies to mergers that lead to unlawful monopoly acquisition or maintenance); *see United States v. Grinnell Corp.*, 384 U.S. 563, 576 (1966) (describing unlawful and exclusionary practices by which the defendant used to

create a monopoly, including a series of acquisitions, restrictive agreements, and certain pricing practices).

11 US Dep't of Just., *Justice Department Sues Monopolist Google for Violating Antitrust Laws* (Oct. 20, 2020), www.justice.gov/opa/pr/justice-department-sues-monopolist-google-violating-antitrust-laws.

12 Niels J. Rosenquist, Fiona M. Scott Morton, & Samuel Weinstein, *Addictive Technology and Its Implications for Antitrust Enforcement*, 100 N.C. L. Rev. 477–78 (2022) (discussing competition for non-addictive models); Am. Compl. at 20, 41, *FTC v. Facebook, Inc.*, No. 1:20-cv-03590-JEB (D.D.C. filed Aug. 19, 2021) (discussing WhatsApp's non-advertising model).

13 *See generally* Robert Bork, The Antitrust Paradox 72–88 (Free Press 1978); *Cont'l T.V., Inc. v. GTE Sylvania, Inc.*, 433 U.S. 36, 56–58 (1977); Herbert Hovenkamp, *Is Antitrust's Consumer Welfare Principle Imperiled*, 45 *Iowa J. Corp. L.* 65, 66 (2019).

14 *See* Gregory Day & Abbey Stemler, *Infracompetitive Privacy*, 105 *Iowa L. Rev.* 61, 78 (2019).

15 Gregory Day, *Antitrust, Attention and the Mental Health Crisis*, Minn. L. Rev. (forthcoming) (manuscript at 26) (on file with SSRN) (in several antitrust cases involving tech companies courts dismissed the cases applying the efficiency and high-cost rationale); *see e.g. Philadelphia Taxi Ass'n, Inc. v. Uber Techs., Inc.*, 886 F.3d 332, 338 (3d Cir. 2018) (dismissing a case against Uber); *Kinderstart.com LLC v. Google, Inc.*, No. C06-2057JFRS, 2007 WL 831806, at 26 (N.D. Cal. Filed Mar. 16, 2007) (questioning whether the nature of "free" services can even give rise to antitrust litigation).

16 Niels J. Rosenquist, Fiona M. Scott Morton, & Samuel Weinstein, *Addictive Technology and Its Implications for Antitrust Enforcement*, 100 N.C. L. Rev. 474 (2022).

17 This is unless the monopolist has deprived consumers of a choice between competing products. *See* Gregory Day & Abbey Stemler, *Are Dark Patterns Anticompetitive?*, 72 Ala. L. Rev. 1 (2020); *Berkey Photo, Inc. v. Eastman Kodak Co.*, 603 F.2d 263, 287–88 (2d Cir. 1979); *In re. Keurig Green Mt. Singleserve Coffee Antitrust Litig.*, 383 F. Supp. 3d 187, 215–16 (S.D.N.Y. 2019) (finding antitrust liability when a monopolist combines product withdrawal with some other conduct, in effect coercing consumer behavior rather than persuading consumers on the merits); *see also United States v. Microsoft Corp.*, 253 F.3d 34, 65 (D.C. Cir. 2001) (finding that Microsoft designed Windows 98 in a way that made it difficult for users to change the default browser to something other than Internet Explorer, thereby harming competition by deterring consumers' choice).

18 Gregory Day, *Antitrust, Attention and the Mental Health Crisis*, Minn. L. Rev. (forthcoming) (manuscript at 2–3) (on file with SSRN).

19 Gregory Day & Abbey Stemler, *Are Dark Patterns Anticompetitive?*, 72 Ala. L. Rev. 1, 27 (2020) (few if any firms have incurred antitrust liability in the United States exclusively for eroding privacy).

20 Zephyr Teachout, Break 'Em Up: Recovering Our Freedom from Big Ag, Big Tech, and Big Money 251 (St. Martin's Press 2020) (arguing that "we need to organize an antitrust movement for our time").

21 Lina M. Khan, *Amazon's Antitrust Paradox*, 126 *Yale L.J.* 710 (2017).

22 Robinson Meyer, *How to Fight Amazon (before You Turn 29)*, The Atlantic (Jul./Aug. 2018), www.theatlantic.com/magazine/archive/2018/07/lina-khan-antitrust/561743/;

David Streitfeld, *Amazon's Antitrust Antagonist Has a Breakthrough Idea*, N.Y.
Times (Sep. 7, 2018), www.nytimes.com/2018/09/07/technology/monopoly-antitrust-
lina-khan-amazon.html.

23 Prior to her appointment to the FTC, Lina Kahn joined the faculty at Columbia Law
School, where she became part of a group of law professors called the Neo-
Brandeisians who rejected antitrust law's focus on price and economic values. *See
generally* Mason Marks, *Biosupremacy: Big Data, Antitrust, and Monopolistic
Power over Human Behavior*, 55 U.C. Davis L. Rev. 513, 568 (2021) (describing
the Neo-Brandeis movement); *see e.g.* Tim Wu, The Curse of Bigness: Antitrust
in the New Gilded Age 128–29, 136 (Columbia Global Reports 2018).

24 Samuel D. Warren & Louis D. Brandeis, *The Right to Privacy*, 4 Harv. L. Rev. 193
(1890); *Carpenter v. United States*, 138 U.S. 2206 (2018); *In re. Facebook Biometric
Info. Privacy Litig.*, 522 F. Supp. 3d 617 (N.D. Cal. 2021).

25 Samuel D. Warren & Louis D. Brandeis, *The Right to Privacy*, 4 Harv. L. Rev. 193
(1890) (writing that the right to privacy has been part of the common law all along).

26 Niels J. Rosenquist, Fiona M. Scott Morton, & Samuel Weinstein, *Addictive
Technology and Its Implications for Antitrust Enforcement*, 100 N.C. L. Rev. 438,
465, 467 (2022).

27 Gregory Day, *Antitrust, Attention and the Mental Health Crisis*, Minn. L. Rev.
(forthcoming) (on file with SSRN).

28 *See generally* John Newman, *The Myth of Free*, 86 Geo. Wash. L. Rev. 513, 524–26
(2018) (investigating the economics of "free"); *see also* Makan Delrahim, US Dep't
of Just., *"Blind[ing] Me With Science": Antitrust, Data, and Digital Markets*
(Nov. 8, 2019), ("[W]e cannot afford to be overly formalistic in assessing the potential
harms that may be attendant to these kinds of business practices. Today, the extraction
of monopoly rents may look quite different than it did in the early 20th century"");
Mason Marks, *Biosupremacy: Big Data, Antitrust, and Monopolistic Power over
Human Behavior*, 55 U.C. Davis L. Rev. 513, 573 (2021) (arguing that when people
access "free" online services, they usually pay with their data instead of currency.
Consequently, at the very least, antitrust regulators should expand the concept of
consumer welfare to accommodate the cost of deceptive data collection).

29 Gregory Day & Abbey Stemler, *Are Dark Patterns Anticompetitive?*, 72 Ala.
L. Rev. 1 (2020); *United States v. Microsoft Corp.*, 253 F.3d 34, 65 (D.C. Cir. 2001).

30 Thom Lambert, *Why the Federal Government's Antitrust Case against Google
Should – and Likely Will – Fail*, Truth on the Market (Dec. 18, 2020), https://
truthonthemarket.com/2020/12/18/why-the-federal-governments-antitrust-case-
against-google-should-and-likely-will-fail/. *See also* James C. Cooper, Joshua D.
Write, & John M. Yun, *Testimony on the "State of Competition in the Digital
Marketplace" before the U.S. House of Representatives, Committee on the
Judiciary, Subcommittee on Antitrust, Commercial, and Administrative Law*, Geo.
Mason U. L. & Econ. Rsch. Paper Series 25–27 (Apr. 17, 2020) (noting that
Facebook and Instagram exponential growth in users and output is not anticompe-
titive under antitrust law); Ariel Katz, *The Chicago School and the Forgotten
Political Dimension of Antitrust Law*, 87 U. Chi. L. Rev. 413, 414 (2020) (summar-
izing the critics' position: "considering anything other than a narrow set of purely
economic variables such as prices and output would 'politicize' antitrust law, thereby
undermining its efficacy and legitimacy"); Mason Marks, *Biosupremacy: Big Data,
Antitrust, and Monopolistic Power over Human Behavior*, 55 U.C. Davis L. Rev.
513, 568 (2021) (stating that critics of the Neo-Brandeisians argue that focusing

antitrust on non-economic goals will undermine economic growth by discouraging vigorous competition).

31 Cat Zakrzewski, *Bipartisan Proposals in House Would Mean Major Changes for the Way Tech Giants Operate*, WASH. POST (Jun. 11, 2021), www.washingtonpost.com/technology/2021/06/11/antitrust-legislation-curbs-silicon-valley/.

32 Bhaskar Chakravorti, *Antitrust Isn't the Solution to America's Biggest Tech Problem*, HARV. BUS. REV. (Oct. 2, 2020), https://hbr.org/2020/10/antitrust-isnt-the-solution-to-americas-biggest-tech-problem. Antitrust authorities did succeed in breaking up Bell in 1982. In addition, some scholars believe that cases like Microsoft eventually produced successful outcomes. *See e.g.* Alec Stapp, *The Ghosts of Antitrust Past: Part 2 (IMB)*, TRUTH ON THE MARKET (Feb. 3, 2020), https://truthonthemarket.com/2020/02/03/the-ghosts-of-antitrust-past-part-2-ibm.

33 Gaia Bernstein, *Incentivizing the Ordinary User*, 66 FLA. L. REV. 1275, 1294 (2015).

34 Compl. at 73, *New York v. Facebook, Inc.*, No. 1:20-cv-03589-JEB (D.C.C. filed Dec. 9, 2020), ECF No. 4, 15–16.

35 Niels J. Rosenquist, Fiona M. Scott Morton, & Samuel Weinstein, *Addictive Technology and Its Implications for Antitrust Enforcement*, 100 N.C. L. REV. 464 (2022); Justine Fuga, *Trading Public Nuisance for Product Safety: Reviving the Office of Technology Assessment*, 13 DREXEL L. REV. 489, 492 (2021); Tom Wheeler, *Facebook Says It Supports Internet Regulation. Here's an Ambitious Proposal That Might Actually Make a Difference*, TIME (Apr. 5, 2021), https://time.com/5952630/facebook-regulation-agency/; Steve Lohr, *Forget Antitrust Laws. To Limit Tech, Some Say a New Regulator Is Needed*, N.Y. TIMES (Oct. 22, 2020), www.nytimes.com/2020/10/22/technology/antitrust-laws-tech-new-regulator.html.

36 Gaia Bernstein, *Incentivizing the Ordinary User*, 66 FLA. L. REV. 1275, 1310–12 (2015).

37 Harry Brignull, *Harry Brignull*, https://brignull.com/; Harry Brignull, *How Do Dark Patterns Work?*, www.darkpatterns.org/.

38 FED. TRADE COMM'N, BRINGING DARK PATTERNS TO LIGHT: AN FTC WORKSHOP (Apr. 29, 2021), www.ftc.gov/system/files/documents/public_events/1586943/ftc_darkpatterns_workshop_transcript.pdf (Harry Brignull testifying).

39 Harry Brignull, *Hall of Shame*, DARK PATTERNS, www.darkpatterns.org/hall-of-shame.

40 FED. TRADE COMM'N, *FTC to Ramp up Enforcement against Illegal Dark Patterns That Trick or Trap Consumers into Subscriptions* (Oct. 28, 2021), www.ftc.gov/news-events/press-releases/2021/10/ftc-ramp-enforcement-against-illegal-dark-patterns-trick-or-trap; Detour Act, H.R. 6083, 117th Cong. § 3 (2021).

41 These states include: California, Cal. Consumer Priv. Act (CCPA) § 1798.140; Colorado, C.R.S.A. § 6-1-1303; and Connecticut, S.B. 1202.

42 *See e.g.* Cal. Consumer Priv. Act (CCPA) § 1798.140 (2018) (defining a dark pattern as a "user interface designed or manipulated with the substantial effect of subverting or impairing user autonomy, decision-making, or choice, as further defined by regulation").

43 *See* Jamie Luguri & Lior J. Strahilevitz, *Shining Light on Dark Patterns*, 14 J. LEGAL ANALYSIS 43 (2021) (focusing on dark patterns that involved monetary injuries).

44 FED. TRADE COMM'N, *FTC to Ramp up Enforcement against Illegal Dark Patterns That Trick or Trap Consumers into Subscriptions* (Oct. 28, 2021), www.ftc.gov/news-events/press-releases/2021/10/ftc-ramp-enforcement-against-illegal-dark-patterns-trick-or-trap.

45 *See* Jamie Luguri & Lior J. Strahilevitz, *Shining Light on Dark Patterns*, 14 J. Legal Analysis 43, 53 (2021) (providing a taxonomy of black patterns).

46 *See* Fed. Trade Comm'n, Bringing Dark Patterns to Light: An FTC Workshop (Apr. 29, 2021), www.ftc.gov/system/files/documents/public_events/1586943/ftc_darkpatterns_workshop_transcript.pdf. While some stress that a dark pattern design needs to be intentionally designed and benefit bad actors to the detriment of the consumer, most definitions of dark patterns focus on the impact on autonomy and decision-making. *See generally* William Rinehart, Caden Rosenbaum, & Amanda Ortega, *"Bringing Dark Patterns to Light" FTC Workshop Public Comment*, The Ctr. for Growth & Opportunity Utah State U. (Jun. 22, 2021), www.thecgo.org/research/bringing-dark-patterns-to-light-ftc-workshop-public-comment/ (providing a narrower definition of dark patterns based on intent).

47 Jamie Luguri & Lior J. Strahilevitz, *Shining Light on Dark Patterns*, 14 J. Legal Analysis 43, 46, 48, 103 (2021).

48 Nicholas Kardaras, Glow Kids: How Screen Addiction Is Hijacking Our Kids – and How to Break the Trance 20–22 (St. Martin's Press, 2016); Joe Pring, *New Study Reveals the Most Addictive Video Games on the Market*, We Got This Covered (Jan. 13, 2020), https://wegotthiscovered.com/gaming/study-reveals-addictive-video-games/.

49 Fed. Trade Comm'n Act, 15 U.S.C. § 45; Child.'s Online Priv. Prot. Act of 1998, 15 U.S.C. § 6501–6505.

50 Fed. Trade Comm'n, FTC Policy Statement on Deception (Oct. 14, 1983), www.ftc.gov/system/files/documents/public_statements/410531/831014deceptionstmt.pdf.

51 Fed. Trade Comm'n, *Snapchat Settles FTC Charges That Promises of Disappearing Messages Were False* (May 8, 2014), www.ftc.gov/news-events/press-releases/2014/05/snapchat-settles-ftc-charges-promises-disappearing-messages-were.

52 Daniel J. Solove & Woodrow Hartzog, *The FTC and the New Common Law of Privacy*, 114 Colum. L. Rev, 583, 628–37 (2014).

53 Kyle Langvardt, *Regulating Habit-Forming Technology*, 88 Fordham L. Rev. 129, 141–44 (2019).

54 The FTC could also regulate these manipulative designs as an "unfair practice." But an unfair practice needs to cause a substantial injury to consumers (which is usually assessed in monetary terms) and must undergo a cost-benefit analysis. This makes regulating a manipulative design as an unfair practice more challenging than regulating it as a deceptive practice. *See* Jamie Luguri & Lior J. Strahilevitz, *Shining Light on Dark Patterns*, 14 J. Legal Analysis 43, 87–89 (2021); Kyle Langvardt, *Regulating Habit-Forming Technology*, 88 Fordham L. Rev. 129, 164–66 (2019).

55 Gretchen A. Ramos & Darren Abernethy, *Additional U.S. States Advance the State Privacy Legislation Trend in 2020*, 10 The Nat'l L. Rev. (Jan. 27, 2020), www.natlawreview.com/article/additional-us-states-advance-state-privacy-legislation-trend-2020; Anupam Chander, Margot E. Kaminski, & William McGeveran, *Catalyzing Privacy Law*, 105 Minn. L. Rev. 1733, 1737 (2021).

INDEX